Meeting the Needs of Ethnic Minority Children

of related interest

Group Work with Children and Adolescents
A Handbook
Edited by Kedar Nath Dwivedi
ISBN 1 85302 157 1

The Child's World
Assessing Children in Need
Edited by Jan Horwath
ISBN 1 85302 957 2

A Multidisciplinary Handbook of Child and Adolescent Mental Health for Front-line Professionals
Nisha Dogra, Andrew Parkin, Fiona Gale and Clay Frake
Foreword by Panos Vostanis
ISBN 1 85302 929 7

Effective Ways of Working with Children and their Families
Edited by Malcolm Hill
ISBN 1 85302 619 0

Permanent Family Placement for Children of Minority Ethnic Origin
June Thoburn, Liz Norford and Stephen Parvez Rashid
ISBN 1 85302 875 4

The Construction of Racial Identity in Children of Mixed Parentage
Mixed Metaphors
Ilan Katz
ISBN 1 85302 376 0

'Race', Housing and Social Exclusion
Edited by Peter Somerville and Andy Steele
ISBN 1 85302 849 5

Immigration Controls, the Family and the Welfare State
A Handbook of Law, Theory, Politics and Practice for Local Authority, Voluntary Sector and Welfare State Workers and Legal Advisors
Steve Cohen
ISBN 1 85302 723 5

Meeting the Needs of Ethnic Minority Children – Including Refugee, Black and Mixed Parentage Children

A Handbook for Professionals
Second Edition

Edited by Kedar Nath Dwivedi

Foreword by Richard Williams

Jessica Kingsley Publishers
London and Philadelphia

First edition published in 1995 by Jessica Kingsley Publishers
This edition published in the United Kingdom in 2002
by Jessica Kingsley Publishers Ltd
116 Pentonville Road
London N1 9JB, England
and
325 Chestnut Street
Philadelphia, PA 19106, USA
www.jkp.com

Copyright © Jessica Kingsley Publishers 2002

Library of Congress Cataloging-in -Publication Data
Meeting the needs of ethnic minority children : including refugee, Black, and mixed parentage children : a handbook for professionals / edited by Kedar N. Dwivedi,--2nd ed.
p. cm.
Includes bibliographical references and index.
ISBN 1-85302-959 9 (pbk.)
1. Children of minorities--Services for--Great Britain. 2. Children of immigrants--Services for--Great Britain. 3. Child Welfare--Great Britain. I. Dwivedi, Kedar Nath.

HV751.A6 M44 2002
362.7'089'0941--dc21   2002025471

British Library Cataloguing in Publication Data
A CIP catalog record for this book is available from the British Library

ISBN 1 85302 959 9

Printed and Bound in Great Britain by
Athenaeum Press, Gateshead, Tyne and Wear

Contents

With the warmest affection and best wishes
this book is dedicated by the editor
to his grandson Siddharth Dwivedi

Foreword

Anyone who has survived childhood has enough information to last him the rest of his days. (Flannery O'Connor)

This book sits at the conjunction of two major issues for society. They are according young people the position that they deserve and ensuring that we reap the benefits of struggling to become a truly multicultural world. Avoiding the enormous pitfalls associated with each of these great challenges is a major endeavour.

I am deeply honoured by Kedar Dwivedi's invitation to write this foreword. As I prepared to do so, I was reminded of the enormity of the tasks that face us. It think it likely that most of us would be offended by a suggestion that we fail to afford children and childhood the priority they deserve. Yet, the challenge remains of assisting society to realize the vital importance of investing adequately in childhood experience and the cultures of young people as they grow up and of focusing on children the more concrete resources of adult time, effort and finance. It is not just how much resource and effort we put in, but how we do so. Time and again, the pull away from centring our services on children towards illusions formed out of well-intentioned adult goals for children trips up our thinking and actions. It is not that these adult intentions are wrong, but we do require a better balance with listening to and caring for children, if we are to avoid failure, alienation and exclusion. Progress is being made and there are new opportunities.

As I write this foreword, I have three documents open before me on my desk. They are the drafts of this, Kedar Dwivedi's edited text, the *Strategy for Child and Adolescent Mental Health for Wales* published in 2001 by the National Assembly for Wales's Minister for Health, Social Services and Children, and a draft of a report on research to gain the views of ethnic minority children and their families on child and adolescent mental health services. Reading them together has been a privilege. As I did so, I was struck by resonances between their contents. I became more aware of the powerful cultural themes embedded within myself and our services. These matters have the ability to enrich the lives of young people, if we get them right, but the power to disqualify and sustain inequity, if we do not.

Policies such as clinical governance and evidence-based practice could provide us with the impetus and frameworks for work towards getting right the cultural themes covered in this book, but only if we allow ourselves to do so. Clinical governance is defined by the Department of Health in England as 'A framework through which NHS organizations are accountable for continuously improving the quality of their services and safeguarding high standards of care by creating an environment in which excellence in clinical care will flourish.' But reading this book prompts me to ask if, when creating that environment, we will allow ourselves to look at the cultures of our service organizations and the communities we serve as well as more closely regulating services and the professions. And, as we develop evidence-based practice, will we be able to juxtapose evidence drawn from study of the humanities, ethics and culture with that derived from the sciences?

The Welsh Strategy defines the qualities of child-centred services. It sets out Wales's intent and direction for child and adolescent mental health services and includes as one of its three aims 'Partnership with families, substitute families and all those who care for children.' Delivering child-centred services built on partnership will require much greater cultural awareness, sensitivity and skills than we have been enabled to show so far.

This is the second edition of a book that has already established its place and value. It directs our attention to ethnic minorities and the differences in culture that are now represented in most countries and the various ways in which accumulated experience and skills might benefit delivery of better services. But its contents also provoke consideration of assumptions we make about how adults construe children and their families and the cultures in which we rear them.

As Fateh and colleagues say in Chapter 6, many definitions of culture tend to foster a view of inheriting or being 'born into one's culture, as if it is a top coat that we don'. But, as they say, 'culture constructs us and our sense of who we are, and on the other hand we construct it.' They believe that 'Cross-cultural work, then, should be used critically not only to understand the meaning of suffering and emotions in other cultures but also to recognize the particularity of our own cultural understanding of suffering and emotions. Without this, we cannot begin to develop a truly cross-cultural approach to therapy.'

The conclusion of Fateh and colleagues that 'Talking about culture is like talking about everything else too' reminded me of just how deeply embedded can be our values and assumptions about ourselves as well as others. They made me think about the nature of the tasks implied by deciding to make services more sensitive and responsive to all clients. The point they make is reinforced by Banhatti and Bhate, who say in Chapter 3: 'It then becomes important that professionals dealing with the child are able to look through the smokescreen of cultural factors (their own and the child's) to identify pathological or maladaptive patterns of behaviour or symptoms.' This collection will help readers to do just that. As well as providing information, it will also provoke you to think about yourself and who you are and the assumptions and values you take with you in what you do.

I read the report on the opinions of ethnic minority young people and their families at much the same time as I read the drafts of this book. Banhatti and Bhate summarize the 'Ethnocultural factors [that] play a significant role in utilization of psychiatric services'. In their opinion, these factors include 'Communication difficulties due to language barrier, disparity between cultural beliefs of professionals and clients' and 'Stigma attached to mental illness'. I found examples of all of these in the opinions expressed to the researchers. In his introductory chapter, Kedar Dwivedi groups the factors impinging on young people from ethnic minorities and their needs for and use of services as stemming from risks that affect all children, risks relating to racism and risks consequent on dislocation.

Dwivedi describes this book as using 'a framework for looking at where they are coming from', 'In order to make sense of the interactions between professionals and ethnic minority children' and to emphasize the urgency of the 'need for adequate service provision beyond mere rhetoric'. Evidently, we have a demanding journey before us if we want to design and deliver services that are appropriately culturally sensitive and which do go beyond rhetoric, but this excellent book will help. If we want to change what we are and do, then we could do nothing better than invest our efforts, backed up by the resources required, in young people for they will be the culture-carriers of tomorrow and, if their voices are heard, they will also provoke us, the adults, to reflect and act today. Read on!

Richard Williams
Professor of Mental Health Strategy
University of Glamorgan

Preface

There are now a considerable proportion of children living in the United Kingdom and elsewhere who belong to minority ethnic groups. As the 'melting pot' concept of a single culture resulting from the blending of different ethnic groups has sensibly given way to a pluralistic view of recognizing and accepting differences among groups, the Children Act 1989 emphasizes the need for sensitivity to children's cultural, ethnic and linguistic requirements. There is a huge variety of professionals involved in helping, caring for, educating, looking after and advocating for children, such as solicitors, childcare social workers, residential workers, educational therapists, child psychologists, teachers, probation officers, education welfare officers, child psychiatrists, paediatricians, school doctors, school nurses, health visitors, nursery nurses, community psychiatric nurses, child psychiatric nurses, art therapists, play therapists, family therapists, group therapists, child psychotherapists, occupational therapists and so on. As we found that these professionals working with ethnic minority children were looking for a practical, comprehensive and integrated book, we felt that this would be a worthwhile effort. Many professionals, in fact, often find themselves at a loss as to how to understand and meet these children's different needs and the first edition of this book (published in 1996) went a long way to help.

Since the publication of the first edition, many important developments have taken place in this field, for example, the publication of the Macpherson Report, the creation of the Ethnic Issues Committee within the Royal College of Psychiatrists and several examples of good practices beginning to meet at least some of the needs of ethnic minority children. The second edition is therefore an attempt to keep up with the developments and an opportunity to include new chapters and revise some of the original chapters in the light of the recent developments.

Acknowledgements

It was a great pleasure for both Dr Ved Prakash Varma and me to edit the first edition of this book, as we were extremely fortunate in receiving quality contributions from all the authors. It was a real privilege to put together the work of such an extraordinary group of multidisciplinary experts. Dr Varma has now retired from editing and has therefore not been able to join me in preparing this edition. I extend all good wishes to him. The additional chapters and revisions of some of the original ones have been of excellent quality and I am extremely grateful to all the contributors. I am immensely thankful to Jessica Kingsley, Amy Lankester-Owen, Claudia Conway and the rest of the publishing team for their unfailing support. I am equally thankful to the readers for considering to make use of the material. I am sure that readers will find the book helpful in meeting the needs of not only ethnic minority children but most others as well.

I would like to take this opportunity to thank my colleagues in the service for their dedication and commitment, including Claire Allen, Karen Amos, Dawn Bailham, Brenda Baldwin, Rajeev Banhatti, Mary Barnes, Mary Battison, Amit Biswas, Cazz Broxton, Sue Buckland, George Butler, Dan Buys, Sheila Catchpole, Susie Chapman, Lynda Davies, Gina Der-Kevorkian, Denise Ewing, Brenda Fletcher, Linda Flower, Nein Gardner, Peter Harper, Avril Hart, Amanda Hayle, Sarah Hogan, Jo Johnson, Frances Jones, Tania Kiana, Elisabeth Lamont-Hoffman, Natasa Ljubomirovic, Anthony Maister, Sharon Mallon, Adrian Marsden, Carol Passingham, Jan Pawlikowski, Sandra Roberts, Sachin Sankar, Annette Schlosser, Paul Sellwood, Angela Shanly, Vyvienne Tippler, Michael Van Der Eijk, Annie Waldsax, Melanie Westley, Katie Wheatley, Phillipa Williams and Margaret Wysling. It has also been a pleasure to be associated with the child psychiatry colleagues from neighbouring services, such as Geoff Brown, Kusay Hadi, Raj Kathane, Theo Mutale, James Pease, Louise Quinn, Tony Roberts and Vinod Sharma, to name only a few.

Similarly, I am grateful for the support of the consultant colleagues and the management team of the Child Health Directorate, such as Fran Ackland (Clinical Director), Bob Butcher, Laith Chandrakantha, Lesley Cockerill, Jackie Coles, Jane Coles, Sue Collier, Janet Collinson, Peter Daish, Tracey Davis, Joy Dinnage, Nick Griffin, John Hewertson, Sita Jayakumar, Helen Jessop, Val McDonald, Kate MacIntosh, David Moscrop, Susan Price, Linda Scott, Sheila Shribman (Medical Director),

Damienne Sinclair, Fiona Thompson and Christine Walker; psychiatric consultant colleagues: Suheib Abu-Kmeil, Wasi Ahmad, David Berry, Amit Bhattacharyya, Mohan Bonthala, Jaikar Jani, Harnek Masih, Ram Mudaliar, Alex O'Neil-Kerr, Julie Roberts and Brian Timmins; public health consultant colleagues such as Paul Crosford, John Forde, Silas Sebugwawo, and the Chief Executive of the Northampton General Hospital National Health Service (NHS) Trust, David Wilson, to name just a few. My special thanks to Malcolm Robinson, Kristi Smith and Ruth Thurston-Ward from the Princess Marina Hospital library. And I am particularly thankful to Naina Sadrani, my secretary.

The warmth and support from my wife Radha, my sons Amitabh and Rajaneesh, my daughter-in-law Amrita and my delightful grandson Siddharth have been immensely invigorating for me in this project.

Kedar Nath Dwivedi

CHAPTER 1

Introduction

Kedar Nath Dwivedi

Children come in contact with a variety of professionals, such as health visitors, general practitioners (GPs), teachers, school nurses and school doctors. Many children also come in contact with professionals such as youth workers, social workers, education welfare officers, educational psychologists and various child health and child mental health specialists and other professionals, all of whom vary in how much professional contact they have with children. A school teacher and a child, for example, will have plenty of opportunities to get to know each other, their likes, dislikes, opinions and feelings. This has an enormous potential to influence and colour the other's perceptions such as that of the child's parents, culture, and various aspects of the child's life. A GP, on the other hand, may depend largely on the parents to understand their child. Thus, the relationships between the child, parents and professionals (Figure 1.1) can vary a great deal from situation to situation.

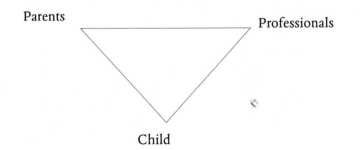

Figure 1.1 Triadic relationships

Determinants of Professional Attitudes and Practices

The attitudes and practices of professionals are the product of a variety of factors. In addition to their psychological background, 'baggage', and their professional training and experiences, the concerns of the state and their cultural ideologies also exert an important influence.

Concerns of the State

In western culture, ill treatment of children was not really recognized as a social problem until the end of the nineteenth century. There are numerous instances of barbarous treatment of children from medieval times including infanticide, mutilation, flogging, starvation and exploitation (Mause 1976). As children were seen as the 'property' of their parents, parents had the full right to treat or punish their children as they saw fit. In 1880 Lord Shaftesbury tried to improve conditions for children at work but left the parental ill treatment of children as beyond the reach of legislation. However, by 1889 the state took steps to intervene to protect children with the passage of the Prevention of Cruelty to and Protection of Children Act 1889. The state intervention consisted primarily of physically removing the child, and this idea of 'rescue' remained the dominant ideology until after the Second World War. The Children and Young Persons Act 1933 was mainly concerned with preventing and controlling delinquency. As evacuation and the dislocation of families due to the war revealed that widespread deprivation and neglect were experienced by numerous children, the Children Act 1948 and the Children and Young Persons Act 1963 emphasized the strength and formative power of the family (Charles and Stevenson 1990). Then an increased awareness of incidents of child abuse led to the Children Act 1975, enabling local authorities to make legal application to free abused children for adoption. During the 1980s,

> Professionals working in child protection and hence representing the State, have been criticized on the one hand for too little intervention, too little attention to children's welfare and allowing children, such as Jasmine Beckford, Tyra Henry and Kimberly Carlile to die; whilst on the other hand, they have been accused of intervening unnecessarily in the families, with removing children without sufficient cause and with a lack of sensitivity to parents' rights, as was believed to have happened in Cleveland. (Charles and Stevenson 1990, pp.5–6)

The Children Act 1989 recommends giving full consideration to the racial origin and ethnic, cultural, religious and linguistic background of the child. The Act also requires the court to find out and consider the wishes and feelings of the child giving due regard to the child's age and understanding.

Cultural Ideology

In western culture, an enormous emphasis is placed on independence, autonomy, self-determination, separation, individuation and self-expression. Although social dependence had an honourable status in Europe until the fifteenth century it then began to be seen as a cause of grave social problems. However, the process of colonization created more dependency in the colonies. The American War of Independence epitomized independence as the most cherished value and established dependency as a despicable state. The ideal of independence thus began to be held as the goal for personal growth in western culture and permeated all aspects of it.

Parents are therefore often at pains to make their children independent as quickly as possible, with an emphasis on early training (Roland 1980). Even the psychoanalytic literature conditioned by this preoccupation emphasizes the crucial place of separation, individuation and autonomy. Clear, open and direct expression of one's opinions, views and feelings is considered to be a manifestation of this process.

In such a cultural context, a professional's responses to the needs for guidance, advice and counsel can become rather awkward, indirect and disguised, taking on almost an art form. Even the non-professional ordinary social interactions are often influenced by this ideology. Pande (1968) observed how requesting, telling, instructing or worse still ordering someone to do something even as trivial as closing a door requires camouflaging (e.g. 'Do you want to close the door?') to make it appear as if motivation originated in the recipient of the request rather than the requester. In psychotherapy too, where one needs and seeks guidance and counsel from a mentor on life's difficult situations, the therapist, instead of telling the patient, has to offer 'interpretation' in which the therapist's own point of view is embedded. Thus the therapist gradually manages to influence the value system and major life themes of the patient in a culturally nourished mutual illusion that the decisions reached are those essentially of the patient.

It is a commentary on deeper human needs that a society which above all prizes self direction and independence in life, and which is quite sensitive to the intrusion of personal belief systems of one individual upon another, has had to invent the institution of psychotherapy. Among other things, psychotherapy copes with needs that are perhaps more forthrightly met with by other societies that are oriented toward interdependence rather than toward independence. (Pande 1968, p.426)

Influences on children

Ethnic minority children are exposed to stresses that can affect any child, for example, that of demanding school work, getting on with other family members, health issues, life events, social conflicts and financial matters leading to anxiety, depression, conduct disorder, post-traumatic stress and other mental disorders (Dwivedi 2000a; Dwivedi and Varma 1997a, 1997b; Horne and Sayger 1990). In addition, children from ethnic minorities can experience two other sources of stress, one related to racism and the other to their dislocated family background (Dwivedi 1993a, 1996a, 1996b). For ethnic minority families the impact of dislocation, loss of the extended family and that of other significant social networks along with the experience of racism and the undermining of their value systems by major institutions can produce serious consequences.

Race, racialization and racism

'Race is an essentially biological concept based on those distinctive sets of hereditary phenotypical features that distinguish varieties of mankind' (Smith 1986, p.189). In fact, no race possesses a discrete package of genetic characteristics (Cooper 1984). Moreover there is more genetic variation within than between races, and the genes responsible for morphological features such as skin colour, which are the usual basis of racial groupings, are very few and atypical (Hill 1989). The enumeration of races has depended upon the purpose of such classification and the classifications have left out several unclassified groups such as the Kalahari bushpeople or pygmies (Mausner and Dramer 1985). Thus the concept of race as an objective category has very little credibility and is essentially incorrect. However, the process of categorization on racial lines does still continue.

In reality, 'race' is a social construction in which the variations between the groups said to be 'races' are emphasized more than the variations within the groups, in spite of the fact that these variations are continuous and not discrete (Thomas and Sillen 1979). Dalal (1993) clarifies the context for this phenomenon:

> we live in a historical era that began in the sixteenth century, during which Imperial Europe colonized the rest of the world. The colonizer used various myths, phantasies and ideologies to maintain a division between the colonizer and the colonized. (Dalal 1993, p.277)

The Second World War contained the most repugnant consequences of this process. The practices of racial discrimination, whether deliberate or unintentional, and the beliefs based on racial prejudice are referred to as 'racism'. Prejudice literally means prejudging. A person who holds views about an individual, or group of people, which are not based on knowledge, and is unwilling to change these views even when presented with clear evidence that they are factually wrong, is a prejudiced person.

The racial frame of reference includes assumptions and myths about other cultures and can become an organizing principle of popular consciousness (Carter and Williams 1987). It leads to a tendency to suppress or dismiss minority cultures in the name of integration. 'Racism affects black children – but it also affects white children, who may be growing up with a false sense of their own superiority and acquiring views based on unacceptable stereotypes if they are not shown alternative ways of thinking and behaving' (Pugh 1994, p.xi). Cultural racism

> seeks to justify racist attitudes and practices in cultural terms. The culture of minority groups is seen as deficient in social customs, manners, appropriate attitudes etc. and holding them back. If they refuse to turn their back on their own culture, then any 'discrimination' is their own fault. (Massey 1991, p.34)

The national representative survey by the Policy Studies Institute (Coker 2001) found 20–26 per cent of the 'white' participants admitting to prejudice against ethnic minorities. 'Racism is the belief that some races or ethnic groups are superior to others, which is then extended to justify actions that create inequality' (Bhopal 2001). Ideological impositions are also clearly a kind of cultural imperialism and a form of institutional racism. The Macpherson Report (Home Office 1999) defined institutional racism as 'the collective failure of an organisation to provide an appropriate and professional service to people because of their colour, culture or ethnic origin' (p.28). Institutional racism is the way in which society's institutions operate to the continued advantage of the majority either intentionally or unintentionally (Halstead 1988).

A larger proportion of coloured people than white suffer from social and economic disadvantages such as unemployment, poor jobs, poor housing and fewer opportunities for education and training in the UK. Government statistics show that black and minority people are twice as likely to be unemployed compared with white people. The media, particularly the popular press, can also be biased in the way they report racial incidents and issues. The Home Office estimated that there were 130,000 racial attacks annually. Poor wages, night shifts, long working hours, overcrowding and bad housing all increase the risk of health problems and impact on their children's psychological development (Braun 1997). Racism can lead to direct or indirect racial discrimination, abuse, inequality and disadvantage as regards employment, housing, educational and training opportunities, access to health care, welfare, local amenities, environmental quality and to the undermining of their culture, identity and self-image. It may leave children and their families feeling hopeless when they experience bullying and racial abuse in schools, playgrounds and other places. Racism denigrates and dehumanizes communities leading to lowering of individuals' self-esteem, sense of worthlessness and depression (Fernando 1988). The ethnic minority children's emotional difficulties can be further exacerbated by professionals who unwittingly conflate cultural differences with psychopathologies. The damage to self-identity of ethnic minority children in such a climate is often extremely deep and difficult to repair (Dwivedi 1993b, 1993c).

Fragmentation of extended family network

Another source of stress for the ethnic minorities is their disrupted extended family background. In a culture where the emotional support from one's extended family, especially in times of stress, is the essential ingredient of any coping strategy, the fact of migration and dislocation deprives many ethnic minority families of that healing support. Such a fragmentation of social structure also makes them vulnerable to losing their cultural strength. They have already embarked upon a process of ethnic redefinition. This has often meant loss of their traditional arrangements and the creation of new ones but these new arrangements may still not fit in with their new context (Perelberg 1992). A study in Tower Hamlets has shown that the Bangladeshi respondents experienced more serious life events and reported more symptoms than their indigenous neighbours (MacCarthy and Craissati 1989). Similarly a survey by the Confederation of Indian organizations revealed an alarmingly high rate of emotional distress within South Asian communities and little outlet for their expression (Beliappa 1991).

Ethnicity and culture

The King's Fund classed all disadvantaged people as 'black' believing that the experience of racism is most important (McKenzie and Crowcroft 1994). Dalal (1993) has looked at its source:

> Colour was used as the primary visible signifier to distinguish 'us' from 'them'. In order to do this successfully it was necessary for the hallucinatory whitening of all the peoples of Europe including the Roman, the Greek, the Celt, and of course Jesus Christ, so that they could be distinguished from the 'coloured'. It was this that generated the political category 'black'. The categories 'black' and 'white' are hallucinations. (Dalal 1993, p.278)

The Commission for Racial Equality (CRE) used the term 'ethnic minorities', believing that cultural and religious differences are important. Thus there is now a tendency to use the notion of 'ethnicity' more than that of race implying shared or common features such as social background or origin, language, culture, tradition and religion. Ethnicity includes *culture*. Culture was defined in the nineteenth century as 'that complex whole which includes knowledge, belief, art, morals, law, custom, and any other capabilities and habits acquired by man as a member of society' (Tylor 1871, p.13). It contains the system of rules for governing behaviour, and of beliefs or a web of meaning for making sense of experiences. Thus it organizes our cognitive, emotional and behavioural functions in both subtle and obvious ways, though the cultural values and assumptions may remain outside our awareness (McGoldrick, Pearce and Giardano 1982). McGoldrick (1982) describes the ethnic group as those who perceive themselves as alike by virtue of their common ancestry, real or fictitious, and who are so regarded by others. People from different ethnic groups also tend to experience and express their distress differently (Patel 1994). However, ethnic boundaries can be very imprecise and fluid. The word ethnic is often abused by referring to coloured populations as 'ethnic populations' or 'ethnic families', as if others do not have any ethnicity! It is also frequently confused with nationality or with migrant status.

In spite of the conceptual confusion, race and ethnicity are commonly used variables in research. According to the National Library of Medicine nearly 2500 papers just on medical research were indexed each year under the headings of 'ethnic groups' or 'racial stocks' on Medline. However,

> The categories of race or ethnic group are rarely defined, the use of terms is inconsistent, and people are often allocated to racial or ethnic groups, arbitrarily. Some researchers use the original classification and class Asians as 'Caucasian', though modern definitions often class 'Asians' as 'black'. (McKenzie and Crowcroft 1994, p.286)

Family processes

Children are subject to both overt and disguised influences not only from the professionals around them but also from their social network, the media and of course their family members. The intensity of family relationships both financial and emotional makes it more conducive to organize each other's experiences and fantasies. The family members are in fact in an ideal position (just like the situation of hypnosis) to transmit suggestions to individuals within the family. Children can carry a playful and flexible boundary between the outer and the inner reality and can enjoy the company of playmates invisible to others. Their parents can easily join in the revivification of events complete with special smells, sights, laughters, sighs, tears and chills. Their words and sounds experienced during childhood can deeply reverberate within, ever after (Dwivedi 1993b; Ritterman 1983). A great many such influences take place outside conscious awareness.

Perelberg (1992) has explored the links between culture and the patterns of interactions between families with the help of the intervening concepts of social structure, social organization and family maps. Social structure and social organization are the form and processes respectively taken by the historical and sociological relationships. Family maps are a set of ideas that guide emotions and behaviour in everyday life. The patterns of interactions between the individuals within the family involve meaning, emotion and behaviour and contain within themselves an image of the whole expressing the family organization. Thus family maps link the family organization with the family interactions. The map can contain the conflicting ideas and expectations held by different generations. Culture influences the family maps and family processes. A differentiated map contains differentiated or segregated roles, tasks and activities and has a sociocentric view of individuals in a role relationship, while the undifferentiated (symmetrical, egalitarian or democratic) family map has the egocentric emphasis on the autonomy of the individual.

Many ethnic minority parents react to what they perceive and fantasize in the western culture in a way that leads to conflict. For example, many Asian parents bombarded by the images of romantic courtship and of violent, drugged, excessively sexualized and senseless scenes of youngsters on the media may feel panicky and overprotective towards their offspring. Youngsters' attempts to resist this can easily lead to further escalation of parental protectiveness and the involvement of professionals. The triadic relationship between the child, parents and professionals can then become polarized culminating even in suicidal behaviours.

The interplay between professionals, parents and children

The professionals (such as teachers, social workers, counsellors and various health professionals) aim at fostering independent views and opinions along with skills in self-expression so that their children appear to have their own voices. When such a voice is separate, different from and even opposite to their parents and other relatives, it creates a strong illusion of being really independent (Dwivedi 1996b). The rebellion of young people against institutions and their becoming nonconformist becomes understandable in such a cultural context. If a child or an adolescent does not express such independent views, it raises concerns and may lead to a professional's intervention, often with the assumption that the youngster's family may have been repressive and over-restrictive thus preventing self-expression. Because of their cultural conditioning, the professionals perceive their role as that of facilitators of individuality, self-expression and independence. Many may, therefore, feel passionate about 'rescuing' such children.

The helping professionals are also subject to the cultural conditioning of their own social group. It is difficult to step outside one's belief systems and to be open to other cultural possibilities because such differences and ambiguities can be threatening and can lead to questioning of one's very methods of coping, treating or handling the situation. Even if there is a genuine willingness to respect other cultural values of interdependence, heightened sensitivity to each other's feelings and the significance of mastering narcissistic individuality, it is difficult to do so without adequate preparation, development and training. It is only then that the resonance between the child and the parents as regards their feelings, views, attitudes and wishes is not automatically read as evidence of pathology.

This is why Dayal (1990) points out that the emotional availability of many professionals to ethnic minority families is often very limited. Some fail to respond on the grounds that they cannot understand the cultural ways of ethnic minority families (Fernando 1988), while others look for and quickly find 'cultural conflict' types of explanation. Devereux (1953) called this 'culturistic pseudo insight' whereby one attributes to the culture what is actually an explanation of the individual personality. If a professional is unable to appreciate this fully, it leads to distancing of the child either from the professional or from the parents through the mechanism of projective identification.

Projective identification

The concept of projective identification is extensively described and illustrated in the psychoanalytic literature (Cashdan 1988; Ogden 1979). It helps to comprehend the subtlety of interpersonal influences outside each other's conscious awareness and is believed to consist of three parts: (1) a fantasy of some quality, attribute or emotion which is stripped off from oneself, and (2) projected onto someone else, along with (3) considerable interpersonal pressure to comply with the projection. The mounting pressure makes the person onto whom the stripped-off parts are projected identify unconsciously with what is projected, and the recipient of the pressure is induced to think, feel and behave accordingly.

For example, the primitive, oppressive and other aspects of the Victorian extended family life from the cultural past can be stripped off and projected onto the family map of an ethnic minority group. Ethnic minority cultures are therefore described in a way which make them seem bizarre or backward or imply that their problems are somehow caused by the nature of their culture (Mares, Henley and Baxter 1985). The very fabric of society appears to be permeated by such an attitude manifesting itself in education, media, history books, social work, counselling and psychotherapy literature, and children's storybooks. It is such an atmosphere of Eurocentric imperialistic cultural ideology that leads to many Asian youngsters, at times of distress and when needing help, ending up identifying with such projections (through the process of projective identification) and presenting to the professionals with problems in a way that is more likely to elicit a sympathetic response, for example, a complaint of ill-treatment, fear of arranged marriage and so on (S. Ahmed 1986). Goldberg and Hodes (1992) demonstrate how self-poisoning by a number of Asian adolescent girls symbolizes the acting out of the view of the dominant group that the minority is 'poisonous' or 'harmful'.

The attitudinal balance in triadic relationships

Heider (1946, 1958) proposed a model to comprehend the process of attitudinal balance in triadic relationships. Accordingly in any triadic relationship the constellation is in a state of balance (Figure 1.2) when (1) all three parties are in a positive relationship with one another, (2) all three parties are in a negative relationship with one another (although this is a vacuous balance), or (3) the relationship of any one dyad is positive and the other two dyads are negative. If we take the example of a triadic relationship between father, mother and child, it can be in a state of balance when (1) all three love each other, so that there is no pressure from within the system for change and each relationship is supportive of the other relationship within the system (Figure 1.2a), (2) all three hate each other; although this is a vacuous balance, each relationship still supports the other relationships within the system (Figure 1.2b), or (3) any two of the dyads are negative and one positive, for example, mother and the child may love each other but both hate the father who hates them in turn (Figure 1.2c).

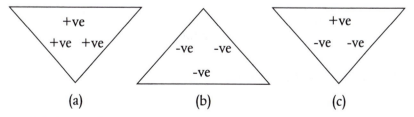

Figure 1.2 States of balance

Some children can get caught in legal proceedings and can come in contact with court welfare officers, social workers, guardians *ad litem*, solicitors and so forth who try to assist the court in finding out and considering the wishes and feelings of the children. Sometimes a great deal of the court's time has to be spent in ascertaining how much of the child's apparent feelings and wishes in relation to individual parents are expressed as a result of the subtle pressures put upon the child by one or other of the parents and how much they are truly independent. More often than not one is really unsure.

When only one of the dyads is negative and the other two dyadic relationships are positive, the constellation is in a state of imbalance. Thus the attitudinal balancing process comes into sharp focus as the parental conflicts influence their relationships with their child. In order to please one parent the child may develop a negative relationship with the other. For a child to love both parents when they hate each other (Figure 1.3) is to be in a state of attitudinal imbalance with constant systemic pressure attempting to shift the relationships in the direction of balance. If both parents love the child who loves them both but the parents themselves hate each other, there is a continuous pressure from within the system to shift the relationships so that either the sole negative relationship becomes positive or one of the positive relationships becomes negative. For example, the child may wish for the parents to change their attitude and become positive towards each other. Similarly the parents may put pressure on the child's relationship with the other parent to turn it into a negative. Any of these changes will be able to balance the system.

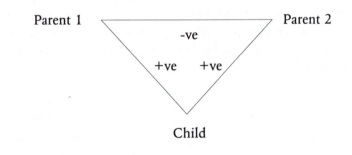

Figure 1.3 A state of imbalance

The same principle can be applied to the relationships between the parent, professional and some aspect of culture. If it is an aspect of the culture that the parent considers to be the most essential ingredient for proper growth and development and the professional considers it to be most obstructive, they may be entrenched in their attitudes towards it. If the relationship between the professional and the parent is positive, it is not likely to last long, because the situation is in a state of imbalance (two positives and one negative). They may wish for the other to see some sense and change their attitude but if that does not happen their relationship towards each other may then become negative in order to balance the system.

A similar triadic dynamic can arise between the professional, parents and the child (Figure 1.4). So a strongly negative relationship in any of the three dyads (parent–professional, professional–child and child–parent) will exert a strong pressure on the other two positive dyads so that at least one of them (usually the weak one) will turn into a negative. The evolution of a professional's relationship with the child is thus greatly influenced by (and influences in turn) the parent–child and the professional–parent relationships. One can extend this kind of analysis to look at the relationship between child, professional and an aspect of culture as well (e.g. feeding: see Dwivedi 2000b). If the professional has a fixed negative attitude towards the aspect of culture, the system can be balanced only by the child changing his or her attitude (in the negative direction) either towards that aspect of the culture or towards the professional or both. A child's identity is thus such a fluid process. This is why Dalal (1998, p.190) points out that 'identity is not a possession, but rather it is a phenomenon that is embedded in a network of social interactions and relations. This shows up the usual notion of identity for what it is – a reification, something that has been abstracted out of a living continuum of interchanges'.

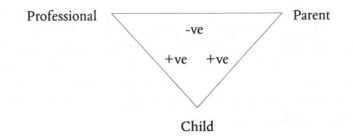

Figure 1.4 Another state of imbalance

Service Provisions

The publication of the Macpherson Report (Home Office 1999) high-lighted the systemic, institutional racial inequality and injustice through public services. There is a growing recognition of the acute need to improve services to minority ethnic groups (Dwivedi 1999). Meeting the needs of ethnic minority children requires setting up of community outreach work, interpreter and translation services, culturally sensitive therapeutic family and other work and also giving voice to subjugated narratives. Also professional development needs to incorporate the perspective of difference and diversity aiming to raise not only cultural awareness by gaining knowledge but also cultural sensitivity through experiences that challenge one's respective cultural identities and their influence on understanding and acceptance of others.

The agenda of equality and inclusion needs to incorporate the whole spectrum of concepts ranging from access, opportunity, entitlement, targeting, promotion, positive discrimination and anti-discrimination.

Health including mental health

Cultural, linguistic, socio-economic and political factors seem to have a greater influence on how people present to and interact with the healthcare system than they do on the nature or symptoms of mental disorders. Planning and policy must focus on removing language-specific and culture-specific barriers to effective treatment (Bhugra and Bahl 2000). The CRE launched in 1992 the *Race Relations Code of Practice in Primary Health Care Services* with the aim of facilitating fair access in provision of services (Commission for Racial Equality 1992). The Code had been drawn up in consultation with general practitioners, family health service authorities (FHSAs), community health councils, regional and district health authorities and a wide range of other related health bodies. However, when 600 FHSAs were contacted by the CRE in 1993, only 29 out of the 600 indicated that they were planning to implement the code. Similarly a survey of the opinions of ethnic minority populations in Buckinghamshire revealed that only 3.9 per cent correctly identified the purpose of the Patient's Charter, 40 per cent of the patients asked others to make their appointment to see the general practitioner and 65 per cent of patients who needed an interpreter were never offered one (Leisten and Richardson 1994).

> Despite the commitment by both professionals and managers to provide ethnically sensitive and culturally appropriate services the overall experience of psychiatric services by Black and South Asian people in this country remains largely negative and aversive. (Sashidharan 2001, p.244)

Lack of adequate resources to meet the mental health needs of any population (Dwivedi 1996c) has not helped the development of services for ethnic minority populations either. There is a poor service uptake of child mental health services by the ethnic minority families. This may be because of a variety of factors such as the clash of cultural values, lack of awareness of the role of professionals or lack of faith in such services, a sense of alienation, communication difficulties and so on. Cultural ideologies have an impact on all aspects of life ranging from one's purpose of life to their help-seeking behaviours. For example, developing states of mind that are conducive to transcending narcissistic preoccupations and achieving enlightenment in this life or a future lifetime can be the most important purpose of life for a Hindu, Jain or Buddhist (Dwivedi 1990, 1994a, b, c; Dwivedi and Prasad 2000). A therapeutic paradigm going against the grain of such an overarching aim may become rather incongruent. An outcome study of Bangladeshi families attending a child psychiatric service in London revealed that the congruence in problem definition between family and therapists was linked with good outcome as rated by the family (Hillier et al. 1994).

The mental health professionals may act as if the minority communities never had anything like psychotherapeutic approaches until western science came along and invented it. Many cultures have had an extensive body of therapeutic knowledge and practices regarding relationships, feelings and mental health (Dwivedi 1980, 1997a). For example, in the Indian literature of 500 BC there is a sophisticated and advanced systematic treatment of the nature of consciousness, something that began to happen in modern western science in the nineteenth century (Reat 1990). There are numerous accounts of interface between Buddhism (for example) and modern therapeutic interventions available in the literature (Brazier 1995; Claxton 1986; De Silva 1984; Epstein 1995; Fromm, Suzuki and De Martino 1974; Kabat-Zinn 1996; Kwee and Holdstock 1996; Pickering 1997; Rosenbaum 1998; Schwartz 1998; Welwood 1985).

Thus one may set up services that may not be culturally sensitive to ethnic minorities and wait for them to come. Then when they do not come, the professionals wonder why (Sue and Sue 1990). It is highly welcome that some child and adolescent mental health services have now made a start by employing outreach or link workers for ethnic minority families. Such good practices need to be adequately resourced and spread across the UK. It is important that the entire responsibility of the issue is not dumped on such workers but they are seen as resources to help improve the whole service by sensitizing it.

Whether it is counselling (D'Ardenne and Mahtani 1999), art therapy (Campbell *et al.* 1999), parenting enhancement (Kemps 1997), group therapy (Coward and Dattani 1993; Mistry and Brown 1997) or family therapy (Barratt *et al.* 1999; Krause 1998), it needs to be culturally congruent and sensitive, considering, among other things, value systems, body language, channels of communication, metaphorical, narrative and indirect communications and so on (Dwivedi 1997b, 2000c). It is ironic that Gans (1994) advocates the use of indirect communication to manage better one's turbulent countertransference as well.

> As a group, we therapists tend to underestimate the toxicity of the emotional field in which we work. Radiologists wear lead aprons, surgeons wear masks, and dentists now wear gloves. Are we guilty of taking insufficient precautions even while we read of our colleagues' vulnerability to suicide, sexual violations of patients, and addiction? The truth is that we sometimes do need temporary, partial insulation from the emotional maelstrom that constitutes countertransference. (Gans 1994, p.126)

Education

Research looking at the experiences of ethnic minority children in nursery and primary schools highlighted that it is not only children who behave in racist manner but also some of their teachers (Wright 1992). They not only held negative stereotypes but also were aware of the racial harassment and reluctant to deal with it. The introduction of educational reforms such as local management of schools (LMS), therefore, produced a mixed feeling in the ethnic minority parents.

> Some black parents have welcomed the national curriculum and national testing as a guarantee that their children will not be fobbed off with a second rate curriculum or suffer discriminatory subjective assessments by prejudiced teachers. Others have seized on the possibilities of LMS for ensuring that black people's voices

can no longer be disregarded by the schools. (Hatcher 1989, p.24)

It is the space between the policy and the classroom practices that provides the real opportunities for multicultural and antiracist education (Smith 1989) although there is an enormous potential for improvement at the level of policy too. The decision of Cleveland Education Authority to allow a parent to exercise choice on racist grounds arose from the Education Reform Act 1988. This in fact established the primacy of education legislation over race relations legislation and opened the way for racial segregation in schools. Such segregation was believed to have contributed to recent communal riots in the north of England.

Mehra (1998) has found an alarmingly high rate of exclusion of Asian children, in addition to that of black children, from schools. However, at least at the policy level, there seems to be an emphasis now on the agenda of inclusion, anti-bullying, antiracism, multicultural education, personal and social education, citizenship, healthy school initiatives and so on, but in practice it is usually neglected due to the preoccupation with the agenda of literacy and numeracy.

Social care

The Children Act 1989 emphasizes the concept of 'parental responsibility' rather than that of 'parental rights' and requires the views of the children to be actively sought. The Act also makes it unlawful to ignore the crucial aspects of racial origin and cultural, ethnic, religious and linguistic background of the child in the process of any decision-making. However, the professional practices and perceptions including the definitions of what is 'normal' or 'deviant' have so far been largely white and Eurocentric. If such professional perceptions and practices continue, the Act can easily work against the best interest and protection of the ethnic minority child. The instrument of 'race, culture, religion and language' can be easily abused to perpetuate the dominance of professional control as a manifestation of their perception of ethnic minority families as culturally deficient, dysfunctional or pathological, from whom the children need to be rescued on the one hand, to a justification of non-intervention even when a child desperately needs intervention and protection, so that the professional could appear to be culturally sensitive in case abuse is culturally acceptable!

like the Race Relations Act 1976, the Children Act 1989 may end up with little or no impact in promoting the welfare and protecting the interest of the black child, if the interest and welfare of the black child are left to the rhetoric of the Act and not transferred into social work action. (B. Ahmed 1991, p.III)

According to Roys (1988), the notion of 'cultural pluralism' has not been difficult to accept for the policy-makers and practitioners because of the traditional social work ideal of respecting individual differences. However, there seems to be little evidence of this in appropriate and adequate service provision (Association of Directors of Social Services 1983; Commission for Racial Equality 1989), because of the assumption that the needs arising out of religious and cultural differences should be met from within the existing resources (Barn 1993).

Partnerships

Research on racial bullying and abuse of children stresses the importance of producing integrated and coordinated strategies, involving a range of agencies in health, education, social care, law enforcement, housing and so on to combat racist abuse across schools, communities and neighbourhoods (Barter 1999). There is also a growing recognition of the need for 'joined-up thinking', joint commissioning and partnership between various departments. There has been an establishment of a Children and Young People's Unit at the national level with the agenda of inclusion. Similarly, initiatives such as Sure Start, On Track, Connexions, Children's Fund and so on acknowledge the needs of ethnic minority children, at least in principle.

A guide to this book

This chapter is an attempt to introduce the themes elaborated further in the book. In order to make sense of the interactions between professionals and ethnic minority children, it uses a framework for looking at where they are coming from with an emphasis on the acute need for adequate service provision beyond mere rhetoric. Chapter 2 on 'Culture and personality' (Dwivedi) examines the way in which culture influences a variety of institutions and processes such as psychotherapy, parenting, child development and the development of personality, personhood and psychopathology with the help of examples from Indian culture in contrast to the western. The chapter also illustrates how cultural components mutually support each other, for example, the emphasis on dependability, interdependence, extended family life, indirect communication and freedom from self in eastern culture and on independence, nuclear family life, direct and clear communication and attachment to self in western culture. There is no attempt to describe different cultural patterns, for which one needs to consult other texts (for example, Lau 2000).

In Chapter 3 on 'Mental health needs of ethnic minority children', Rajeev Banhatti and Surya Bhate look at the effect of ethnicity, especially when associated with a minority status, on children's development which can sometimes lead to psychopathology. The mental health issues, in the context of the stresses on ethnic minority families and some of the childhood psychiatric disorders, have been illustrated with case examples. Both preventive and curative aspects at individual clinical and group (organizational) levels have been addressed. In Chapter 4 on 'Family therapy and ethnic minorities', Annie Lau highlights the cultural differences in family organizations, their knowledge, beliefs and rituals through family life cycles and offers some valuable guidelines for assessment and therapy along with a case example.

In Chapter 5 on 'Children, families and therapists: clinical considerations and ethnic minority cultures', Begum Maitra and Ann Miller examine the meeting between the psychological therapist and the ethnic minority families as a meeting between two cultures which may contain a conflict between potentially opposing and possibly irreconcilable views of childhood. With the help of a number of informative case examples they also highlight the significance of the process whereby this meeting is negotiated. In Chapter 6 on 'Can talking about culture be therapeutic?', the Asian Service Team from Marlborough Family Service, London, share their good practice with the readers. In this chapter they describe how talking and thinking about culture entered into the clinical work of a team of systemic psychotherapists.

In Chapter 7 on 'What is a positive black identity?', Nick Banks argues the case for identity work with black children and offers practical suggestions. In Chapter 8 on 'The emergence of ethnicity: a tale of three cultures', John Burnham and Queenie Harris point out that ethnicity is not a static entity but a narrative which is constantly emerging through the relationships between people, groups of people and nations. They describe for the professionals the flexible use of a conceptual framework of the Co-ordinated Management of Meaning from the social constructionist tradition. Through the case study of a Chinese family they explore some of the issues for children as they negotiate changes in family and cultural processes.

In Chapter 9 on 'Antiracist strategies for educational performance: facilitating successful learning for all children', Gerry German describes the experiences of black and Asian children in the education system and suggests ways of improving their educational performance by actual implementation of antiracist strategies and by creating a learning environment that would facilitate successful learning for all children. In Chapter 10 on 'Mixed-race children and families', Nick Banks looks at the historical factors surrounding mixed race children and families and how these combine with the contemporary social context to affect the psychological dynamics and social pressures within such families. With the help of case studies the chapter also considers mixed-race children who find themselves separated from a parent with an acrimonious relationship with the other parent.

In Chapter 11 on 'Adoption of children from minority groups', Professor Harry Zeitlin examines the complex issues involved, with the hope that this will help evolve practices that are least damaging to the children but are conducive to their comprehensive growth. In Chapter 12 on 'Residential care for ethnic minority children', Harish Mehra, through the moving case example of Gurvinder, highlights the issues for social work practice, particularly in residential childcare.

In Chapter 13 on 'Practical approaches to work with refugee children', Jeremy Woodcock highlights the multidimensional nature of work with refugee children and how to work as a practitioner from a human rights perspective. They will never get a good enough service until they are regarded first and foremost as children, rather than as aliens and strangers. To do that means public services need to reach out. In Chapter 14 on 'Community and youth work with Asian women and girls', Radha Dwivedi provides an excellent account of a piece of community and youth work with Asian women and girls in a small town. Similarly in Chapter 15 on 'A conceptual framework of identity formation in a society of multiple cultures', a team from Casey Family Programs looks at the unfolding of ethnic identity development within the context of their foster care system. Casey Family Programs is a Seattle-based private operating foundation providing a range of services including fostering, adoption, kinship care, legal guardianship, family preservation and reunification.

References

Ahmed, B. (1991) 'Setting the context: race and the Children Act 1989.' In S. Macdonald (ed) *All Equal under the Act.* London: Race Equality Unit.

Ahmed, S. (1986) 'Cultural racism in work with Asian women and girls.' In S. Ahmed, J. Cheetham and J. Small (eds) *Social Work with Black Children and their Families.* London: Batsford.

Association of Directors of Social Services (ADSS) (1983) *Social Services and Ethnic Minorities: Report of a Questionnaire Survey on Social Services Departments and Ethnic Minorities.* London: ADSS.

Barn, R. (1993) *Black Children in the Public Care System.* London: Batsford.

Barratt, S., Burck, C., Dwivedi, K., Stedman, M. and Raval, S. (1999) 'Theoretical bases in relation to race, ethnicity and culture in family therapy training.' *Context 44*, 4–12.

Barter, C. (1999) 'Children and racism.' *Young Minds Magazine 40*, 17–18.

Beliappa, J. (1991) *Illness or Distress: Alternative Models of Mental Health.* London: Confederation of Indian organizations.

Bhopal, R. (2001) 'Racism in medicine: the spectre must be exorcised.' *British Medical Journal 322*, 1503–1504.

Bhugra, D. and Bahl, V. (eds) (2000) *Ethnicity: An Agenda for Mental Health.* London: Gaskell.

Braun, D. (1997) 'Parent education programmes.' In K.N. Dwivedi (ed) *Enhancing Parenting Skills.* Chichester: John Wiley.

Brazier, D. (1995) *Zen Therapy.* London: Constable.

Campbell, J., Liebman, M., Brooks, F., Jones, J., Ward, C., Spurlock, C. and Spurlock, I. (1999) *Art Therapy, Race and Culture.* London: Jessica Kingsley.

Carter, B. and Williams, J. (1987) 'Attacking racism in education.' In B. Troyna (ed) *Racial Inequality in Education.* London: Tavistock.

Cashdan, S. (1988) *Object Relations Therapy: Using the Relationship.* London: W.W. Norton.

Charles, M. and Stevenson, O. (1990) *Multidisciplinary is Different: Child Protection Working Together, Part II: Sharing Perspectives.* Nottingham: Nottingham University.

Claxton, G. (ed) (1986) *Beyond Therapy.* London: Wisdom.

Coker, N. (ed) (2001) *Racism in Medicine: An Agenda for Change.* London: King's Fund.

Commission for Racial Equality (CRE) (1989) *Race Equality in Social Services Departments: A Survey of Opportunity Policies.* London: CRE.

Commission for Racial Equality (1992) *Race Relations Code of Practice in Primary Health Care Services.* London: CRE.

Cooper, R. (1984) 'A note on the biological concept of race and its application in epidemiological research.' *American Heart Journal 108*, 715–723.

Coward, B. and Dattani, P. (1993) 'Race, identity and culture.' In K.N. Dwivedi (ed) *Group Work with Children and Adolescents: A Handbook.* London: Jessica Kingsley.

Dalal, F.N. (1993) '"Race" and Racism: an attempt to organize difference.' *Group Analysis 26*, 277–293.

Dalal, F. (1998) *Taking the Group Seriously.* London: Jessica Kingsley.

D'Ardenne, P. and Mahtani, A. (1999) *Transcultural Counselling in Action*, 2nd edn. London: Sage.

Dayal, N. (1990) 'Psychotherapy services for minority ethnic communities in the NHS: a psychotherapist's view.' *Midland Journal of Psychotherapy 11*, 28–37.

De Silva, P. (1984) 'Buddhism and behaviour modification.' *Behaviour Research and Therapy 22*, 6, 661–678.

Devereux, G. (1953) 'Cultural factors in psychoanalytic therapy.' *Journal of American Psychoanalytic Association 1*, 629–655.

Dwivedi, K.N. (1980) 'Indian notions in counselling situations.' *BAC Counselling News 32*, 10–14.

Dwivedi, K.N. (1990) 'Purification of mind by Vipassana meditation.' In J. Crook and D. Fontana (eds) *Space in Mind.* Shaftesbury: Element.

Dwivedi, K.N. (1993a) 'Coping with unhappy children who are from ethnic minorities.' In V. Varma (ed) *Coping with Unhappy Children.* London: Cassell.

Dwivedi, K.N. (1993b) 'Confusion and underfunctioning in children.' In V.P. Varma (ed) *How and Why Children Fail.* London: Jessica Kingsley.

Dwivedi, K.N. (1993c) 'Emotional development.' In K.N. Dwivedi (ed) *Groupwork with Children and Adolescents.* London: Jessica Kingsley.

Dwivedi, K.N. (1994a) 'Mental cultivation (meditation) in Buddhism.' *Psychiatric Bulletin 18*, 503–504.

Dwivedi, K.N. (1994b) 'The Buddhist perspective in mental health.' *Open Mind 70*, 20–22.

Dwivedi, K.N. (1994c) 'Social structures that support or undermine ethnic minority groups: eastern value systems.' *Context 20*, 11–12.

Dwivedi, K.N. (1996a) 'Children from ethnic minorities.' In V. Varma (ed) *Coping with Children in Stress.* Aldershot: Arena.

Dwivedi, K.N. (1996b) 'Race and the child's perspective.' In R. Davie, G. Upton and V. Varma (eds) *The Voice of the Child: A Handbook for Professionals.* London: Falmer.

Dwivedi, K.N. (1996c) 'Services to meet the mental health needs of children.' *Child Psychiatry On-Line* http://www.priory.com/journals/psych/service.htm

Dwivedi, K.N. (1997a) 'Management of anger and some eastern stories.' In K.N. Dwivedi (ed) *The Therapeutic Use of Stories.* London: Routledge.

Dwivedi, K.N. (ed) (1997b) *The Therapeutic Use of Stories.* London: Routledge.

Dwivedi, K.N. (1999) 'Editorial.' *Context 44*, 2–3.

Dwivedi, K.N. (ed) (2000a) *Post-traumatic Stress Disorder in Children and Adolescents.* London: Whurr.

Dwivedi, K.N. (2000b) 'Cultural aspects of feeding: some illustrations from the Indian culture.' In A. Southall and A. Schwartz (eds) *Feeding Problems in Children.* Oxford: Radcliffe Medical Press.

Dwivedi, K.N. (2000c) 'Therapeutic powers of narratives and stories.' *Context 47*, 11–12.

Dwivedi, K.N. and Prasad, K.M.R. (2000) 'The Hindu, Jain and Buddhist communities: beliefs and practices.' In A. Lau (ed) *South Asian Children and Adolescents in Britain.* London: Whurr.

Dwivedi, K.N. and Varma, V.P. (eds) (1997a) *A Handbook of Childhood Anxiety Management.* Aldershot: Ashgate.

Dwivedi, K.N. and Varma, V.P. (eds) (1997b) *Depression in Children and Adolescents.* London: Whurr.

Epstein, M. (1995) *Thoughts without Thinker: Psychotherapy from a Buddhist Perspective.* New York: Basic Books.

Fernando, S. (1988) *Race and Culture in Psychiatry.* London: Croom Helm.

Fromm, E., Suzuki, D.T. and De Martino, R. (1974) *Zen Buddhism and Psychoanalysis.* London: Souvenir.

Gans, J.S. (1994) 'Indirect communication as a therapeutic technique: a novel use of countertransference.' *American Journal of Psychotherapy 48*, 1, 120–140.

Goldberg, D. and Hodes, M. (1992) 'The poison of racism and the self poisoning of adolescents.' *Journal of Family Therapy 14*, 51–67.

Halstead, M. (1988) *Education, Justice and Cultural Diversity: An Examination of the Honeyford Affair 1984–85.* London: Falmer.

Hatcher, R. (1989) 'Anti-racist education after the Act.' *Multicultural Teaching 7*, 3, 24–27.

Heider, F. (1946) 'Attitudes and cognitive organization.' *Journal of Psychology 21*, 107–112.

Heider, F. (1958) *The Psychology of Interpersonal Relations.* New York: John Wiley.

Hill, A.V.S. (1989) 'Molecular markers of ethnic groups.' In J.K. Cruickshank and D.G. Beevers (eds) *Ethnic Factors in Health and Disease.* London: Wright.

Hillier, S.A., Loshak, R., Rahman, S. and Marks, F. (1994) 'An evaluation of child psychiatric services for Bangladeshi parents.' *Journal of Mental Health 3*, 327–337.

Home Office (1999) *The Stephen Lawrence Inquiry: Report of an Inquiry by Sir William Macpherson of Cluny.* London: The Stationery Office.

Horne, A.M. and Sayger, T.V. (1990) Treating Conduct and Oppositional Disorders in Children. Oxford: Pergamon.

Kabat-Zinn, J. (1996) *Full Catastrophe Living.* London: Piatkus.

Kemps, C.R. (1997) 'Approaches to working with ethnicity and cultural differences.' In K.N. Dwivedi (ed) *Enhancing Parenting Skills: A Guide for Professionals Working with Parents.* Chichester: John Wiley.

Krause, I.B. (1998) *Therapy across Culture.* London: Sage.

Kwee, M.G.T. and Holdstock, T.L. (eds) (1996) *Western and Buddhist Psychology: Clinical Perspectives.* Delft: Eburon.

Lau, A. (ed) (2000) *South Asian Children and Adolescents in Britain.* London: Whurr.

Leisten, R. and Richardson, J. (1994) *Access to Health: A Minority Ethnic Perspective.* Northampton: Nene College.

MacCarthy, B. and Craissati, J. (1989) 'Ethnic differences in response to adversity: a community sample of Bangladesh and their indigenous neighbours.' *Journal of Social Psychiatry and Psychiatric Epidemiology 24,* 196–201.

McGoldrick, M. (1982) 'Ethnicity and family therapy.' In M. McGoldrick, J.K. Pearce and J. Giardano (eds) *Ethnicity and Family Therapy.* New York: Guilford.

McGoldrick, M., Pearce, J. and Giardano, J. (eds) (1982) *Ethnicity and Family Therapy.* New York: Guilford.

McKenzie, K.J. and Crowcroft, N.S. (1994) 'Race, ethnicity, culture and science: researchers should understand and justify their use of ethnic groupings.' *British Medical Journal 309,* 6950, 286–287.

Mares, P., Henley, A. and Baxter, C. (1985) *Healthcare in Multicultural Britain.* Cambridge: Health Education Council and National Extension College.

Massey, I. (1991) *More than Skin Deep: Developing Anti-racist Multi-cultural Education in Schools.* London: Hodder and Stoughton.

Mause, L. De (ed) (1976) *The History of Childhood.* New York: Souvenir.

Mausner, J.S. and Dramer, S. (1985) *Epidemiology: An Introductory Text.* Philadelphia, PA: Saunders.

Mehra, H. (1998) 'The permanent exclusion of Asian pupils in secondary schools in central Birmingham.' *Multicultural Teaching 17,* 1, 42–48.

Mistry, T. and Brown, A. (1997) *Race and Groupwork.* London: Whiting and Birch.

National Library of Medicine (1994) Medline Silver Plater 3.11 CD-ROM. *Medline Express 1989–1.* Bethesda, MD: National Library of Medicine.

Ogden, T. (1979) 'On projective identification.' *International Journal of Psychoanalysis 60*, 357–373.

Pande, S.K. (1968) 'The mystique of western psychotherapy: an eastern interpretation.' *Journal of Nervous and Mental Diseases 146*, 6, 425–432.

Patel, V. (1994) 'The cross-cultural assessment of depression.' *Focus on Depression 2*, 1, 5–8.

Perelberg, R.J. (1992) 'Familiar and unfamiliar types of family structure: towards a conceptual framework.' In J. Kareem and R. Littlewood (eds) *Intercultural Therapy: Themes, Interpretations and Practices*. Oxford: Blackwell Scientific.

Pickering, J. (ed) (1997) *The Authority of Experience*. Richmond, Surrey: Curzon.

Pugh, G. (1994) 'Foreword.' In I. Siraj-Blatchford, *The Early Years: Laying the Foundations for Racial Equality*. Stoke-on-Trent: Trentham.

Reat, N.R. (1990) *Origins of Indian Psychology*. Berkeley, CA: Asian Humanities Press.

Ritterman, M. (1983) *Using Hypnosis in Family Therapy*. London: Jossey-Bass.

Roland, A. (1980) 'Psychoanalytic perspectives on personality development in India.' *International Review of Psychoanalysis 1*, 73–87.

Rosenbaum, R. (1998) *Zen and the Heart of Psychotherapy*. Philadelphia, PA: Brunner Mazel.

Roys, P. (1988) 'Social services.' In A. Bhat, R. Carr-Hill and S. Ohri (eds) *Britain's Black Population: A New Perspective*, 2nd edn. The Radical Statistics Race Group. Aldershot: Gower.

Sashidharan, S.P. (2001) 'Institutional racism in British psychiatry.' *Psychiatric Bulletin 25*, 244–247.

Schwartz, J.M. (1998) *A Return to Innocence*. New York: HarperCollins.

Smith, J. (1989) 'Anti-racist practice after the Act: what are the ways forward?' *Multicultural Teaching 7*, 3.

Smith, M.G. (1986) 'Pluralism, race and ethnicity in selected African countries.' In J. Rex and D. Mason (eds) *Theories of Race and Ethnic Relations*. Cambridge: Cambridge University Press.

Sue, D.W. and Sue, D. (1990) *Counselling the Culturally Different*. New York: John Wiley.

Thomas, A. and Sillen, S. (1979) *Racism and Psychiatry*. New York: Citadel.

Tylor, E.B. (1871) *Primitive Culture*. London: John Murray.

Welwood, J. (ed) (1985) *Awakening the Heart: East/West Approaches to Psychotherapy*. Boston, MA: Shambhala.

Wright, C. (1992) 'Early education: multiracial primary school classrooms.' In D. Gill, B. Mayor and M. Blair (eds) *Racism and Education*. London: Sage.

Chapter 2

Culture and Personality

Kedar Nath Dwivedi

Every society reproduces its culture – its norms, its underlying
assumptions, its mode of organising experience – in the
individual, in the form of personality. (Lasch 1980, p.34)

Introduction: Perspective of difference and difference of perspectives

There has been a great deal written in western anthropological literature
about human differences. In the past this was heavily influenced by the
tradition of 'environmental humouralism'. Such a theory assumed that
different groups developed their characteristic inborn temperaments
due to living for long periods in different geographical environments.
Thus during the mid-eighteenth century Linnaeus divided humankind
into four major races around an implicit geographical wheel of colour
and other morphological features and temperament. Accordingly these
were: Americanus (rufus, cholericus, rectus) in the west, Europaeus
(albus, sanguineus, torosus) in the north, Asiaticus (luridus,
melancholicus, rigidus) in the east and Afer (niger, phlegmaticus, laxus)
in the south (Marsella and White 1982). Although the concept of 'race'
as an objective category is essentially incorrect and has very little credibility, racial categorization or the process of racialization continued.
'The colonizer used various myths, phantasies and ideologies to maintain a division between the colonizer and the colonized' (Dalal 1993,
p.277). This led to an explosive proliferation of anthropological studies.
Ethnology became a branch of anthropology that studied racial characteristics. The science of determining the strength of the faculties by the
size and shape of the skull was called phrenology. Such pseudo-scientific

speculations continued throughout the nineteenth century and even into the twentieth century.

In the twentieth century, however, an alternative explanation of human differences began to be put forward in terms of 'cultural determinism'. Thus in the aftermath of a world war, a 'culture and personality movement' was born in the context of a multi-ethnic make-up of twentieth-century North American society. By the 1950s, it too came under severe attack as the same racial prejudices had continued in the guise of cultural determinism. Vernon's (1969) survey of culture and intelligence is a typical example of such a Eurocentric approach. He concludes:

> Cultural groups and subgroups are exceedingly varied, and so also must be their effects on the intellectual growth of their members. A number of attempted classifications or typologies are examined, and it seems reasonable to regard the Puritan ethic of the western middle class as producing the greatest development of intelligence, in contrast, both to western lower class and to the 'less civilised' cultures. (Vernon 1969, p.219)

There has now been a revival of interest in culture, society, self, personhood and personality connections and a renaissance in cross-cultural formulations of these relationships. The 'old culture and personality movement' (Stocking 1986) was essentially Eurocentric, while the 'new culture and personality' approach aims to go beyond Eurocentrism by attempting to understand cultures and personality from indigenous ideological perspectives and explore the ways in which culturally contrasting people conceptualize their human nature.

> People around the world do not all think alike. Nor are the differences in thought that do exist necessarily to be explained by reference to differences or 'deficits' in cognitive processing skills, intellectual motivation, available information, or linguistic resources. It is well known in cognitive science that what one thinks about can be decisive for how one thinks (e.g. Wason and Johnson-Laird 1972). What's not yet fully appreciated is that the relationship between what one thinks about (e.g. other people) and how one thinks (e.g. 'contexts and cases') may be mediated by the world premise to which one is committed (e.g. holism) and by the metaphors by which one lives (Lakoff and Johnson 1980). (Shweder and Bourne 1982, p.133)

In the past, 'culture' had been defined as 'that complex whole which includes knowledge, belief, art, law, custom, and any other capabilities and habits acquired by man as a member of society' (Tylor 1871, p.1). Now there is a greater emphasis on the cultural worldview. Geertz (1973), in fact, conceptualizes culture as a 'web of meaning'.

> That people lose control over their lives, that people become depressed, unhappy and withdraw into a world of their own, unbounded by constraints of time. space and reality, that people abandon their will to live, seek oblivion in alcohol, resort to uncontrollable and meaningless acts of cruelty and violence, that people are haunted by feelings of guilt, remorse, fear and shame, are all common human experiences which exist around us. The problem is not that these problems do not exist; they exist everywhere. The problem is *how* one construes them meaningfully. For it is the construing of an experience, its interpretation, and the meaning one assigns to the experience which involves making all sorts of assumptions. *It is those assumptions which often are culture-specific.* Not the experience itself as has been mistakenly assumed by the cultural relativists. (Laungani 1992, p.233, original emphasis)

In order to illustrate the above, this chapter focuses, by way of an example, on differences mainly between eastern, particularly Indian, and western cultures.

> In many western societies, 'successful' families are signified by the presence of dominant cultural values of independence, autonomy, self-determination, separation, individuation, self-expression, self-sufficiency, assertiveness and competition, clear and direct verbal communication (Dwivedi and Varma 1996; Lau 1996). In other societies i.e. Eastern Europe, the East and Far East, these values would be an anathema and run counter to moral and religious values. Instead, family life stresses loyalty, interdependence, harmony, co-operation, and non-verbal and indirect communication through the use of symbols (Lau 1996). As mentioned earlier, professionals observe through their own cultural filters, and therefore should be attentive as to how and why they need to influence the skills of parents with whom they have become involved. (Kemp 1997, p.67)

Self and freedom from self

From the eastern, particularly Buddhist perspective, the existence of a deep-rooted sense of 'self' is not only a product of illusory processes but also the root cause of all our suffering. All physical and mental phenomena are transient in nature; however, the rapidity of their change creates an illusion of continuity, solidity, entity and agency or a sense of self. Working towards enlightenment means attempting to cut through these illusory processes in order to achieve freedom from 'self' (Dwivedi and Prasad 2000). Although the Buddhist concept of *anatta* (lack of self) and the Hindu core doctrine of *atman* (soul or self, but not as identified with body, sense or mind) 'are mutually exclusive and polarised, *both of them together* radically contrast with any of the western perceptions of the self, from the Judaeo-Christian to the general systems and cybernetics-informed notions of self' (Bharati 1985, p.203, original emphasis). Individuation, separation and autonomy are actually rather privileged in western and Eurocentric cultural contexts.

> In many other cultural contexts this is perceived as a primitive mode of relating and various cultures through milennia of maturation have developed ways of transcending such naturally occuring narcissistic tendencies (Dwivedi 1994 a, b, 1995a, 1996a). However, because of the emphasis in Western psychological and sociological theorising on the importance of individuation and autonomy, this transcendence has itself been labelled as primitive and pathological enmeshment. This can be clearly seen in the family therapy literature... Di Nicola (1997) outlines how the 'myth of independence' influences family therapy and psychiatric theory and practice. (Barratt *et al.* 1999, p.6)

'In Western cultures, individuality is the prime value and relatedness is secondary in the sense that a person has the choice of whether to make certain relationships with other entities or not' (Tamura and Lau, 1992, p.330). As it is essentially a work and activity-centred culture, relationships such as marital, family, friends, colleagues and so on have to be developed by working for these on the basis of shared commanalities (Pande 1968). Relationships of the individual to society are viewed from an 'egocentric' perspective, for example focusing on the reproduction of individuals rather than on the reproduction of relationships with an emphasis on separateness, clear boundaries, individuality and autonomy within the relationships. In eastern cultures there is a 'sociocentric' conception of these relationships and a person is seen as a part of the embedded interconnectedness of relationships (Shweder and Bourne 1982; Strathern 1992).

Parsons (1964) pointed out that the bridge between personality and culture is the super ego acquired through the process of social interaction. Hsu (1985, p.27) emphasizes that 'meaning of being human is found in interpersonal relationships, since no human being exists alone' and criticizes the western concept of personality as rather restrictive. Such a concept, instead of seeing the individual in a web of interpersonal relationships, focuses on the individual's deep core of complexes and anxieties. In fact, the nature of the interpersonal relationships, in such a viewpoint, is seen merely as indicators of the expression of this core.

Self-control from the western point of view is seen to come from within the person, while the eastern perspective has a more ecological view considering the individual in a wider system of cosmic (including both physical and social) relationships as evident in the humoural theory of Ayurvedic medicine (Krause 1995; Lutz 1988). The eastern view of person is, therefore, essentially transactional and transformational:

> Persons – single actors – are not thought in South Asia to be 'individual', that is, indivisible, bounded units, as they are in much of western social and psychological theory as well as in common sense. Instead, it appears that persons are generally thought by South Asians to be 'dividual' or divisible. To exist, dividual persons absorb heterogeneous material influences. They must also give out from themselves particles of their own coded substances – essences, residues, or other active influences – that may then reproduce in others something of the nature of the persons in whom they have originated. (Marriott 1976, p.111)

Culture and child-rearing practices

Trawick writes: 'child rearing is one area of life in which cultural, social, psychological and biological patterns converge and find simultaneous expression in single acts' (Trawick 1990, p.49). As childhood experiences do influence the shaping of personality and also determine the likelihood of the nature and extent of its disorders, and as the cultural and environmental factors influence child-rearing practices, culture has an enormous influence over personality through child-rearing practices. Minturn and Lambert (1964), emphasizing the role of environmental factors on child-rearing, suggest that child-training practices are based mainly upon conditions in the natural and social environment that make them necessary for survival. These practices are then rationalized and justified by a structure of beliefs and values designed to support them.

> It now appears that the pressures impinging upon the growing child are much more in the nature of by-products of the horde of apparently irrelevant considerations that impinge upon the parents. These considerations of household composition, size of family, work load etc., determine the time and energy that mothers have available to care for children. They determine the range and content of mother–child relations and the context in which these relations must take place. (Minturn and Lambert 1964, p.291)

Thus environmental factors can be responsible, at least to some extent, for shaping the cultural ideologies of the place, but the cultural ideologies can take on a life of their own and continue despite the changes in the environment (vestigial evolution of behaviours) and can have an important influence on shaping the environment. To think of cultural ideologies only as a product of environmental factors would be extremely naive and an insult to the human capacity for considering and shaping one's social structures and human welfare. In fact, cultural ideologies greatly influence the way one interprets and responds to the environment and to the personal experiences.

Cultural assumptions and ideologies have an enormous impact on child-rearing practices and in any stable society there is also a reciprocity between the social structures of child rearing and that of other institutions governing adult lives. Child-rearing practices are in a way the most important manifestations of cultural assumptions.

Independence and dependability

Roland (1980) highlights differences in early child-rearing practices between the western and Indian cultures. Since the Industrial Revolution in western culture, 'independence' is viewed as the cherished ideal and 'dependence' is seen as a despicable state. Although the process of colonization meant making others dependent, being dependent began to be seen as a stigma, a shameful state of being and the cause of a grave social problem. The parents are therefore often at pains to make their children independent as soon as possible. Similarly professionals working with their clients consider that fostering independence is the most important aspect of their work. Children are expected to have their own voices, preferably different from that of their parents (Dwivedi 1996b). For adolescents, leaving home is considered to be a very important developmental task (Lau 1990).

In contrast, eastern cultures place more emphasis on 'dependability'. The parents are usually at pains to ensure that their children grow up in an atmosphere where parents are a model of dependability. Such a goal leads to an atmosphere of indulgence, physical closeness, common sleeping arrangements, immediate gratification of physical and emotional needs and a rather prolonged babyhood. From the western point of view this could be seen as a culture of spoilt children. However, it leads to the creation of very strong bonds and provides an inner sense of security and strength. As separation experiences for very young children are considered traumatic and therefore avoided, there is very little need for transitional objects. The care-givers intend to be always there. Similarly the commercial play materials are not seen as important, as the purpose of play and interpersonal interactions of parenting is to create a feeling of contentment rather than achievement. The young ones are there to be loved just for 'being' there rather than 'doing' the right things. Kumar (1992), when visiting India, was most moved by their attitude towards children. 'Indians have a loving and tolerant attitude towards children even under the most trying circumstances' (Kumar 1992, p.1582).

> I once told the grandmother next door that in the West children sleep separately from their parents right from birth. Ammaji threw up her arms in horror. 'The poor little darlings! They must be so frightened, all by themselves. A child should sleep with his parents until he is at least five years old'... The practice of young children sharing the parents' bed is widespread in Eastern countries. Dr Spock would have been horrified. Dire consequences were predicted for children who sleep in the same bed with their parents. I've never observed any such consequences; in fact, Indian children are generally well adjusted and happy. Thumb sucking is rare, as are night terrors or sleepwalking. Indian toddlers never seem to need a favourite blanket or teddy bear to take to bed – why should they when they can cuddle up to their mothers at night? Perhaps the grandmother next door is right: children in Western countries are frightened of sleeping alone, and they try to tell us by

thumb-sucking, teddy bears and sleepwalking. (Kumar 1992, p.1582)

Similarly DeVos (1985), describing child-rearing practices in Japanese culture, writes:

> Mothers tend to 'suffer' their children rather than to forbid or inhibit their behaviour by using verbal chastisement or even physical punishment. The child, while this form of discipline is going on, learns gradually the vulnerability of the loved one and that control of an offender is exercised not by doing any thing to the offender but by self-control. (DeVos 1985, p.155)

Nuclear and extended family dynamics in relation to proactive training in overcoming narcissism

Another manifestation of cultural embedding of interconnectedness of relationships is the value placed upon extended family life. For example, in India most people spend the formative years of their early childhood in an extended family setting. The cultural ideal of filial loyalty and fraternal solidarity stipulates common economic and social life, common residence, ritual activities and cooking arrangements. The joint celebration of religious festivals, family rituals and traditional ceremonies within the extended family circle helps to consolidate the family ties further. In the pure form of 'extended family' the brothers (along with their wives and children) live together with their parents. Nowadays in actual practice, this pure form of extended family is not so common. However, its variants such as the 'joint family', where some of the brothers (with their wives and children) live together without their parents, and the 'intergenerational family', where the parents live together with one of their grown-up children (and their spouse and children), are still very common. In any case, for most children, one or other form of extended family is the immediate 'society' which they encounter as they grow up and the indulgent attitude towards them is pervasive throughout the extended family circle.

> One might assume that this indulgent approach to child behaviour would result in very naughty children. Yet it doesn't, Indian children are generally well behaved. My theory is that Indian children get so much attention from a host of loving relatives that they do not need to act out for attention. (Kumar 1992, p.1582)

It is the cultural ideal of mastering narcissism that can be best achieved through growing up in an extended family system. On the other hand, it is impossible for an extended family system to be sustained without proactive training in mastering narcissism through extended family life. As the biggest danger to an extended family is the possibility of its fracuturing along the boundaries around nuclear units because the natural tendency of love is to be concentrated towards one's own, an extra ideological effort is required to redirect it across the nuclear family boundaries.

> For the strength and cohesion of the extended family depend upon certain psychosocial diffusion; it is essential that nuclear cells do not build up within the family, or at the very least, that these cells do not involve intense emotional loyalties that potentially exclude other family members and their interest. Thus, the principles of Indian family life demand that a father be restrained in the presence of his own son and divide his interest and support equally among his own and his brother's sons. (Kakar 1981, p.131)

Trawick (1990) describes how in an extended Tamil family that she studied, the mother first fed all the other children while her own son whimpered. Only when others had been served did she serve her own son. Trawick also noticed how repeated efforts had to be made to encourage children to share food and play materials in order to foster love between them across nuclear units.

> Annan would often seat the two boys opposite each other on his two knees with a single toy between them, that he tried to make them share. When the two boys went out with their mothers, each woman would carry the other's son. The mothers themselves shared the kind of love that they hoped their sons would share... All of them, including my own, were 'our children', and if I needed to distinguish between them, I should refer to them by name. In the extreme, this mixture of yours and mine into ours became reversal again – mine were called yours, and yours mine. So when I wrote to Ayya's sister Porutcelvi that my second child had been born, she wrote back, 'I can't wait to see my new son'. (Trawick 1990, pp.52–58)

One of the cultural forces that also helps prevent fracturing of extended families along nuclear lines is the strongly held ideology in the Indian culture that 'love grows in hiding'. Therefore, in order to make true love grow properly, it must be kept hidden. Thus, a mother's love for her child (the strongest and the most highly valued of all loves in the Indian culture) must be kept hidden and contained. Many women, therefore, show great affection for others' children but avoid (at least in public) expressing intense love for their own children. Some may even spurn their own children, forcing their affection outward. Sometimes it can take the form of downgrading the loved one, especially a very precious child, for example by giving them a very ugly name, or the mother pretending not to care for the child. Similarly in the marital relationship there is a mutual avoidance between spouses at least in public including the avoidance of mentioning the spouse's name.

It is not only the boundaries around the nuclear units that are subjected to cultural editing but also those in gender relationships and in intergenerational hierarchical structures that are transformed by the cultural influences in a paradoxical manner. Although the wife of a family patriarch pays

> a formal, and often perfunctory deference to her husband, especially in front of strangers, she may exercise considerable domestic power, not merely among the other women of the household, but with her husband, and she often makes many of the vital decisions affecting the family's interests. (Kakar 1981, p.118)

Similarly the intergenerationally hierarchical relationships are no exceptions to this paradoxical reality. Trawick (1990, p.42) writes, 'When I told her it was an American custom to let people lead their own lives, she said simply, "Tappu" (that is a mistake). After some time I learned that if you cared about people, you would interfere'. In fact, the most important qualitiy of the 'head' or the superior of the family is that of acting in a nurturing way so that the 'subordinates' either anticipate his or her wishes or accept them without questioning. It is emancipation and renunciation through which the individuals within the family establish the superiority of their love and aim to express it in the form of *metta* or loving kindness, *mudita* or empathic joy, *karuna* or compassion and *upekkha* or equanimity (Dwivedi 1990, 1992, 1994c). The paradox of love turns the acts of humility into pride, of servitude into respect, and the master into a slave.

> Thus, although family relationships are generally hierarchical in structure, the mode of the relationship is characterised by an almost maternal nurturing on the part of the superior, by filial respect and compliance on the part of the subordinate and by a mutual sense of highly personal attachment. (Kakar 1981, p.119)

The other social institutions too, in such a culture, reflect the hierarchical structure of the extended family system sustained by the complementary mode of nurturing. Child-rearing practices aimed at fostering dependability, rather than independence, attempt to create an atmosphere whereby children can model upon their parents and grow up to become model dependable parents themselves for their children and also to look after their elderly parents. The twelfth blessing of the Mangala Sutta, in Buddhism, is about passing on one's wealth to one's children and the eleventh blessing is about taking care of one's parents (Jureegate 1993).

> The concept of long term intergenerational recipriocity is communicated to children at an early age, in a very direct and explicit manner … The idea that parent–child reciprocity involves a life-span calculus was prominent in these people's thoughts about old age. To make one's home with adult children was not associated with emotions like shame or guilt, such as have been reported for American elderly people unable to conform to our cultural ideal of self-reliance and independent living in the later years of life. On the contrary, these Indian elders typically displayed pride in having offspring who could and did support them in comfort with grace and loving concern'. (Vatuk 1990, pp.66–68)

In western culture, the ideal is that of self-reliance and independent living even during the later years of life. The parents do not want to be a burden on their children's independence in their old age. An elderly person usually thinks that the most important thing in their life is that they do not become a burden on anyone as becoming dependent has acquired a rather prejorative connatation. To make a home with one's grown-up children is therefore associated with intense shame and guilt. The 'fear of dependency in old age is rooted in a deeply inculcated need for self-reliance and self-sufficiency, not only to retain the respect of others but, most important, to retain respect for oneself' (Vatuk 1990, p.84). Children too do not think of looking after their parents in their old age because they do not see their parents looking after their own parents.

When social values dictate that the children should not be expected to look after their parents in their old age, they should not come asking for money either.

Cultural construction, regulation and expression of emotion

As pointed out by Bateson, Mead and Benedict in the 1930s, emotions are culturally and socially constructed (see Krause 1998). The western construction of emotion has been in opposition to rational logic. It is also linked with its construction of gender (e.g. men as rational and women as emotional) (Barratt *et al.* 1999). On the other hand, the Indian construction of emotion according to the theory of *Rasa* (established several millennia ago and outlined in Bharat's famous *Treatise on Dramatology* of 200 BC) is in terms of extract, flavour, essence or juice. The aesthetic forms can act as catalysts and activate, refine or transform our already present emotion (de Bary *et al.* 1958; Dwivedi and Gardner 1997).

> In the Indian culture, as early as the sixth century BC a systematised and coherent theory of consciousness became available, something that did not begin to happen in western culture until the nineteenth century AD (Reat 1990). In the eastern way of thinking there is no state of emotionlessness, as there is no state of weatherlessness; however, these emotions are normally preconscious and we become aware of them only when they intensify and break through our consciousness. Eastern meditative practices of expanding one's consciousness aim to get in touch with otherwise preconscious emotions. (Dwivedi 2000a, p.1)

Not only the construction of emotion but also its location, meaning, expression and maturation may vary from culture to culture. For example, according to the theory of Rasa, emotions are grounded not only in the self but also in play, music, food and scent. Food, in such a cultural context, contains not only nutrients but also emotion and morality. Its purity (in an emotional and moral sense) may in fact be more important than its nutrient value (Dwivedi 2000b). Parkes (1998) describes the cultural differences in the emotional expression of grief and the price that has to be paid for its repression.

There are at least four aspects of emotional development described; emotional differentiation, self-regulation, desomatization and utilization. These developments among other things are influenced greatly by culture and parenting (Dwivedi 1993a, 1996c, 1997a).

> Human beings by virtue of their shared genetic heritage, are equipped with such phylogenetically adapted response packages from infancy. These patterns of emotional responses change in various ways (such as self-regulation and differentiation) in the context of maturation, development, socialisation and training. The responses contain within them a propensity towards certain actions that regulate the situations that trigger them. (Dwivedi 1997b, p.3)

Concepts and experience of emotional distress and disorder (e.g. anxiety, depression etc.) are therefore also linked to culture.

> One of the child's major responsibilities is to learn to adjust to the group or groups of which the child is the member. Depending on the ease or difficulty with which success is achieved in adjustment or failure, anxiety may be aroused. In other words, culture could, in some respects, be considered responsible for anxiety. Change may take place over centuries or even within a decade. For Sinha (1962), culture is basic to anxiety. (Lokare 1997, pp.201–202)

Similarly, certain circumstances, depending upon the cultural context and their mediation of meaning, may lead to a recursive shrinking repertoire of responses, a state of depression, in which the spiralling loop becomes narrow and constricted over time (Lewis and Miezitis 1992).

Differences in child-rearing practices may also be in relation to the training in dealing with one's own feelings and in becoming sensitive to others' feelings. DeVos (1980, 1985), describing Japanese culture, emphasizes their 'field independent' cognitive style on the one hand and a strong evidence of conforming behaviour in school and elsewhere, and a refinement of interpersonal concerns with acute sensitivity to what others are thinking, on the other.

Roland (1980) observes that in Indian culture, as toddlers mature and receive training in urinary and faecal continence, they are also expected to develop emotional continence and a capacity gradually to self-regulate their affect (Dwivedi 1993a). Unlike the western ideal of self-expression, eastern cultures aim to express feelings in such a way that it is not harmful either to oneself or to others. This, therefore, influences the style of communication placing more value on indirect and metaphorical communication rather than direct and clear communication as emphasized in western culture. One of the most important aspects of spiritual training is in better handling of one's feelings through expanding one's consciousness, getting in touch with one's emotions at the subtlest levels, accepting them, discerning their transitory nature and transmuting them by harnessing their energy to one's advantage, sometimes described metaphorically as 'tiger taming' (Rimpoche 1987).

Direct and indirect communication

There is a great value placed upon clear and direct communication within western culture. In a household one can imagine a scenario where mother is on the telephone, father has just arrived home and is reading a newspaper and their daughter walks towards him with a runny nose. Father is feeling neglected and angry with his wife on the telephone for going on and on for ages. However, he does have a few options about the way he communicates his feelings e.g. to be direct or indirect, clear or masked. For example he may (1) shout at his daughter to wipe her nose (*indirect*); (2) say to his wife: 'What the hell is going on in this house?' (*direct but masked*); (3) communicate to his wife exactly what he feels and why (*direct and clear*). The last option would be the most culturally congruent.

The eastern emphasis on self-regulation of emotion, empathy and avoiding hurting others' feelings requires development of a style that places more value on indirect, hypothetical and metaphorical communication turning it into an art form (Dwivedi 1993b, 1996b). Similarly, the postmodern therapeutic framework has begun to place a greater value on indirect communication clearly acknowledging and utilizing its enormous therapeutic and protective powers (Bowen and Robinson 1999; Dwivedi 1997c, 2000c; Smith and Nylund 1997).

Child development

Various cultural components, it seems, mutually support each other, such as the emphasis on dependability, extended family life, indirect communication, interdependence and so on in eastern culture and the emphasis on independence, nuclear family life and direct and clear communication in western culture. Together their impact on child development is bound to be substantial.

In a study of cultural values and traditions influencing the development of coping styles of 6–14 year olds in Thailand and the USA, McCarty *et al.* (1999) found support for a model of coping development in which culture and stressor characteristics interact, with societal differences most likely to be found in situations where culture-specific norms become salient. Similarly in a study of cross-cultural coping strategies, Olah (1995) found that adolescents in European countries more frequently reported assimilative coping strategies (attempts to change the environment to their own benefit e.g. problem-focused, confrontative, task-oriented etc.) than boys and girls in India and Yemen, who preferred emotion-focused solutions (i.e. accommodative). Gilani (1999), in a study of 80 dyads of British (white) and Pakistani mothers and their adolescent daughters (age range 17–18.5 years), found that Pakistani mothers and daughters expressed more intimacy, relational harmony, connectedness and mutuality and less individuality than British mothers and daughters.

Ekblad (1988) has looked at the influence of child-rearing on aggressive behaviour in a transcultural perspective. Hackett and Hackett (1993) in their study in Manchester found more stringent expectations on the part of the Gujarati community in most of the areas of child behaviour examined, reflecting narrower and more exacting ideas of normality. This might lead one to expect more children to be labelled as deviant but the rate of disturbance was found to be lower than the English.

Personality and pathology

Personality is 'that which characterizes an individual and determines his unique adaptation to the environment' (Harsh and Schrickel 1950). As studied by the modern western psychologist, it is conceptualized as an integrated whole which can be viewed from different directions, for example, temperament, attitudes, morphology, physiology, needs, interests, aptitudes and so on. However, in studying personality, the characteristics that affect an individual's ability to get along with other people and with oneself are given greater significance. Personality features (such as types, traits, dimensions) highlight some inner consistency over time, as well as some generality, so that predictions can be made of behaviour likely to occur in a variety of contexts (Guilford 1959).

A personality can be described by its position on a number of scales or dimensions, each of which represent a trait. A person can be characterized according to the profile of different traits. There have been a large number of studies to delineate different categories of traits or personality variables. Another approach has been to classify people into a few types by thinking in terms of some central themes or styles of life (such as extroversion versus introversion) that characterize some individuals so well. Such theories of personality types have been around from ancient times and persist even today in one form or another.

For example, the Buddhist meditation masters (since the sixth century BC) taught specific meditation techniques depending upon the particular personality of the trainee. Buddhism recognizes that there are three fundamental dimensions underlying the behaviour of all unenlightened human beings in varying degrees: craving versus faith, hatred versus intelligence and confusion versus speculation. These factors condition almost everything that we do and the way we dress, relate, work, think and so on (Mann and Youd 1992). This approach resonated with the humoural theory of Ayurvedic medicine. Ayurveda has been the ancient and traditional system of medicine in India and still has an enormous influence on their day-to-day life (Rai and Dwivedi 1988). The golden period of Ayurveda corresponded with the rise of Buddhism in India (Dwivedi 1994a). In Ayurvedic medicine the humoural approach to diagnosis, treatment and health promotion is based upon three fundamental humours (*Vaat*, *Pitt* and *Kaf*) resonant with the Buddhist approach (Clifford 1984). Similarly in the Greek system of (Unani) medicine human temperaments were classified on the basis of the body humours: sanguine, phlegmatic, melancholic and choleric.

As there are a variety of approaches to comprehending the notion of personality today, there are also a variety of ways of assessing it (Vernon 1963). Such assessments can take the form of (1) unstructured or structured interviews, (2) self-report rating scales or personality inventories such as Minnesota Multiphasic Personality Inventory, Cattell's 16 PF Questionnaire, Eysenck Personality Inventory, Edwards Personal Preference Schedule, (3) projective tests such as Thematic Apperception Test, Rorschach Inkblot Test and (4) behavioural observations. In actual practice the personality inventories appear to be the most commonly used tools both for clinical and for occupational (such as the recruitment of managers with certain personality traits) purposes.

People can differ very widely as regards their profiles of personality traits but could still be regarded as normal. However, in some individuals certain traits can be sufficiently maladaptive and abnormal, constituting a 'personality disorder'. These traits can also cause enormous subjective distress.

As there are many ways of classifying personality, there are similarly many ways of classifying and assessing personality disorders. However, the classification systems based upon the *International Classification of Diseases* (ICD-10) (World Health Organization 1992) and the *Diagnostic and Statistical Manual of Mental Disorders* (DSM-IV) (American Psychiatric Association 1994) are the most commonly used.

Cultural approach to self is also reflected in pathological processes. Littlewood (1995) points out that eating disorders were once identified exclusively with western societies but when these occur among South Asian women including those living in the west, these arise as manifestations of self-renunciation rather than the western ideal of self-cherishing and fear of fatness. Lasch (1980), commenting on the recent changes within the western culture, writes:

> Every age develops its own peculiar forms of pathology, which express in exaggerated form its underlying character structure. In Freud's time, hysteria and obsessional neurosis carried to extremes the personality traits associated with the capitalist order at an earlier stage in its development – acquisitiveness, fanatical devotion to work, and a fierce repression of sexuality. In our time, the preschizophrenic, borderline, or personality disorders have attracted increasing attention, along with schizophrenia itself. (Lasch 1980, p.41)

There appears to be a rising tide of narcissistic disorders in western culture.

> We hear more and more that we live in a narcissistic society... 'Protect yourself from the demands of others and take care of yourself first'. Even where no pathological problem exists, narcissistic traits of grandiosity and idealisation are encouraged as behaviour norms... Faced with diminished sense of responsibility, more and more of us have turned inward, increasingly toward self-fulfilment... Now, however, important parts of our society regard narcissism as a goal, not a problem. Many who feel they are living according to the norms of society now end up in therapy confused over their feelings of emptiness, isolation, and desperation. (Solomon 1990, pp.30–31)

Ethnic identity and acculturation

Although the cultural ideals do influence the overall picture, in real life there are enormous variations. Colonial influences have placed varying degrees of acceptance on local practices (e.g. modes of dress and address) leading to dying out of some and adoption of other practices which are inappropriate in the context of the local climate and culture. Due to global communication and influences of other cultures and their media, it is now becoming hard for the cultural transmission of traditional values to take place smoothly whether in the east or the west, even within societies where those values actually originated. Their transmission to ethnic minority children growing up in another culture (e.g. in the west) is, therefore, much harder, as it can very easily be undermined by other cultural ideologies (Dwivedi 1993c, 1994b, 1995b).

> The sad truth is that no one can simply construct for themselves 'an identity'. Culture is both inherited and has to be recreated through experience so that it may reside within the individual in memory and feeling. It is the product of experience and history represented in individuals through our internalised parents and by the values and traditions they have passed on to us. Ethnic minority children are born into a society which often differs markedly in its social and family organization and they themselves may experience different types of care and upbringing. (Andreou 1992, pp.147–148)

The vicissitudes of crossing cultures are vividly described by Storti (1989). The process of acculturation is therefore immensely significant. A study of 506 adolescents from Vietnam, Pakistan, Turkey and Chile, living in Norway, found that family values, acculturation strategies and social group identity could account for 12–22 per cent of the observed variance in psychological well-being (symptoms outcome, life satisfaction and self-esteem). On the whole, social group identity showed the strongest predictive power (Sam 2000). Similarly, an American study (Smith *et al.* 1999) of 100 male and female early adolescents, ranging from 11 to 13 years old, from different racial/ethnic backgrounds, found that ethnic identity and self-esteem are distinct but related contributors to young people's perceptions of their ability to achieve academically, to find meaningful careers and to value prosocial means of goal attainment.

A school-based survey of 3071 students (including those of African, Mexican, Vietnamese and European descent) in a south-west metropolitan area in the USA found that a stronger sense of belonging to one's own ethnic group was associated with more positive attitudes toward out-groups (Romero and Roberts 1998).

Conclusion

Although 'culture and personality movement' as an alternative explanation of human differences was born in the aftermath of a world war, the same racial prejudices as before continued in the guise of cultural determinism. The 'new culture and personality' approach, therefore, aims to understand cultures and personality from indigenous ideological perspectives and explore the ways in which culturally contrasting people conceptualize their human nature. As an illustration, this chapter has focused on eastern, particularly Indian, and western cultures. It seems that various cultural components mutually support each other, such as the emphasis on dependability, extended family life, indirect communication, interdependence and so on in the eastern culture and the emphasis on independence, nuclear family life and direct and clear communication in the western culture. Cultural ideologies have an enormous impact on a variety of institutions and processes including parenting, psychotherapy, child development and development of psychopathology. In a multicultural society, the processes of acculturation and ethnic identity formation (also see chapters by Rodriguez *et al.* and by Banks in this volume) have significant bearing on mental health.

References

American Psychiatric Association (APA) (1994) *Diagnostic and Statistical Manual for Mental Disorders: Fourth Edition.* Washington, DC: APA.

Andreou, C. (1992) 'Inner and outer reality in children and adolescents.' In J. Kareem and R. Littlewood (eds) *Intercultural Therapy.* Oxford: Blackwell Scientific.

Barratt, S., Burck, C., Dwivedi, K., Steadman, M. and Raval, H. (1999) 'Theoretical bases in relation to race, ethnicity and culture in family therapy training.' *Context 44*, 4–12.

Bharati, A. (1985) 'The self in Hindu thought and action.' In A.J. Marsella, G. DeVos and F.L.K. Hsu (eds) *Culture and Self: Asian and Western Perspectives.* London: Tavistock.

Bowen, B. and Robinson, G. (1999) *Therapeutic Stories.* Canterbury: AFT
Publishing.

Clifford, T. (1984) *Tibetan Buddhist Medicine and Psychiatry.* Wellingborough:
Aquarian Press.

Dalal, F.N. (1993) 'Race and racism: an attempt to organise difference.' *Group
Analysis 26*, 277–293.

de Bary, W.T., Hay, S., Weiler, R. and Yarrow, A. (1958) *Sources of Indian
Tradition.* New York: Columbia University Press.

DeVos, G.A. (1980) 'Ethnic adaptation and minority status.' *Journal of
Cross-Cultural Psychology 11*, 1, 101–124.

DeVos, G.A. (1985) 'Dimensons of the self in Japanese culture.' In A.J. Marsella,
G. DeVos and F.L.K. Hsu (eds) *Culture and Self: Asian and Western Perspectives.*
London: Tavistock.

Di Nicola, Y. (1997) *A Stranger in the Family: Culture, Families and Therapy.* New
York and London: W.W. Norton.

Dwivedi, K.N. (1990) 'Purification of mind by Vipassana meditation.' In J.
Crook and D. Fontana (eds) *Space in Mind.* Shaftesbury: Elements.

Dwivedi, K.N. (1992) 'Eastern approaches to mental health.' In T. Ahmed, B.
Naidu and A. Webb-Johnson (eds) *Concepts of Mental Health in the Asian
Community.* London: Confederation of Indian organizations (UK).

Dwivedi, K.N. (1993a) 'Emotional development.' In K.N. Dwivedi (ed) *Group
Work with Children and Adolescents: A Handbook.* London: Jessica Kingsley.

Dwivedi, K.N. (1993b) 'Confusion and under-functioning in children.' In V.P
Varma (ed) *How and Why Children Fail.* London: Jessica Kingsley.

Dwivedi, K.N. (1993c) 'Coping with unhappy children who are from ethnic
minorities.' In V.P. Varma (ed) *Coping with Unhappy Children.* London:
Cassell.

Dwivedi, K.N. (1994a) 'The Buddhist perspective in mental health.' *Open Mind
70*, 20–21.

Dwivedi, K.N. (1994b) 'Social structures that support or undermine families
from ethnic minority groups: eastern value systems.' *Context 20*, 11–12.

Dwivedi, K.N. (1994c) 'Mental cultivation (meditation) in Buddhism.' *Psychiatric
Bulletin 18*, 503–504.

Dwivedi, K.N. (1995a) 'Self.' In *Working with Families in Multi-ethnic Society:
Conference Proceedings.* London: Institute of Family Therapy and Transcultural
Psychiatry Society.

Dwivedi, K.N. (1995b) 'Stress in children from ethnic minorities.' In V.P.
Varma (ed) *Coping with Stress in Children.* Aldershot: Arena.

Dwivedi, K.N. (1996a) 'Culture and personality.' In K.N. Dwivedi and V.P. Varma (eds) *Meeting the Needs of Ethnic Minority Children*. London: Jessica Kingsley.

Dwivedi, K.N. (1996b) 'Race and the child's perspective.' In R. Davie, G. Upton and V.P. Varma (eds) *The Voice of the Child: A Handbook for Professionals*. London: Falmer.

Dwivedi, K.N. (1996c) 'Facilitating the development of emotional management skills in childhood: a programme for effective self regulation of affect.' In D.R. Trent and C.A. Reed (eds) *Promotion of Mental Health, Volume 6*. Aldershot: Ashgate.

Dwivedi, K.N. (ed) (1997a) *Enhancing Parenting Skills*. Chichester: John Wiley.

Dwivedi, K.N. (1997b) 'Introduction.' In K.N. Dwivedi and V.P. Varma (eds) *Depression in Children and Adolescents*. London: Whurr.

Dwivedi, K.N. (ed) (1997c) *The Therapeutic Use of Stories*. London: Routledge.

Dwivedi, K.N. (2000a) 'Introduction.' In K.N. Dwivedi (ed) *Post-traumatic Stress Disorder in Children and Adolescents*. London: Whurr.

Dwivedi, K.N. (2000b) 'Cultural aspects of feeding: some illustrations from the Indian culture.' In A. Southall and A. Schwartz (eds) *Feeding Problems in Children*. Oxford: Radcliffe Medical Press.

Dwivedi, K.N. (2000c) 'Therapeutic powers of narratives and stories.' *Context* 47, 11–12.

Dwivedi, K.N. and Gardner, D. (1997) 'Theoretical perspectives and clinical approaches.' In K.N. Dwivedi (ed) *The Therapeutic Use of Stories*. London: Routledge.

Dwivedi, K.N. and Prasad, K.M.R. (2000) 'The Hindu, Jain and Buddhist communities: beliefs and practices.' In A. Lau (ed) *South Asian Children and Adolescents in Britain*. London: Whurr.

Dwivedi, K.N. and Varma, V.P. (eds) (1996) *Meeting the Needs of Ethnic Minority Children*. London: Jessica Kingsley.

Ekblad, S. (1988) 'Influence of child rearing on aggressive behaviour in a transcultural perspective.' *Acta Psychiatrica Scandinavica*, supplement no. 344, 78, 133–139.

Geertz, C. (1973) *The Interpretation of Cultures*. New York: Basic Books.

Gilani, N.P. (1999) 'Conflict management of mothers and daughters belonging to individualistic and collectivistic cultural backgrounds: a comparative study.' *Journal of Adolescence 22*, 853–865.

Guilford, J.P. (1959) *Personality*. New York: McGraw-Hill.

Hackett, L. and Hackett, R. (1993) 'Parental ideas of normal and deviant child behaviour: a comparison of two ethnic groups.' *British Journal of Psychiatry 162*, 353–357.

Harsh, C.M. and Schrickel, H.G. (1950) *Personality Development and Assessment.* New York: Ronald Press.

Hsu, F.L.K. (1985) 'The self in cross cultural perspective.' In A.J. Marsella, G. DeVos and F.L.K. Hsu (eds) *Culture and Self: Asian and Western Perspectives.* London: Tavistock.

Jureegate, S. (1993) 'Where there's a will.' *The Light of Peace 5*, 2, 30–31.

Kakar, S. (1981) *The Inner World: A Psychoanalytic Study of Childhood and Society in India,* 2nd edn. Delhi: Oxford University Press.

Kemp, C. (1997) 'Approaches to working with ethnicity and cultural differences.' In K.N. Dwivedi (ed) *Enhancing Parenting Skills: A Guide for Professionals Working with Parents.* Chichester: John Wiley.

Krause, I-B. (1995) 'Personhood, culture and family therapy.' *Journal of Family Therapy 17*, 363–382.

Krause, I-B. (1998) *Therapy across Culture.* London: Sage.

Kumar, K.T. (1992) 'To children with love'. *British Medical Journal 305*, 1582–1583.

Lakoff, G. and Johnson, M. (1980) *Metaphors We Live By.* Chicago: University of Chicago Press.

Lasch, C. (1980) *The Culture of Narcissism.* London: Norton (Abacus).

Lau, A. (1990) 'Psychological problems in adolescents from ethnic minorities.' *British Journal of Hospital Medicine 44*, 201–205.

Lau, A. (1996) 'Family therapy and ethnic minorities.' In K.N. Dwivedi and V.P. Varma (eds) *Meeting the Needs of Ethnic Minority Children.* London: Jessica Kingsley.

Laungani, P. (1992) 'Cultural variations in the understanding and treatment of psychiatric disorders: India and England.' *Counselling Psychology Quarterly 5*, 3, 231–244.

Lewis, M.D. and Miezitis, S. (1992) 'Emotional development and depression.' In S. Miezitis (ed) *Creating Alternatives to Depression in Schools.* Seattle, WA: Hogrefe & Huber.

Littlewood, R. (1995) 'Psychopathology and personal agency: modernity, culture change and eating disorders in South Asian societies.' *British Journal of Medical Psychology 68*, 45–63.

Lokare, V. (1997) 'Cultural aspects of anxiety in children.' In K.N. Dwivedi and V.P. Varma (eds) *A Handbook of Childhood Anxiety Management.* Aldershot: Arena/Ashgate.

Lutz, C. (1988) *Unnatural Emotions: Everyday Sentiments on a Micronesian Atoll and their Challenge to Western Theory.* Cambridge: Cambridge University Press.

McCarty, C., Weisze, J.R., Wanitramani, K., Eastman, K.L., Suwanlert, S., Chaiyasit, W. and Band, E.B. (1999) 'Culture, coping, and context: primary and secondary control among Thai and American youth.' *Journal of Child Psychology and Psychiatry 40*, 5, 809–818.

Mann, R. and Youd, R. (1992) *Buddhist Character Analysis*. Bradford on Avon: Aukana.

Marriott, McK. (1976) 'Hindu transactions: diversity without dualism.' In B. Kapferer (ed) *Transaction and Meaning: Directions in the Anthropology of Exchange and Symbolic Behaviour*. Philadelphia, PA: Institute for the Study of Human Issues.

Marsella, A.J. and White, G.M. (eds) (1982) *Cultural Conceptions of Mental Health and Therapy*. Dordrecht: Reidel.

Minturn, L. and Lambert, W.W. (1964) *Mothers of Six Cultures: Antecedents of Child Rearing*. New York: John Wiley.

Olah, A. (1995) 'Coping strategies among adolescents: A cross-cultural study.' *Journal of Adolescence 18*, 491–512.

Pande, S.K. (1968) 'The mystique of western psychotherapy: An eastern interpretation.' *Journal of Nervous and Mental Disease 46*, 425–432.

Parkes, C.M. (1998) 'Understanding grief across cultures.' *Psychiatry in Practice*, Winter, 5–8.

Parsons, T. (1964) *Social Structure and Personality*. Glencoe, IL: Free Press.

Rai, P.H. and Dwivedi, K.N. (1988) 'The value of Parhej and sick role in Indian culture.' *Journal of the Institute of Health Education 16*, 2, 56–61.

Reat, N.R. (1990) *Origins of Indian Psychology*. Berkeley, CA: Asian Humanities Press.

Rimpoche, D.A. (1987) *Taming the Tiger*. Eskdalemuir: Dzalendra.

Roland, A. (1980) 'Psychoanalytic perspectives on personality development in India.' *International Review of Psychoanalysis 1*, 73–87.

Romero, A.J. and Roberts, R.E. (1998) 'Perception of discrimination and ethnocultural variables in a diverse group of adolescents.' *Journal of Adolescence 21*, 641–656.

Sam, D.L. (2000) 'Psychological adaptation of adolescents with immigrant backgrounds.' *Journal of Social Psychology 140*, 1, 5–25.

Shweder, R.A. and Bourne, E.J. (1982) 'Does the concept of the person vary cross-culturally?' In A.J. Marsella and G.M. White (eds) *Cultural Conceptions of Mental Health and Therapy*. Dordrecht: Reidel.

Sinha, D. (1962) 'Cultural factors in emergence of anxiety.' *Eastern Anthropologist 15*, 21–37.

Smith, C. and Nylund, D. (eds) (1997) *Narrative Therapies with Children and Adolescents*. New York: Guilford.

Smith, E.P., Walker, K., Fields, L., Brookins, C.C. and Seay, R.C. (1999) 'Ethnic identity and its relationship to self-esteem, perceived efficacy and prosocial attitudes in early adolescence.' *Journal of Adolescence 22*, 867–880.

Solomon, M.F. (1990) 'Narcissistic vulnerability in marriage.' *Journal of Couples Therapy 1*, 3/4, 25–38.

Stocking, G.W. (ed) (1986) *Malinowski, Rivers, Benedict and Others: Essays on Culture and Personality.* Madison, WI: University of Winconsin Press.

Storti, C. (1989) *The Art of Crossing Cultures.* Yarmouth, ME: Intercultural Press.

Strathern, M. (1992) *After Nature: English Kinship in the Late Twentieth Century.* Cambridge: Cambridge University Press.

Tamura, T. and Lau, A. (1992) 'Connectedness versus separations: applicability of family therapy to Japanese families.' *Family Process 31*, 4, 319–340.

Trawick, M. (1990) 'The ideology of love in a Tamil family.' In O.M. Lynch (ed) *Divine Passions: The Social Construction of Emotion in India.* Berkeley, CA: University of California Press.

Tylor, E.B. (1871) *Primitive Culture.* London: John Murray.

Vatuk, S. (1990) 'To be a burden on others: dependency anxiety among the elderly in India.' In O.M. Lynch (ed) *Divine Passions: The Social Construction of Emotion in India.* Berkeley, CA: University of California Press.

Vernon, P.E. (1963) *Personality Assessment.* London: Methuen.

Vernon, P.E. (1969) *Intelligence and Cultural Environment.* London: Methuen.

Wason, P.C. and Johnson-Laird, P.W. (1972) *The Psychology of Reasoning.* London: Batsford.

World Health Organization (WHO) (1992) *The ICD-10 Classification of Mental and Behavioural Disorders: Clinical Descriptions and Diagnostic Guidelines.* Geneva: WHO.

Chapter 3

Mental Health Needs
of Ethnic Minority Children

Rajeev Banhatti and Surya Bhate

Introduction

It is now generally accepted that promoting mental health is inseparable from treating mental ill health. Hence mental health needs can be conceptualized as existing on a continuum starting from primary prevention, proceeding along secondary (detection and treatment of disorder) and ending with tertiary (rehabilitation, preventing recurrence).

When we start to think about 'mental health' needs of ethnic minority children, it is useful to develop an understanding of common or basic needs universal to any child irrespective of ethnicity and then to see the effect of ethnic minority status and any other variables on his or her development. Unfortunately, most of the western psychiatric literature has essentially evolved from an ethnocentric, mostly Eurocentric position. Hence a major task for current and coming generations of psychiatrists will consist of developing a multidimensional and flexible postmodern understanding about these issues. Though desirable, this may be a long way away. Till then maybe we need to raise awareness about our own positions as observers and the effect of our own ethnicity on what we 'construct' as 'scientific truth'.

Ethnicity is a complex concept encompassing biological (e.g. skin, eye, hair colour), psychological (sense of belonging, attitudes), social (language, cultural heritage, customs) and legal (immigration status, nationality) aspects. The categories used by the Office for National Statistics (ONS 1998) are based on an arbitrary mixture of skin colour and nationality (e.g. Black Caribbean, African and Other, Indian, Pakistani, Bangladeshi, Chinese, Other Asian, Other Other, White).

It is useful to understand the differences and parallels between different variables like race, culture, ethnicity, nationality and immigration status (McKenzie and Crowcroft 1996). Race, though scientifically not a valid concept, suggests biological characteristics while culture is the way social perceptions and norms are formed and passed from groups to individuals. Ethnicity encompasses both biological and non-biological differences between groups. Nationality and immigration status, like culture but unlike race, can change over time and so can ethnicity in some but not all aspects. Singh (1997) has rightly stressed the need for precision when using ethnicity and related terms in research.

One can generate some questions to help conceptualize something as complex as ethnicity in the context of mental health needs. What will be the mental health needs of a Muslim child growing up in India or a Hindu or Christian child in Pakistan? How will this compare with the needs of an Indian Muslim or an Indian Hindu child growing up in the UK? If we substitute London, Inverness or Llandudno in place of the UK, it is clear that the needs of all these children can in some ways be quite different depending on a complex tapestry of various biopsychosocial and legal aspects of their surroundings. Their ethnicity *per se* will be just a small variable (itself a mixture of many discrete variables) interacting and at times dependent on other variables.

In this chapter an attempt has been made to look at what we know about the effect of ethnicity, especially when associated with a minority status, on children's development, which can sometimes lead to psychopathology, and what can be done to provide for these children at individual (clinical) and group (organizational) levels. Though we have focused more on aspects specific to the UK, an attempt has been made to take into account more general process issues and lessons evident from international research findings. In addition illustrative case studies have been included.

Influence of Ethnic Minority Status on Psychosocial Development in Childhood

Ethnic minority status can be newly acquired as a result of immigration to a country where the majority have a different ethnicity or be historically derived from relocation centuries ago. Muslims or Parsis in India would be examples of the latter type while many eastern Europeans in the UK would be of the former one. Different ethnicities can be associated with different languages and cultures but similar physical appearance e.g. various white Europeans; or with similar language and culture but different physical appearance e.g. many second- or third-generation Asians or African Carribeans in the UK or USA.

Not all ethnic minorities suffer deprivation. Some ethnic minorities can compare more favourably on variables like affluence, employment and educational status when compared with the majority e.g. whites in South Africa, Zimbabwe and in a very different context Parsis in India. So it is important not to stereotype minorities as always being associated with disadvantage or deprivation. However, whenever this appears to be the case it is now becoming clear that focusing on social variables (poverty, rundown overcrowded housing, unemployment, political injustice, racism) or psychological ones (e.g. low self-esteem, psychosocial reality of facing racism and resultant anger, frustration or learned helplessness) rather than biological ones ('lazy' or 'criminal' genes, 'criminal races' or dangerous pseudoscience like phrenology) is more fruitful, constructive and effective in changing things for the better for people in general rather than for a privileged few.

Though ethnic minority status can be a shared variable for two children, different contexts can influence their development in very different ways. Parental cultural beliefs and attitudes, geographical location, financial status, opportunities to mix with peers and relatives belonging to the same minority community are a few such contextual variables one can think of. Sometimes exposure to experiences that are different and often negative by minority populations as compared to the indigenous majority peers can lead to a feeling of having less control over one's environment (external locus of control), helplessness, low self-esteem and negative self-concept. Some work done in the USA shows that this is not inevitable and the context is an important factor which affects outcome. Ethnic minority status *per se* is not related to lower self-concept if readily identifiable models for the self can be found among the minority group (Powell 1985).

Apart from identification with positive role models, the child's positive perception of parental nurturance has been found to be associated with emotional well-being in many cultures. Interestingly parental perception about themselves does not have a similar relationship to the child's well-being. Some (now) minority cultures, such as that associated with Native Americans, were adaptable and eco-friendly, emphasizing the importance of sharing, respecting nature and accepting natural order of life, disease and death. However, children raised in this culture faced a major disadvantage when they had to face the majority American culture emphasizing fierce competition, individual greed and consumerism.

Cultural beliefs about illness, disorder, help-seeking behaviour and stigma attached to certain symptoms are often transmitted through parents to children influencing the nature and timing of psychopathology. Hackett and Hackett (1993) have described the difficulties that abound in studying cross-cultural child psychiatry. Influence of culture on parental expectations from children, ideas of normal and deviant behaviour and culture-specific considerations of 'caseness' are some of the difficulties in comparing like with like. In their research they found that Gujarati parents attached greater weight to items concerned with aggression and obedience, but less to items concerned with lying and fears as compared with indigenous English parents. There was no difference in parental perceptions of self-care items, items concerning nightmares and sleep-walking.

Banks (2000) has given useful guidance on this aspect in a recent government publication. Dutt and Phillips (2000) have also dealt with issues surrounding assessment of black children in need at length and given useful practice guidelines.

It then becomes important that professionals dealing with the child are able to look through the smokescreen of cultural factors (their own and the child's) to identify pathological or maladaptive patterns of behaviours or symptoms.

Migration and the ethnic minority child

Migration can involve a complex mixture of variables depending on the origin and destination of the person or family involved. Some variables can increase vulnerability of the people concerned towards physical or psychological disorder mediating through stress while some others can act as protective factors. An example of the risk variables would be an unwelcoming or 'hostile' host culture, language, religions and lifestyle changes acting as barriers to smooth acculturation; a protective variable would be a relatively safer host environment as compared with persecution at place of origin.

While grown-ups may have variable degree of choice and control over migration, children often have to accompany them or arrive on the scene after migration has taken place. Diane Abbott (a black Member of Parliament (MP) from London) has described how she could not understand the complex meaning attached to the term 'respect' as used by her father ('children today have no respect!') till she visited rural Jamaica.

The child growing up as an ethnic minority child faces direct effects of that experience and in addition indirect effects through parents of successful or not so successful parental adaptation to the host culture.

Current Situation in the UK

Migration of Jewish people from Russia in the late nineteenth century, as a result of the pogroms; that of African Caribbeans and South-east Asians in the 1950s and 1960s when thriving industry in the UK wanted workers, and political upheaval in Uganda in the 1970s formed the majority of original ethnic minority populations in the UK. During the latter half of the 1990s many eastern European refugees migrated to the UK as a result of wars involving 'ethnic cleansing' in their own countries. More recently white-collar information technology workers mainly from India are also being targeted to make up the shortfall of UK workforce as are nurses from Spain and teachers from various countries.

Recent UK data show that ethnic minority populations are concentrated in the more urbanized parts of the country. Nearly half of all people in Great Britain of ethnic minority origin live in Greater London, compared with less than one in ten of the white population.

Nearly three-quarters of the ethnic minority population (referred to as non-whites even in the official article found on the ONS website) live in the metropolitan counties of Greater London, Greater Manchester, West Yorkshire and West Midlands compared with less than a quarter of the white population. Further variation is evident when one breaks these categories into different ethnic groups.

Approximate population of Great Britain (1998) (in millions): total 56.7, Whites 53.0, Ethnic minorities 3.7, Black Caribbean 0.5, Black African 0.3, Black-Other 0.29, Indian 0.94, Pakistani 0.56, Bangladeshi 0.23, Chinese 0.16, Other Asian (non-mixed) 0.19, Other Other (including mixed) 0.4.

A website such as www.statistics.gov.uk is a useful reference to keep up with changing datasets such as Census 2001.

Identity and Mental Health

It is often assumed that the more that children identify with their ethnicity in terms of skin colour (black/white) or culture (Indian, African, European, English) the more emotionally healthy they will be. However, an interesting study from Sweden shows that this is not always true. Cederblad *et al.* (1999) explored the mental health of a teenager/young adult group that was transracially adopted and hence visibly different in physical appearance from their parents. In the study 147 families and their 211 adopted children who were 13 years of age or older at the time of investigation were interviewed in their homes. Good-quality measures were used to compare these adolescents' mental health and self-esteem with non-adopted Swedish youngsters of the same age. The adoptees had good mental health and self-esteem. The pre-adoption conditions were more important than the age of arrival in itself for the risk of later maladaptation. Those who were most engaged in questions about their identity and felt mostly non-Swedish had more behaviour problems. This association between identity and mental health disappeared in older subjects (18–27 years of age).

The majority (about 90%) of the adoptees felt mostly Swedish; 70 per cent did not feel any connection to their country of origin. It is quite possible that rather than the content of one's identity it is the ease with which one embraces it that decides its adaptive value to the person. On the other hand there is a significant body of research which clearly shows that positive evaluation and closer identification with one's own ethnic group ('high ethnic affirmation')was predictive of positive attitudes about other ethnic (including the majority) groups (Romero and Roberts 1998). In one study of boys and girls from different ethnic groups, gender differences proved more powerful predictors of beliefs around self-expression, family relationships and male/female roles than cultural affiliation (McDermott *et al.* 1983).This study compared Japanese American and Caucasian families in Hawaii. However, it would be unwise to generalize from the findings of this one study as one commonly comes across adolescents who are clearly strongly influenced by their culture of origin.

Epidemiology of Psychiatric Disorders

Epidemiology is concerned with the study of both the distribution of a disorder or illness in human populations and the factors that influence that distribution. The data generated can lead to improved scientific understanding of risk factors and mechanisms associated with disorders as well as more efficient service provision.

Studies done in the Indian subcontinents indicate a prevalence rate of psychotic disorders of 3–11 per cent among indigenous children (Lal and Sethi 1977; Verghese and Beig 1974). However, these workers have used older classifications and included mental retardation and other developmental disorders making it difficult to compare their findings with prevalence rates of disorders found in Indian children in more recent studies.

There were very few studies looking at prevalence rates of psychiatric disorder in ethnic minority children in the UK until very recently. Two recent studies (Kramer, Evans and Garralda 2000; Meltzer *et al.* 2000) will be described in some detail after looking at earlier findings of interest.

Rutter, Yule and Berger (1974) surveyed 10 year olds in inner London. They found that West Indian children showed a lower rate of disorder based on parent interview than indigenous (white) children (18% versus 25%). However, based on teacher interview the same children showed a higher rate of disorder (38% versus 28%) mostly consisting of conduct disorder, restlessness and poor concentration. Non-sanctioned school absence was by contrast higher in indigenous students. West Indian girls in the same study showed a much higher rate of disorder – conduct disorder rather than emotional disorder – as compared with indigenous girls. Rutter *et al.* (1974) concluded that two probable explanations were societal and racial discrimination and greater educational retardation in West Indian children as compared with indigenous children.

Earls and Richman (1980) found a similar prevalence rate of overall disorder when comparing preschoolers born to mothers who had been born in the West Indies. West Indian mothers suffered more disadvantages like poor housing or separation from their own parents and they were more educated and worked longer hours.

Symptom patterns were somewhat different in these children. West Indian children were faddy eaters, difficult to settle at night, more fearful and with speech articulation problems. Indigenous children were more likely to soil, wet the bed and have tempers.

Butler and Golding (1986) found similar findings in West Indian children at the age of 5 when followed up from birth by administering questionnaires to health visitors. Again, these families suffered on a wide range of social indices like overcrowding, lone parents, more siblings and poverty, which have been uniformly associated with higher prevalence of mental disorder in the recent survey published by the Office for National Statistics, UK.

An exception to this is the Indian children who appear to show a lower prevalence rate of mental disorder compared with African Caribbean, Pakistani, Bangladeshi or even white indigenous children. This finding has been uniform in studies done in the 1970s, 1980s and 1990s (Butler and Golding 1986; Hackett, Hackett and Taylor 1991; Kallarackal and Herbert 1976; Meltzer *et al.* 2000).

A much higher rate of two-parent households, very high value put on education, family unity and discipline are findings that are likely to have been instrumental in these lower prevalence rates in Indian children. Different (less aggression, more obedience) expectations of children and different child-rearing practices among Gujarati parents as compared with indigenous parents have been demonstrated (Hackett and Hackett 1993).

In an interesting study, Goodman and Richards (1995) compared prevalence rates of different psychiatric disorders in British-born African Caribbean black children and indigenous white children in South London. Autism (classical and atypical), psychosis and conduct disorders were significantly more common in the black children whereas emotional disorders were more common in white children. Hyperkinesis and other disorders were slightly more common in white children.

A biological factor like puberty occurring on average approximately six months earlier in African Caribbean children was suggested to explain a 'brought forward' effect at least for psychosis. Pervasive and complex effect, of social disadvantages, mainly racial discrimination, was suggested and a need for effective action to break the continuity of some findings (especially relating to conduct disorders) evident from older studies was highlighted.

Some noteworthy findings of this study include:

- higher academic self-esteem in pre-pubertal black girls which starts going down in teenage years in contrast to white counterparts
- more family warmth and less dysfunction in African Caribbean families in spite of social disadvantage
- lower incidence of school refusal and higher value placed on education by African Caribbean parents.

A survey of mental health of children and adolescents in Great Britain by the ONS on behalf of the Department of Health (Meltzer *et al.* 2000) has recently been published. It has used ICD-10 (World Health Organization 1992) to make four groups of disorders: emotional disorders, conduct disorders, hyperkinetic disorders and less common disorders (pervasive developmental disorders (PDDs), psychosis, tics, eating disorders and other psychiatric disorders). A sample of 10,438 children aged 5–15 years were effectively surveyed using parent interviews (99.7%), child interviews/assessments (95.3%) and teacher questionnaires (80.3%).

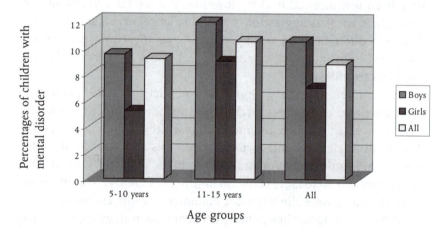

Figure 3.1: Prevalence of any mental disorder by age and sex

As you can see from Figure 3.1 prevalence of mental disorder was approximately 11 per cent in boys, 7.5 per cent in girls and overall 9.5 per cent.

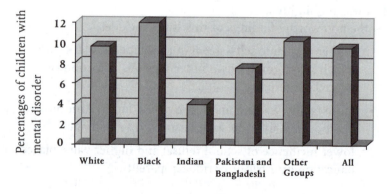

Figure 3.2: Prevalence of any mental disorder by ethnicity

Prevalence of mental disorder by ethnicity (Figure 3.2) showed a distinctly lower rate (4%) in Indian children as compared with Pakistani and Bangladeshi (7.5%), white (9.5%), others (10%) and black (12%).

Even though one could not be certain of it, there were indications that factors relating to age (older children), sex (boys), number of children in the household (four or five), unemployment and lower social class were associated with higher prevalence rate while ethnicity *per se* was not.

In another study, Kramer Evams and Garralda (2000) looked at a Central London Child and Adolescent Clinic during 1991 and 1992. This was a case note study. Some findings were as follows:

- one in ten children were born outside the UK
- English was second language in 13.5% children
- attenders originated from 43 different countries
- there was a trend for more developmental disorders and fewer psychiatric disorders in the Asian group
- comparable service access was a somewhat unusual finding when the groups were divided into White, Asian, Black and Others.

A confounding factor was that ethnicity of white children was often not recorded in notes. This is dissimilar to findings of Stern, Cottrell and Holmes (1990) who found underutilization of services by Bangladeshi children in east London, though the populations of these two studies were probably quite different in the relative ethnic mix.

International Trends

Adolescent substance misuse including alcohol, cannabis and other illicit drugs

Many well-conducted recent studies, mostly from the USA, show a complex relationship between adolescent drug use and variables like ethnicity and gender. Close bonds with parents or family were uniformly associated with lower rates of substance misuse. Contrary to the common perception in the USA that substance abuse is a 'minority problem', a review of studies found that whites have higher rates of use, abuse and dependence than other racial or ethnic groups (Smith 1993). Preventive programmes aimed at majority population were also found to reduce smoking and substance use among ethnic minority populations (Botvin

1991). As a discussion of this topic is outside the scope of this chapter, interested readers can refer to original studies (Bhattacharya 1998; Ellickson, Collins and Bell 1999; Moon *et al.* 1999; Oetting *et al.* 1998).

Child sexual abuse

Reported rates of child sexual abuse were similar across four ethnic groups (African Americans, Mexican Americans, Native Americans and non-Hispanic Whites) and amounted to approximately one-third of the 2003 women interviewed. Child sexual abuse was significantly related to depressive symptoms only in non-Hispanic Whites and Mexican Americans while child physical abuse was the strongest predictor of adult depression and the only significant predictor for each ethnic group (Roosa, Reinholtz and Angelini 1999).

Attention deficit and hyperactivity disorder

Ethnic minority status did not influence the rate of diagnosis for attention deficit and hyperactivity disorder (ADHD) in primary health care in the USA but along with female gender and rural residence it lowered the probability of service use. Whether barriers to service use were at the parental or gatekeeper level was not clear (Bussing, Zima and Belin 1998).

Studies have in general showed that ADHD or hyperkinetic disorders are found in all cultures but the prevalence rate can differ considerably, usually being lower in eastern studies (Leung *et al.* 1996).

Conduct Disorder/Delinquency

Most children at some stage are likely to behave in a manner that contravenes the social norm. They are likely to lie, take things which do not belong to them, or display aggression. It is the extent and severity of this behaviour which warrants a psychiatric diagnosis to be made, and DSM-IV (American Psychiatric Association 1994) and ICD-10 classify these. Essentially this behaviour needs to be repetitive, persistent, violate others' basic rights, and to last at least six months. This behaviour includes severe temper tantrums, defiance of rules, anger, spitefulness and vindictiveness. There is also often the initiation of physical fights, cruelty to animals, truancy, running away from home and offences against property. Many of these antisocial behaviours are not illegal, but the use of weapons, cruelty to other people, pyromania, sexual abuse and the confronting of the victims, among others, are antisocial behaviours of higher legal concept. Thus they can be divided into non-delinquent and delinquent conduct disorders.

Compared with the indigenous population, there are lower rates of delinquency among Asian children and higher among those of West Indian origin. Higher rates of delinquency may be linked to higher unemployment (Rutter and Giller 1983). There is concern and belief that discrimination in the courts is so rife that black offenders are twice as likely to receive a prison sentence than whites convicted of the same offence. The study undertaken by Roger Hood (1992) analysed ethnic and white male offenders convicted and sentenced in 1989 in the crown court. He found African Caribbeans were over-represented and received higher rates of custodial sentences, even for offences of a less serious nature, while Asians on the other hand were sentenced to custody less often than either whites or African Caribbeans. In the aftermath of the Stephen Lawrence murder inquiry it was officially acknowledged in the McPherson Report that the Metropolitan Police in London were institutionally racist. It also became clear that racism was a major factor behind failed prosecution. While more people now acknowledge presence of racism in society than before, racism still continues to affect and modify the law and order situation in society in complex ways.

Case Study: John

A 15-year-old African Caribbean youth was recently moved from the south-east of England by the social services department and placed with a special foster carer in the north-east of England. The first three months were uneventful and there was a considerable degree of optimism. The foster carers were taken aback when the police telephoned them to tell them about the arrest of John (assumed name) for the offence of robbery. He was subsequently committed to the court, whereupon the magistrates requested a full psychiatric assessment.

The family background obtained from the voluminous social work records confirmed that John was born to an African Caribbean mother and Ghanaian father after a fleeting relationship. He was one of five children. His biological father left the scene and is said to have a criminal record. The mother suffered from manic-depressive illness which was complicated further by alcohol abuse. John and his siblings were on the At Risk Register and often had to be placed with members of the extended family, with the maternal grandmother often helping out. Eventually he was received into the local authority at the age of 5.

The developmental history suggested that John was born after a breech delivery; his temperament was said to be non-malleable and rigid. Milestones were within normal limits and there were no other major medical problems such as epilepsy or a head injury. But he was separated from his mother on several occasions for a protracted period of time before the age of 3.

John was received into care and placed into a children's home. By the age of 11 he had been in five children's homes (as many of them had closed) and experienced three broken foster placements. His behaviour in primary school was described as disruptive and difficult, with him being cheeky and unwilling and unable to accept adult authority. The move to secondary school, coinciding with the onset of adolescence, brought further management difficulties. He was suspended on several occasions, and ultimately excluded. He began to truant frequently in the company of other children, and there was a suspicion that he may have abused drugs.

Commentary

This case demonstrates that delinquency is a universal phenomenon. John came from a large poor family; he experienced damaging life experiences at critical times in his upbringing, and appeared to be of low to average intelligence. He had been presenting with unmanageable difficult behaviour within and outside the home for many years. The social worker report confirmed his failure to bond with his caretakers, and that he came from a family where there was poor communication, lack of warmth and overt rejection. All these factors are known to contribute to a poor outcome in a child of whatever race or culture.

John's perception that his colour caused the police to treat him as they did rang true, as did the fact that he received a custodial rather than non-custodial sentence from the judiciary. And luckily, it was possible in this instance to argue for a community sentence order, with supervision jointly by the social services and by attendance at the psychiatric clinic. Here attempts were made to help John with his repetitive offending and to deal with his confused identity.

Views on transracial placement and/or adoption are polarized; the opinions of Thoburn are challenged by those of Tizard and Phoenix. Thoburn (1988) argues in favour of delayed placement, if a same-race family cannot be found. Essentially, his concerns are that black children placed with white families fail to develop positive identity and may grow up unable to relate to their country of origin, and white families may not be able to teach black children survival skills in a racist society. Tizard and Phoenix (1989) challenge this concept of positive black identity as too simplistic.

Given the age of John and the absolute commitment and particular strengths of the white foster family, we were able to support him and the family and maintain his placement. For the following year, when the unit was in contact with him, John had managed to remain out of trouble and had began to address some of the issues relating to him.

Eating Disorders

Anorexia Nervosa is a disorder characterized by self-imposed excessive dieting, due to a relentless pursuit of thinness and fear of being fat. The result of this is a varying degree of emaciation with psychiatric sequelae and potential for significant medical consequences. Bulimia Nervosa on the other hand is a condition characterized by binge eating, a sense of loss of control, self-deprecation and purging of ingested food. There is also a preoccupation with body weight, but patients suffering from this condition may not present with or suffer from loss of weight, which is a characteristic of patients with Anorexia Nervosa.

The aetiologies of these conditions are not known, although risk factors are perceived to be of significance, such as the western values of thinness which are particularly prevalent among females. Ballet dancers, actors and fashion models are known to be at a higher risk of developing eating disorders. There is also a familial tendency with a high risk of siblings developing these conditions and this implicates possibly a genetic or environmental influence. Society and the media clearly influence significantly our concept of desirable female shape which during the 1980s and 1990s became more androgenous.

Until recently Anorexia Nervosa was thought to be a culture-bound syndrome peculiar to white western cultures. During the 1990s it became fairly clear that it occurs in many cultures including eastern European countries like Hungary and Poland and among blacks, Hispanics and Asians in the USA and UK. One can argue that this is a manifestation of the spread of western culture to these countries. A recent survey in India showed that up to 50 per cent of adolescents interviewed expressed concern over body image and eating (report in *The Times* 29 November 2000).The child psychiatrist in charge of the survey attributed this to spread of cable television and associated change in cultural values since the mid-1990s.

Crago, Shisslak and Estes (1996) report that younger, heavier, well-educated females from ethnic minority populations who identified with white middle-class values were at an increased risk of developing eating disturbances. However, such studies have been criticized for over-simplifying ethnicity by going by physical genetic or racial features and ignoring mediating effects of many cultural variables.

Anorexia Nervosa has been described in Asian children living in Britain (Bhadrinath 1990; Bryant-Waugh and Lask 1991; Field, Colditz and Peterson 1997; Hill and Bhatti 1995; McCourt and Waller 1995; Mumford and Whitehouse 1988; Ratan, Gandhi and Palmer 1998). Interestingly prevalence of greater body dissatisfaction, concern with dieting and lower body self-esteem was found in those girls that came from more traditional as opposed to westernized cultures. Bryant-Waugh and Lask (1991) have argued that it is the difficulty in reconciling two different cultures (western away from home and traditional eastern at home) rather than exposure to majority western culture in itself that may precipitate the onset of eating disorder.

Case Study: Shamma

A 16-year-old Asian female, Shamma (name changed), was referred by her physician subsequent to an overdose. She had taken 20 tablets of paracetamol in circumstances which led to her immediate referral to hospital. This was her second admission following self-harm and fourth admission to a medical ward. The two medical admissions were related to investigations of epigastric pain following eating and the patient's mother observed that her previously 'healthy' but slightly overweight daughter had lost a significant amount of weight and that she had become less open in her manner.

Her history of food intake confirmed gradual and deliberate avoidance of carbohydrate and fatty food, with refusal to join the family at mealtimes and retching postprandially. She had also become miserable and irritable and began to display challenging behaviour, although she showed willingness to help her mother in the family catering business.

Detailed psychiatric examination as an inpatient revealed two major areas of difficulty. Shamma attributed her overdoses to her family's unwillingness to allow her the freedom that her 'English' friends enjoyed. Her family suspected, but not as yet openly acknowledged, the existence of an English boyfriend. Shamma feared that if her family were to find out about her boyfriend, she would be shipped to Pakistan and forcibly married to a young man of her parents' choice. Her second major area of difficulty was her eating disorder, with her displaying a moderate to severe body image disturbance, believing that she was fat, even though she was 20 per cent below her ideal body weight. She revealed a history of excessive dieting, use of laxatives and exercising to keep her weight down. On direct enquiry she wanted the clinical team to find her a place away from her family to enable her to pursue her education, continue her relationship with her boyfriend and maintain her present body weight. She was unwilling to acknowledge that her body weight was substantially below her ideal body weight. Further enquiries unearthed the possibility of sexual abuse in the past but several attempts by her therapist failed to elicit further details.

Commentary

Shamma is a second-generation 'immigrant' born to Muslim parents of low social class. She was exposed to the western cultural view of desirable body weight as were her Caucasian schoolmates, and the development of Anorexia Nervosa is understandable. Her self-harm attempts happened in the context of the 'forbidden boyfriend', her fear of being taken to Pakistan to be married off against her will and her general inner turmoil.

The multidisciplinary team of the unit comprised only one member from an ethnic minority (the author SB); the rest were from the white majority. Lively debate followed with strong proponents for receiving Shamma into care, helping her to individualize, exercise her right to have a boyfriend as she chose, include the potion of sexual freedom, and ultimately live on her own or with a boyfriend in the community. Conversely arguments were put forward that Shamma may have underestimated the potential difficulties in relating to a white boyfriend about whose background and suitability she knew little, risking racial prejudice and social isolation from her 'community'.

It was agreed to share these views with Shamma and gradually, with her permission, take up specific issues with her family. Reassurance from her family was obtained that she would not be sent to Pakistan to marry for at least the following two years, as was agreement to attend family therapy at the unit regularly to 'understand' their daughter's problems, and help to improve communication. The author saw Shamma and key members of her family, which included grandparents and an uncle, individually.

Two years later, Shamma had obtained high grades in her A levels, although decided not to pursue a university education; she had broken off her relationship with her boyfriend and become engaged to a devout Muslim boy brought up in the UK. It was in this instance possible to avoid inappropriate cultural solutions, and use the knowledge of cultural and religious beliefs to obtain the cooperation of the patient and her family. The temptation to offer her refuge and an opportunity to pursue her 'puppy-love' was avoided, and individual therapy offered her the opportunity to consider and choose options whilst regarding dangers and rewards. The culturally appropriate approach of seeking the involvement of grandparents and an esteemed uncle improved the trust and cooperation of the family. Unfortunately, to date we remain unclear about the question of sexual abuse, as she chose not to reveal any further details.

Service provision and its utilization

Ethnocultural factors play a significant role in utilization of psychiatric services by immigrant populations (Commander *et al.* 1997). Communication difficulties due to language barrier, and disparity between cultural beliefs of professionals and clients are two important such factors. Stigma attached to mental illness is now another well-recognized factor (Byrne 2000). Byrne has described how people from ethnic minorities have to overcome 'double discrimination' (a coincidence of mental illness and minority status) when they seek help for treatment of mental illness for themselves or their children. It is no wonder that their underuse of services is an almost universal reality. This has been addressed only since the late 1990s, reflected in practice guidelines published by the Department of Health (1998), employment of ethnic minority outreach workers, and a council report on training issues related to a multicultural society by the Royal College of Psychiatrists, among other measures.

> Professionals from majority cultures should not lose sight of the fact that all children irrespective of their skin colour and ethnicity require their parents or carers to respond to their fundamental needs like basic care, warmth, stimulation, guidance, boundaries and stability. (Dutt and Phillips 2000, p.38)

One can apply the information gathered from research literature at various levels of practice ranging from day-to-day individual clinical practice to wider organizational service provision issues. One can also think in terms of using the knowledge gained from research at primary, secondary and tertiary levels of prevention of mental disorder.

Primary prevention

1. Increase information and awareness about various minority cultures in schools, public libraries, workplaces and in media. It is important to do this in a sensitive manner emphasizing the need to respect cultural differences while recognizing the common human bond.

2. Ensure inclusion of training modules containing issues about ethnic diversity for professionals from all walks of life e.g. doctors, nurses, teachers, police, judges and lawyers.

3. Acknowledge and celebrate festivals of various minority communities e.g. Id, Diwali, Holi. This can strengthen a sense of uniqueness and identity for ethnic minority children growing in a different majority culture.

4. Use of information leaflets and road shows or open days about mental health issues using various languages congruent to local needs.

5. Awareness and use of interpreters whenever possible. Educate people about their rights and entitlement to public services and benefits.

Secondary prevention

1. Service planners should consult with local community leaders from ethnic minorities during the needs assessment phase to seek guidance on appropriate service structures and

processes including membership of stakeholders' groups (Appleton 2000).

2.   Clinicians should try to use interpreter services whenever appropriate and inform managers of local needs.

3.   Clinicians can use the cultural formulation suggested in DSM-IV on how to assess the impact of cultural factors (related to themselves and the patient) on the clinical interaction and diagnosis (Novins 1997).

4.   Use of questionnaires and scales translated and standardized as appropriate to ethnicity of the patient.

5.   Race Relations Act: professionals have a legal duty under the Race Relations Act 1976 to promote equal opportunities by communicating adequately. The Adoption Act 1976 also requires the court to be satisfied that each parent or guardian fully understands what is involved in adopting a child.

6.   The recording of ethnicity of patients admitted to hospital has been mandatory in the UK since April 1995 – though still widely neglected in actual practice.

7.   Implications of the Human Rights Act (operational from October 2000) are yet to become clear, especially with regard to children, but this along with the new Mental Health Act (likely to be passed in the next few years) would probably influence professional practice significantly.

8.   Novel strategies to engage clients from ethnic minorities if non-attendance is an issue locally. In one study a telephone call prior to the appointment where opportunity to have an extended conversation increased attendance rates (McKay, McCadam and Gonzales 1996).

Tertiary prevention

Rehabilitation of children and adolescents with serious chronic mental disorders, developmental disorders and serious educational special needs will have to be shared between all three sectors, namely health, social care and education. Already joint working and commissioning are becoming the norm. It will be important for planners to be sensitive to needs of local populations while new pathways of care are being formed.

Implications for Individual Professional Practice

A few points have been listed below which have been collated from literature as well as clinical experience. However, individuals can make their own list that is bound to expand with their own clinical experience.

1. The initial process of breaking the ice at the beginning of the interview and establishing rapport and some trust is of paramount importance, especially when dealing with clients from ethnic minorities. Offering the family the opportunity to bring along another person from the community, for example, may be very important for some.

2. Use of interpreters rather than using a child or another family member to translate can avoid many future complications.

3. To listen to the child's or parents' views about the presenting problems without challenging them at least initially can facilitate rapport.

4. Taking one down position whenever stuck or uncertain about anything that comes up in the interview is usually of help (i.e. admitting that the family members may know more than you about a particular issue and can teach or guide you).

5. Remember that avoiding eye contact may be a culturally learnt way of showing respect for one's elders or people in authority positions, rather than due to a shifty or shy nature, sign of anxiety or failure of the professional to form rapport.

6. The clinician should be aware that it would be inappropriate in some cultures for a stranger to ask personal questions or to talk directly to women in the family.

7. The clinician should try to ascertain the nature of presenting problem from the patient's and parents' point of view and also ask about their expectations.

8. Remember the possibility that a child may be getting confused by messages received from teachers and peers that are directly contradictory to cultural and hence parental expectations.

Conclusion

During assessment of parenting one should always be alert to many traps that may lead to erroneous and harmful conclusions that a professional can make if not aware of the impact of culture on parenting practices. Always ask the family or take time to find out answers to any doubts that arise during assessment. Culture has a strong influence on feeding practices, especially with infants (Dwivedi 2000), as well as sleeping arrangements, as is now fairly well known. One should take this into account before drawing conclusions from comparison with the majority culture.

In many cultures older siblings are expected to care for younger siblings. Look for the extent and its impact on both siblings' functioning in various spheres.

In many cultures, including Spanish, children may normally live with parents till their early thirties.

Gender relations and intergenerational hierarchies differ in different cultures. Children may remain quiet and allow parents to speak out of politeness as a cultural practice rather than any psychopathology. In many cultures, e.g. Indian, dependability is valued more than independence in a child.

Acknowledgements

We would like to thank Mrs Seema Banhatti for help with the typing, Karen Amos for help with formatting and the figures, Veann Helyger for reading and correcting a draft, Howard Meltzer for granting permission to use tables from his book and advice, and last but not least, Kedar Dwivedi for his patience and guidance.

References

American Psychiatric Association (1994) *Diagnostic and Statistical Manual for Mental Disorders: Fourth Edition.* Washington, DC: APA.

Appleton, P. (2000) 'Tier 2 CAMHS and its interface with primary care.' *Advances in Psychiatric Treatment 6,* 388–396.

Banks, N. (2000) 'Assessing Children and Families who Belong to Minority Ethnic Groups.' In J. Horwath (ed) *The Child's World.* London: Jessica Kingsley Publishers.

Bhadrinath, B. (1990) 'Anorexia Nervosa in adolescents of Asian extraction.' *British Journal of Psychiatry 156,* 565–568.

Bhattacharya, G. (1998) 'Drug use among Asian-Indian adolescents: identifying protective/risk factors.' *Adolescence 33*, 129, 169–184.

Botvin, G.J. (1991) 'Smoking initiation and escalation in early adolescent girls: one year follow up of a school based prevention intervention for minority youth.' *Journal of the American Medical Women's Associations 54*, 3, 139–143.

Bryant-Waugh, R. and Lask, B. (1991) 'Anorexia Nervosa in a group of Asian children living in Britain.' *British Journal of Psychiatry 158*, 229–233.

Bussing, R., Zima, B.T. and Belin, T.R. (1998) 'Differential access to care for children with ADHD in special education programmes.' *Psychiatric Services 49*, 9, 1226–1229.

Butler, N. and Golding, J. (1986) *From Birth to Five: A Study of Health and Behaviour of Britain's Five year olds*. Oxford: Pergamon.

Byrne, P. (2000) 'Stigma of mental illness and ways of diminishing it.' *Advances in Psychiatric Treatment 6*, 65–72.

Cederblad, M., Hook, B., Irhammer, M. and Mercke, A.M. (1999) 'Mental health in international adoptees as teenagers and young adults: an epidemiological study.' *Journal of Child Psychology and Psychiatry and Allied Disciplines 40*, 8, 1239–1248.

Commander, M.J., Sashi Dharan, S.P., Odell, S.U. and Surtees, P.G. (1997) 'Access to mental health care in an inter-city health district. 1) Pathways into and within specialist psychiatric services and 2) Association with demographic factors.' *British Journal of Psychiatry 170*, 312–320.

Crago, M., Shisslak, C. and Estes, L. (1996) 'Eating disturbances among minority groups: a review.' *International Journal of Eating Disorders 19*, 239–248.

Department of Health (1998) *National Guidance: a Commitment to Improve Modern Social Services*. London: The London Stationary Office.

Dutt, R. and Phillips, M. (2000) 'Assessing Black children in need and their families.' In Department of Health *Assessing Children in Need and their Families: Practice Guidance*. London: Department of Health/The Stationery Office.

Dwivedi, K.N. (2000) 'Cultural aspects of feeding: some illustrations from the Indian culture.' In A. Southall and A. Schwartz (eds) *Feeding Problems in Children: A Practical Guide*. Oxford: Radcliffe Medical Press.

Earls, F. and Richman, N. (1980) 'The prevalence of behavioural problems in three-year-old children of West Indian parents.' *Journal of Child Psychology and Psychiatry 21*, 99–106.

Ellickson, P.L., Collins, R.L. and Bell, R.M. (1999) 'Adolescent use of illicit drugs other than marijuana: how important is social bonding and for which ethnic group?' *Substance Use and Misuse 34*, 3, 317–346.

Field, A.H., Colditz, G.A. and Peterson, I.C.E. (1997) 'Racial/ethnic and gender differences in concern with weight and in bulimic behaviours among adolescents.' *Obesity Research 5*, 5, 447–454.

Goodman, R. and Richards, H. (1995) 'Child and adolescent psychiatric presentations of second generation Afro-Caribbeans.' *British Journal of Psychiatry 167*, 362–369.

Hackett, L., Hackett, P. and Taylor, D. (1991) 'Psychological disturbance and its associations in the children of the Gujarati community.' *Journal of Child Psychology and Psychiatry 32*, 851–856.

Hackett, L. and Hackett, R. (1993) 'Parental ideas of normal and deviant child behaviour: a comparison of two ethnic groups.' *British Journal of Psychiatry 162*, 353–357.

Hill, A.J. and Bhatti, R. (1995) 'Body shape perception and dieting in preadolescent British Asian girls: links with eating disorders.' *International Journal of Eating Disorders 17*, 2, 175–183.

Hood, R. (1992) *Race and Sentencing.* Oxford: Clarendon.

Kallarackal, A.M. and Herbert, M. (1976) 'The happiness of Indian immigrant children.' *New Society 4*, 22–24.

Kramer, T., Evans, N. and Garralda, M.E. (2000) 'Ethnic diversity among child and adolescent psychiatric (CAP) clinic attenders.' *Child Psychology and Psychiatry Review 5*, 4, 169–175.

Lal, N. and Sethi, B. (1977) 'Estimate of mental ill health in children of an urban community.' *Indian Journal of Paediatrics 44*, 55–64.

Leung, P.W., Luk, S.L., Ho, T.P. and Taylor, E. (1996) 'The diagnosis and prevalence of hyperactivity in Chinese schoolboys.' *British Journal of Psychiatry 168*, 4, 486–496.

McCourt, J. and Waller, O. (1995) 'Developmental role of perceived parental control in the eating psychopathology of Asian and Caucasian schoolgirls.' *International Journal of Eating Disorders 17*, 3, 277–282.

McDermott, J.F., Robillard, A., Char, W.F., Hsu, J., Tsing, W. and Ashton, G.C. (1983) 'Re-examining the concept of adolescence: differences between adolescent boys and girls in the context of their families.' *American Journal of Psychiatry 140*, 1318–1322.

McKay, M.M., McCadam, K., Gonzales, J. (1996) 'Addressing the barriers to mental health services for inner-city children and their caretaker.' *Community Mental Health Journal 32*, 4, 353–361.

McKenzie, K. and Crowcroft, N.S. (1996) 'Describing race, ethnicity, and culture in medical research.' *British Medical Journal 312*, 1054.

Meltzer, H., Gatward, R., Goodman, R. and Ford, T. (2000) *Mental Health of Children and Adolescents in Great Britain.* London: The Stationery Office.

Moon, D.G., Hecht, M.L., Jackson, K.M. and Spellers, R.E. (1999) 'Ethnic and gender differences and similarities in adolescent drug use and refusals of drug offers.' *Substance Use and Misuse 34*, 8, 1059–1083.

Mumford, D. and Whitehouse, A. (1988) 'Increased prevalence of bulimia nervosa among Asian schoolgirls.' *British Medical Journal 297*, 718.

Novins, D.K. (1997) 'The DSM-IV outline for cultural formulation: a critical demonstration with American Indian Children.' *Journal of the American Academy of Child and Adolescent Psychiatry 36*, 9, 1244–1251.

Oetting, E.R., Donnermeyer, J.F., Trimble, J.E. and Beauvais, F. (1998) 'Primary socialization theory: culture, ethnicity and cultural identification. The links between culture and substance use.' *Substance Use and Misuse 33*, 10, 2075–2107.

ONS (1998) 'Estimates of the population by ethnic group and area of residence.' Article on website of the office for national Statistics, UK. www.statistics.gov.uk

Powell, G. (1985) 'Self-concepts among African-American students in racially isolated minority schools: some regional differences.' *Journal of American Academy of Child Psychiatry 24*, 142–149.

Ratan, D., Gandhi, D. and Palmer, R. (1998) 'Eating disorders in British Asians.' *International Journal of Eating Disorders 24*, 1, 101–105.

Romero, A.J. and Roberts, R.E. (1998) 'Perception of discrimination and ethnocultural variables in a diverse group of adolescents.' *Journal of Adolescence 21*, 641–656.

Roosa, M.W., Reinholtz, C. and Angelini, N. (1999) 'The relation of sexual abuse and depression in young women: comparisons across four ethnic groups.' *Journal of Abnormal Child Psychology 27*, 1, 65–76.

Rutter, M., Giller, H. (1983) *Juvenile Delinquency: Trends and Perspectives.* Harmondsworth: Penguin.

Rutter, M., Yule, W. and Berger, M., Morton, J. and Bagley, C. (1974) 'Children of West Indian immigrants: I-Rates of behavioural deviance and of psychiatric disorder.' *Journal of Child Psychology and Psychiatry 15*, 241–262.

Singh, S.P. (1997) 'Ethnicity in psychiatric epidemiology: need for precision.' *British Journal of Psychiatry 171*, 305–308.

Smith, E.M. (1993) 'Race or racism? Addiction in the United States.' *Annuals of Epidermiology 3*, 2, 165–170.

Stern, G., Cottrell, D. and Holmes, J. (1990) 'Patterns of attendance of child psychiatry outpatients with social reference to Asian families.' *British Journal of Psychiatry 156*, 384–387.

Thoburn, J. (1988) *Child Placement: Principles and Practice. Community Care Practice Handbook.* Aldershot: Wildwood House.

Tizard, B. and Phoenix, A. (1989) 'Black identity and transracial adoption.' *New Community 15*, 3, 427–437.

Verghese, A. and Beig, A. (1974) 'Psychiatric disturbance in children: an epidemiological study.' *Indian Journal of Medical Research 62*, 1538–1542.

World Health organization (1992) *The ICD-10 Classification of Mental and Behavioural Disorders: Clinical Descriptions and Diagnostic Guidelines.* Geneva: WHO.

Chapter 4

Family Therapy and Ethnic Minorities

Annie Lau

Introduction

Family therapists from a western European ethnocultural background working with ethnic minority families need to pay attention to the tensions in the interface between them and their client families. An understanding and respect for the cultural and religious differences between them and their client families will help therapists to gain credibility, and use culturally determined materials in a way that will enhance the family's problem-solving skills, and mobilize strengths derived from traditional values and practices.

Family therapy assumptions

Family therapists are trained to regard the family unit as the primary focus for assessment and interventions. Behavioural or emotional disturbance in a family member is regarded as symptomatic of family disturbance. All family therapy schools have a basic grounding in family systems theory, which informs both theory and practice. Thus one would look for stress-related changes in the family system in order to understand the causes that led to the precipitation of distress, or disease, in a particular family member. Similarly it would be through exploration of family system characteristics, such as belief systems, role attributions, subsystem alliances, boundaries and authority, that one understands why the family appears to be stuck in a series of maladaptive problem-solving sequences and ends up perpetuating and maintaining the identified patient in a sick or disabled role.

Different family therapy schools would emphasize different aspects of family system in both assessment and intervention. Structural family therapists work in the here and now, use observations of family interactions as a primary means of gathering information about the family, and intervene through empowering in the present by guiding the family through the change process. An example would be unbalancing the system by taking the family past their usual points of lack of problem resolution; directly challenging parental perceptions of the patient that have paralysed parental authority and going for more effective problem-soving in the present.

Both strategic and systemic schools work on underlying rules and belief systems that have led to family paralysis and ineffective functioning. Circular questioning, developed by the Milan School, elucidates differences in perception and understanding by various family members, and the therapist tries to maintain a position of therapeutic neutrality. Strategic family therapists work on the power of the belief system, sometimes by the use of paradoxical interventions. Brief solution-focused approaches regard the problem as an attempted solution gone wrong; the therapist tries to reframe the problem with the family in order to mobilize potential for change.

All the schools are interested in life-cycle issues and developmental tasks, also in stresses that arise from crises in the family life cycle. An understanding of family history, myths and intergenerational patterns is of particular importance to therapists influenced by psychodynamic considerations. In recent years there has been considerable critique of family systems theory for not taking into account disparities of power in the family system such as child abuse or domestic violence. Gender differences and access to power mean that men and women cannot be regarded as having equal weight in their contributions to, say, so-called 'wife-battering'. Feminist writers have stressed that the experiences of men and women are different and that this needs to be taken on board in the process of devising strategies for working with the family.

In a similar vein I suggest that family therapy theory and practice need to be modified in working with ethnic minority families. Existing practice tends to be Eurocentric, based on western European norms and values, which in turn inform practice and research.

Bridging the gulf: acknowledging and working with different culture

A working definition of culture has been offered by Leighton (1981):

> Culture consists in the knowledge, values, perceptions and practices that are

(1) shared among the members of a given society

(2) passed on from one generation to the next (Leighton 1981, p.522).

The components of a culture are interrelated in such a way as to constitute a whole that governs the functioning of the pertinent society. Culture directs the behaviour of individuals within the group, enabling the group to survive.

In cross-cultural family work we need to address the areas of tension in the interface between the therapist and the family from a different ethnocultural and racial background. These will be:

- differences in race
- differences in symbolic and belief systems
- differences in family structure and organization
- differences in language and communication.

Race

Here one needs to consider both conscious and unconscious racial attitudes, also the fact that different racial tensions exist between different racial groups. For example the historical experience of slavery has led to attitudes based on the master–slave dynamic in the tensions between American whites and blacks. Over generations this has led to a lowering of self-esteem in vulnerable clinical populations, with the influence of negative racial stereotypes perpetuating feelings of learned helplessness and despair. It is important that this paradigm, based on the African Carribbean experience, should not be applied indiscriminately to all non-white groups such as Chinese and Vietnamese. So for example, just because black or mixed race children in care will often feel ashamed of being black as this is associated with negative stereotypes, it does not follow that a Chinese, Indian or West African child will have the same psychological difficulties with regard to racial awareness, or even define himself or herself as 'black'. Power disparities between the therapist and the client family may, however, need to be addressed early on in the session.

Differences in symbolic and belief systems

The cultural and religious traditions of a group organize the perception of experience, give shape and form to myths and beliefs, and determine the limits of appropriate behaviour and family roles. The symbolic belief system of the group also provides explanations of health and illness, definitions of normality and deviance, also guidelines for how to be acceptably deviant within a recognized pattern (Lau 1990).

Value orientations that are culturally determined organize the individual's view of the proper relationship between self and context. Differences in basic assumptions between the western and eastern views of self (Lin 1986; Rao 1986) are as follows: the western view emphasizes independence, self-sufficiency, assertiveness and competition, clear and direct verbal communication, while the eastern view emphasizes interdependence, harmony and cooperation in relationships, with more emphasis on non-verbal and indirect communication through the use of shared symbols.

Embedded in the system of cultural meanings for traditional societies is the central role of religious beliefs. Family therapy and the understanding of family systems have developed largely in an areligious, secular context, with the erosion of the authority of the Church in contemporary western society. In religious communities, the authority of religious teaching cannot be discounted by the family therapist. For example, adherence to the principles of the Halacha is a central tenet of individual and family life for Orthodox Jewish communities, and the Rabbi wields considerable personal and community authority. Similar powers are invested in the Imam by Muslim communities.

Family Structure and Organization

Value orientations determine structural relationships; hence family organization following the ideal of the pre-eminence of the group would be along extended family lines, with a primary emphasis on connectedness. For example, in the traditional Chinese family an important organizing principle is filial piety, where loyalties to parents take precedence over loyalties to spouse and children.

Families will need to be located along a continuum between the traditional, hierarchical family with adherence to extended family values and the western, contemporary, egalitarian family. In the non-western European family there are important differences in the construction of 'family' as a concept and the role of the individual within the family. The importance given to interdependence and the need to preserve harmonious family relationships has given rise to structures that do not conform to western European norms, such as extended family groups within the same household. Life-cycle transitions are managed in the context of different rules with regard to authority, continuity and interdependence. In the traditional Asian or Oriental family, relationships are hierarchical between the sexes as well as between the generations. Authority is invested in grandparents or the most senior male members; elder siblings have authority over younger siblings, and responsibility for their welfare. The presence of aged people provides continuity and a link between the generations. Where kinship systems are highly structured, kinship terms delineate the individual's place in the family, including duties and expected obligations, within a system of mutual dependence. Where religion is an important organizing factor, as in Islam, strict religious guidelines may exist for sex-role behaviour including the ideal of segregation of the sexes, particularly after puberty.

Differences in ideas of individual and family competence

Current definitions of family competence used in research into family functioning, for example the Timberlawn study of working-class black families in the USA (Lewis and Looney 1983), are based on nuclear family norms. They do not include, for example, the concept of a network of reciprocal obligations characteristic of ethnic groups with highly structured kinship systems (Lau 1988). It is important to clarify ethnocultural differences in competence for individuals throughout the life cycle, as this has implications for expected stage-specific individual and family tasks.

Preparation for parenting

As part of learning about adult roles, adolescents growing up in a traditional extended family in which three generations are present are exposed to child-rearing practices and learn from examples around them, as well as from 'supervised practice' in helping with the upbringing of younger siblings and cousins. Parenting does not come as a nasty shock. Rather it is an expected and a welcome event, for which their mothers will have prepared them. In contrast, in the industrialized west, parenting may be experienced as an interruption, or a threat to a comfortable lifestyle, rather than a *raison d'être*.

Producing a child, especially a male child, still signifies security for many a young wife in an arranged marriage, and an entry into full social status of the parental couple. In the traditional family the pregnant young wife will also be surrounded by a host of her female kinfolk whose task is to ensure that things go well and that, where necessary, the expectant mother can be relieved of tiring domestic responsibilities.

Infancy and early childhood

Given the importance of interdependence and family connectedness as a goal for the socialization of the young, it should not be surprising that patterns of child-rearing in traditional extended families would be different. The child from a traditional Asian or Vietnamese family could be sleeping with mother or grandmother for many years (Bassa 1978). Indeed co-sleeping arrangements may be preferred in these families even though there may be adequate space for individual bedrooms. Parenting may be shared, and this provides for the young child a wider variety of parental figures, and an increased range of models for age and sex role identifications. Childhood stories, often with religious underpinnings, stress the importance of family, and reinforce family interdependence (Lau 1995). The child learns the overriding importance of being dependable, of being loyal. Through regular participation in family rituals such as meals, outings, festivals, religious events, the child learns its place in the kinship system and the rules governing relationships and expected behaviour. For example, in a well-functioning extended family in the Far East, the young child will have grown up noticing that respect for the grandparents will be shown not only by terms of address, but also by the fact that one often waits for the grandparents to be seated before the meal begins, and that as the elders they have an assumed right to the choicest bits of food.

Middle childhood

The child starting school is taught to accord the teacher with the same respect due to its parents, and that good behaviour in school will reflect well on the family name. An older sibling will be expected to take responsiblity for a younger sibling, or to contribute to the family welfare by, for example, helping in the shop on the weekends. It will be a source of pride to 'so behave that your parents will be proud of you'. Within the family boundary, the child will also learn the importance of manoeuvres for diffusing tension in the family. Through example, the child learns that it is normal and healthy to regard the wider family as an important emotional resource – a temporary refuge from one's angry parents, for example, or a place where one can practise strategies for using on one's parents. Also worries can be shared with a favourite aunt or uncle if one's parents are for any reason emotionally unavailable at the time.

Adolescence

The competent adolescent from a traditional, non-western European extended family background is one who will have been prepared to meet his or her obigations to the family, which often include the obligation to look after one's parents and younger siblings. Within the family the adolescent will have been socialized to know the importance of being dependable, and to be expected to have a behavioural repertoire which includes respectful behaviour to one's elders, and strategies for tension diffusion and conflict avoidance within the immediate and wider family. These skills prepare the young person for adult roles within a value orientation that stresses the importance of maintaining the integrity of the family group. Other issues to do with individuation and separation, as well as distance regulation, will be negotiated differently. Preparation for leaving home is an important difference for adolescents from different ethnocultural groups (Lau 1990).

Marriage

Marriage in traditional families also raises differences in stage-specific family tasks. Where arranged marriage is an expected event in the family life cycle, the wider family has to provide a facilitating environment for stabilizing and nurturing the couple's relationship, particularly in the first year of marriage. There are also gender differences in the levels of adjustment required of the individuals concerned. The new wife moving into a joint household must invest emotionally in the relationship with her mother-in-law and sisters-in-law, and work out power relations within the female network. Competence in these tasks is vital towards ensuring her survival in the new family.

Case study: baby feeding problems

A young family presented with feeding difficulties in their young child of 6 months. This was an Asian family where the mother-in-law lived in the same household as the young couple. Exploration revealed that there was disagreement between the wife and her mother-in-law on feeding routines and weaning practices, arising from different family traditions. The power struggle between the two women had got to the point where the child was becoming distressed and confused, particularly as the young wife was working on a part-time basis, and mother-in-law was involved with childcare.

Case study: adolescent suicidal behaviour

A mixed-race adolescent girl presented with extreme behavioural disturbance, including wrist-slashing and suicidal behaviour. The background history was one of poor relationships with her English mother ever since the family moved to Hong Kong to stay with her Chinese father's extended family. According to the mother, her Chinese in-laws forced her to accept a situation in which she and her husband had to leave the children in Hong Kong with the grandparents, while the couple went back to England to carry on the family business. Each time she saw her daughter again, on a brief visit to Hong Kong, the mother felt an increasing gulf between her and her daughter. It was difficult to relate to her, as the child would speak Chinese and very little English. As a result of mother-in-law's sudden illness and death, the child had to return to England. At this point she had been in a Chinese-speaking environment from age 2 to 8. Mother started shouting at the girl in order to 'get her to understand'. The child turned to her Chinese father for comfort and protection, and the two of them would speak to each other in Chinese. This had the effect of making mother feel increasingly excluded. In addition, the parental relationship was undergoing severe strain; the English wife wanted more physical demonstrativeness, she said, which her husband would not provide. In fact she found it strange that her Chinese in-laws did not touch and hug the way her own family did. The child ended up being the casualty of the conflicts in the parental marriage, as well as the inability of the family system to integrate the foreign daughter-in-law.

African Caribbean family structure

The African Caribbean extended family functions by different rules compared with the extended families of Asia and Africa. Functional relationships are not necessarily defined by formal kinship (Lau 1990; Littlewood and Lipsedge 1982). Contemporary studies of the American black family find a heterogeneity of structure and function. Particular strengths have included role adaptability, strong kinship bonds, a strong religious orientation and church affiliation, and strong work and achievement orientation (Hill 1972). Extended family values are an important element in the family assessment. Traditionally the single parent mother would have depended on male relatives in her own family to provide appropriate male models and authority for her sons. Where the family attends church, religious authority wielded by church elders has been an important source of family support.

Language and Communication

Proper assessment of family needs, vulnerabilities and strengths is difficult where language presents a barrier to communication. If an interpreter is used, he or she needs to be familiar with the therapist's theoretical and conceptual base otherwise important information may be screened out. In my experience, one can gain considerable information through the use of an interpreter, especially where the techniques used involve the therapist asking questions of various family members in order to elucidate differences. Once family transactions (interactions between family members) start to occur, however, it is impossible to slow the action down in order to intervene. In these situations the therapist is unable to gain direct access to information in a family assessment situation, as immediate feedback becomes impossible.

Communicational modes

There may also be differences in expected communication modes. The western-trained therapist's expectation of clear, direct verbal communication is often at variance with cultural rules where direct communication and confrontation are avoided because this may lead to loss of face within the family group (McGoldrick 1982). In the east, a well-known ideal of maturity is the capacity on the part of individuals to tolerate psychic pain and discomfort without 'inflicting' their pain onto the environment. This means qualities like patience and endurance are highly valued, as is silence, contemplation and introspection. Children are praised for 'showing understanding', anticipating the needs of significant others and taking initiative. Thus a child is more praiseworthy if he or she offers tea to a parent on the parent's return from work, without being told to do so. My own mother used to say, 'Empty vessels make the most noise'. Thus children who ask too many questions may well be asked to be quiet and to try to work out some answers by themselves, after which they may then check out the logic of this reasoning with the adult. Western therapists unused to these concepts may well regard these processes as dysfunctional: 'Family members show withdrawal and a lack of communication between them'.

Therapeutic goals

Therapeutic goals may differ between the therapist and the family. The preferred direction of change for families from traditional backgrounds will be in the direction of integration of the family group, rather than towards differentiation and increasing separation of the individual from his/her family (Tamura and Lau 1992). This has potential for conflict for therapists and their supervisors from a different value orientation. Acceptance of these differences in norms implies the use of different therapeutic strategies, with different aims, diffusing and containing conflict rather than amplifying it. Thus a therapist who was working within cultural rules might put more energy into exploring possible areas of agreement, and finding the middle ground. Tamura and Lau (1992) offer case examples where differences in perception and cultural orientation emerged between the therapist, of Japanese ethnic origin, and a western European supervisory team.

Working with families with adolescents

The ethnic family with an adolescent member whose views on autonomy conflict with family norms poses by far one of the most challenging dilemmas for the western therapist. A common response is to 'rescue' the young person, often a girl, from a family that is 'stifling' her. I do not dispute that sometimes it may well be necessary to remove the girl from her family, at least temporarily, especially if there is a serious risk of physical abuse. What often come into play which prematurely punctuates discussion around possible outcomes, however, are beliefs held by western workers about issues like arranged marriages (e.g. they are evil and oppressive patriachal practices) or the role of the adolescent in the family. This often includes the idea that all young people should leave home and set up independent living as soon as possible, or that a young woman needs to be able to make her own choices about sexual partners from around the age of 16. This ignores the psychic reality of the young person, who will have tried to maintain a dual identity in which she maintained a balance between the demands of the school environment and home. I believe one should attempt as far as possible to open up all possibilities for negotiation and airing of differences. This needs to be handled in an atmosphere in which levels of hostility and criticism are managed and kept within tolerable limits. One needs to recognize that in the majority of cases, it will be in the client's long-term interests to be enabled to stay within the family and ethnic community.

Insider therapists

A therapist from a similar ethnocultural background may well find it easier to engage the family, and also be more prepared to engage the cultural material in a way that facilitates therapeutic change. Weiselberg (1992) describes work with Orthodox Jewish families in which the therapist was able to engage the family in trading religious metaphors. Similarly, I have described work with a Chinese family using a cultural ritual that facilitated commitment to change (Lau 1988).

Working with parents

All parents, whatever their ethnic background, have similar expectations of what constitute the results of successful parenting. Indeed, in an address to the National Children's Bureau conference on 'Confident Parents, Confident Children' in 1993, Virginia Bottomley, the then Secretary of State for Health, said all parents expected their children to grow up to be happy, healthy, literate, confident and law-abiding. The difference, however, with working cross-culturally, is that these categories are subject to definitions within the boundaries allowed by the ethnocultural group. Bassa, in making observations on Indian child-rearing practices and identity formation, says, 'Self-fulfilment (i.e.

happiness) is thus to be sought for and found within the family, not in a frantic search for love outside it' (Bassa 1978, p.333). For the traditional Muslim family, literacy will include being able to read the Koran as well as conforming to the requirements of the National Curriculum. Similarly traditional Chinese parents will expect their child to be able to read and write in Chinese. Health may also be defined differently, with different explanatory models, as in the Ayurvedic traditions of India and the classical medical traditions of China. For example a Chinese mother, brought up traditionally in Hong Kong, found it difficult to accept the advice of her health visitor not to give her infant barley water when it was colicky. Her family traditions would suggest that barley water would serve to restore the yin–yang imbalance that ailed the baby. This was however in conflict with the idea, deriving from western medicine, that barley water might introduce another allergen into the baby's diet, on the assumption that the colic was of allergic origin.

Family ritual maintenance

I have found it extremely useful to enquire about the levels of ritualization in ethnic minority families. Family rituals provide support, continuity with family, cultural and religious tradition, and affirm membership for participants. Life-cycle rituals mark and celebrate movement of the individual from one stage of his or her life cycle to another. Where this is a publicly celebrated event, like a naming ceremony for an infant, or the coming of age of an adolescent (e.g. Barmitzvah), the family are also making a public statement to the community. For Jewish parents, it is a declaration that somehow they have succeeded in holding together fragments for the next generation. They have also discharged their duty of responsibility for their child's religious education.

Family rituals, whether religious or secular, provide opportunities for family members to meet on a regular basis and to communicate. The pattern and regularity is important. Do the family eat together, watch television together, go out together? Is there a central family dinner time, are there holiday celebration rituals? Has the impact of immigration and the loss of supportive networks led to a loss of cultural rituals, such as celebration of Chinese New Year? All these factors may have bearing on the meaning and significance to the family of the problem that has precipitated the crisis leading to referral.

Conflicts in mixed marriages

Intergenerational conflict in families with a mixed racial/cultural background may be compounded by the child's sense of confusion regarding racial or ethnic identity. Where the parental subsystem has a poorly maintained boundary, with ineffective emotional containment, the child or young person's frustrations may give rise to a wide range of deviant behavioural disturbances. There may be parental conflict over which family cultural traditions, rituals, values and loyalties are more important; cultural differences in the expected roles of spouses, including kinship obligations, may not have been resolved. The child or young person may end up being triangulated in the parental conflict, or expected to make up for the losses incurred by the parent of ethnic origin in the process of immigration. The young person will end up being unable to resolve the racial diversity in his or her background; it becomes a source of adversity instead of strength.

Refugee families

Families with a refugee background will need to be handled with particular understanding for the traumatic stresses that have been part of the family's recent experience, and allowances made for apparently uncooperative behaviour. Adults will to varying extents carry features of post-traumatic stress disorder, particularly if they have been raped or tortured. My own experience suggests that one can expect a long engagement process, as often these families find it difficult to trust authority and establishment figures, given their previous highly traumatic experiences. Lack of personal networks can lead to crises in daily living e.g. inability to heed the final written demand for payment may lead to the supply of electricity being cut off. Health visitors often report being frustrated as people never seem to be home when they call. It is unfortunately all too common that as soon as a refugee family is housed in the UK, supports are withdrawn and services that may make a difference to the family's adjustment, such as counselling, are not offered. The adults' unresolved losses of personal networks and family, social and financial status, and sense of helplessness and an inability to take control over their own affairs, often leads to a depressive withdrawal from the children and their psychological needs. Where language is a problem, and this is often the case, it means that the parents are inadequately involved with their children's school life. They are then unable to support their children's needs for integration with an appropriate peer group, which would enhance a sense of belonging.

Case study: refugee family problems

An 8-year-old girl from a French-speaking refugee family from Zaire was referred by her GP for 'bizarre behaviour' including apparent auditory hallucinations, lack of concentration and disruptive behaviour in the classroom. She was also described as having learning difficulties, and for the past year had received fairly intensive remedial help to which she had responded well; the school said she was beginning to acquire literacy skills. She was the eldest of four children. The family had enjoyed a comfortable middle-class life back home. The father spoke good English and was a political refugee, now attempting to retrain at a local community college. The mother was extremely isolated. She spoke little English, despite attending English classes. She missed the life back home and had not really wanted to come. They had left two children behind with the grandparents. The identified patient was readily able to tell us that she thought her mother was sad and unhappy at having to be in England, and particularly missed the other children, as well her extended family. The process of leaving had been precipitous and extremely dramatic, with no time for proper leavetaking. We felt the child's behavioural disturbance was a predictable response to the family's sense of loss of practically everything they had taken for granted back home: a good life, adequate accommodation, status and a good job, plus supportive social networks.

The mother felt abandoned by her husband, who was out most of the time at college and also cultivating social networks from which she was excluded. She was reluctant to encourage her children to bring friends home, out of a sense of insecurity and a fear that things may go out of control. She wanted her eldest daughter to demonstrate a capacity for helping her with housework and childcare, and felt ignored and rejected by her. In turn, many of her frustrations were vented on her daughter, who felt that more was expected of her than her same-age peers at school.

The team working with the family consisted of a psychiatrist and a psychiatric social worker. In working with this family we found we had to engage individual members of the family by ensuring that each one had space to articulate their separate concerns and views. This was particularly important for the parents. We also had to work through a French-speaking interpreter, and it was fortunate that both the therapists spoke some French, as this meant we could follow the dialogue between the mother and the interpreter (a French teacher at the school which the children attended) to some extent.

Guidelines for family assessment

While assessing families it would be useful to keep the following questions in mind:

1. What belief systems and values (including religion) influence role expectations, define and set limits of appropriate behaviour?

2. What are the structures relevant to authority and decision-making in the family? Are there formal kinship patterns? What key relationships have important supportive and homeostatic functions? What is the relevant family network to be worked with?

3. What are the stage-specific developmental tasks at different life-cycle stages for this family? How does this family negotiate life-cycle transitions, continuities and discontinuities with the past and present? What are traditional solutions and mechanisms used for conflict resolution and to what extent does the family use them?

4. How is the living unit organized to enable essential tasks to be performed?

5. What activities, including family rituals of ethnocultural and religious origin, maintain and support structural relationships? What traditional networks supported and enabled traditional family tasks to be performed? Which of these networks or rituals have been lost?

6. What are significant stresses and losses arising from the family's own experience, from the environment of origin, or from adaptation to host country? What racial or cultural factors confer advantage or disadvantage in the host culture?

7. The clinical hypothesis must take into account the meaning
    and function of the disturbance for the family, the cultural
    group and the wider community.

8. Therapeutic interventions must engage the authority
    structure in the family and be congruent with the family's
    worldview. For example, it is important to enable the
    identified client and his or her family to work out the right
    balance of separation and attachment consistent with family
    and societal norms. It is often helpful to reframe the problem
    within a developmental context, in order to make it more
    manageable.

Conclusion

Existing therapeutic techniques and methods can be successfully used in
work with ethnic minority families, providing that therapists are sensitive to the importance of respecting cultural rules and prepared to modify their clinical approach. This may mean more flexibility in working
with subsystems such as the group of sisters-in-law, rather than with the
whole family. Ethnic minority families respond more readily to therapists who are directive and assertive (Rao 1986; Tamura and Lau 1992;
Tseng 1975; Yung 1984) as this conforms to traditional expectations of
the learning process. Structural family therapy with its emphasis on
problem-solving in the present has been described as highly successful
with Chinese families in the USA (Yung 1984), where the therapist
works on modifying communication patterns while supportive of parents' traditional beliefs. Gestalt-type work and sculpting was described
by Lau (1988) including the use of metaphors and family rituals (Levick,
Jalali and Strauss 1981; Pesechkian 1986; Scheff 1979). Wolin and
Bennett (1984) link the importance of maintenance of family ritual to
the continuity of family heritage. All these strategies attempt to mobilize
strengths and assert competencies within an ethnocultural context.

References

Bassa, D.M. (1978) 'From the traditional to the modern: some observations on
    changes in Indian child-rearing and parental attitudes, with special reference
    to identity formation.' In E.J. Anthony and C. Chiland (eds) *The Child in his
    Family: Children and their Parents in a Changing World.* New York: John Wiley.
Hill, R. (1972) *The Strengths of Black Families.* New York: Emerson-Hall.

Lau, A. (1988) 'Family therapy and ethnic minorities.' In E. Street and W. Dryden (eds) *Family Therapy in Britain*. Milton Keynes: Open University Press.

Lau, A. (1990) 'Psychological problems in adolescents from ethnic minorities.' *British Journal of Hospital Medicine 44*, 201–205.

Lau, A. (1995) 'Ethnocultural and religious issues.' In C. Burck and B. Speed (eds) *Gender Power and Relationships*. London: Routledge.

Leighton, A.H. (1981) 'Culture and psychiatry.' *Canadian Journal of Psychiatry 26*, 8, 522– 529.

Levick, S.E., Jalali, B. and Strauss, J.S. (1981) 'Onions and tears: a mutidimensional analysis of a counter-ritual.' *Family Process 20*, 77–83.

Lewis, J.M. and Looney, J.G. (1983) *The Long Struggle: Well-Functioning Working-Class Black Families*. New York: Brunner/Mazel.

Lin, T.Y. (1986) 'Multiculturalism and Canadian psychiatry: opportunities and challenges.' *Canadian Journal of Psychiatry 31*, 681–690.

Littlewood, R. and Lipsedge, M. (1982) *Aliens and Alienists*. Harmondsworth: Penguin.

McGoldrick, M. (1982) 'Ethnicity and family therapy: an overview.' In M. McGoldrick, J.K. Pearce and J. Giordano (eds) *Ethnicity and Family Therapy*. New York: Guilford.

Peseschkian, N. (1986) *Positive Family Therapy*. Berlin: Springer-Verlag.

Rao, A.V. (1986) 'Indian and Western psychiatry: a comparison.' In J.L. Cox (ed) *Transcultural Psychiatry*. London: Croom Helm.

Scheff, T.J. (1979) *Catharsis in Healing, Ritual and Drama*. Berkeley, CA: University of California Press.

Tamura, T. and Lau, A. (1992) 'Connectedness versus separateness: applicability of family therapy to Japanese families.' *Family Process 31*, 319–340.

Tseng, W. (1975) 'The nature of somatic complaints among psychiatric patients: the Chinese case.' *Comprehensive Psychiatry 16*, 237–245.

Weiselberg, H. (1992) 'Family therapy and Ultra-Orthodox Jewish families: a structural approach.' *Journal of Family Therapy 14*, 305–330.

Wolin, S. and Bennett, L.A. (1984) 'Family rituals.' *Family Process 23*, 401–420.

Yung, M. (1984) 'Structural family therapy: its application to Chinese families.' *Family Process 23*, 365–374.

Chapter 5

Children, Families and Therapists

Clinical Considerations
And Ethnic Minority Cultures

Begum Maitra and Ann Miller

It is a supposition of cultural psychology that when people live in the world differently, it may be that they live in different worlds. (Shweder 1991, p.23)

Introduction

When therapist and patient meet, assumptions about the nature of problems and solutions are only one set of potentially dissonant belief systems that are conjured up. How each views the other may be dominated (and more so perhaps at the initial contact) by the professional worldview. However, as questions probe the personal spheres, each character is given by the other a personality, a story, a past. The therapist may choose to see this as 'taking a history', as though it were a collage of discoverable, objective facts about the patient. How the child or parent views it is less often considered.

By making the choice to attend, no matter how reluctant the compliance, the parent gives substance to the assumption that it is the parent, or the family, that has the problem; depending on the parent's understanding of where the problem, if any, is located, he or she may believe that the child alone requires therapy. Another view, and one especially relevant to ethnic minority families, might be that the problem lies somewhere between the child/family and other systems, such as western education or health care, that interact with it. Children themselves frequently have little power in directly influencing the course or nature of therapeutic interventions. Referred by adults (parents, teachers or other professionals) and taken to therapy by adults, the child's feelings and wishes are often overlaid by adult fears and hopes. For the ethnic minority family the relationship with western/white systems is yet more complex, and the child's 'voice' may be drowned out completely. Ethnic minority children must face a particularly difficult problem in addition to all those that face their peers, namely that of negotiating a bicultural identity and existence.

Professional curiosity most often concentrates on problems and solutions, or sometimes on pathways to care. It rarely looks for the story the child or parent has discovered about the therapist, and how this has influenced the clinical session. That 'the person of the therapist' has a major impact on therapy has never really been doubted, even when much store was placed on the supposed 'neutrality', clinical dispassion and 'objectivity' of the therapist. Observe the markers of professional identity and status – the use of jargon, patterns of speech and other communication methods (letters, appointment systems, the ritual of professional meetings), and the white coats of the past. We work hard to control how we appear as therapists to our patients. Markers of professional status may be used, among other things, to introduce the patient to a particular world within whose metaphorical language change will, we hope, be effected. However, the growing drive towards demystifying therapy not only makes therapists more visible, but also opens them, as much as their professional discipline, to critical evaluation.

The idea that difference in ethnicity between patient and therapist is significant is indeed true, but if recorded at all, ethnicity is usually seen as a discrete, 'objective' variable (such as age or marital status) and relating to the patient alone. This is, of course, a vast oversimplification. Ethnicity has come to include both the ideas of 'race' or so-called intrinsic difference, and of 'culture' or derived difference. It contains the histories of both the therapist and the patient, and is selectively defined at each encounter between two persons, varying with the context and the need to assert sameness or difference. Thus, when in a foreign land we meet someone who looks like us, we may attempt to discover how much we share. Should the environment be seen as hostile it may be enough that we are 'Asians' together, or we may choose to unite with other people of colour as 'black'. On the other hand if one has painfully acquired a measure of accommodation to the host culture, such as through training as a therapist, one may wish to distance oneself from black groups or to 'pass' as white. With so much personal investment in the identification of one's ethnic group it becomes necessary to examine carefully the various ways in which it is constructed, deconstructed and interpreted in clinical encounters.

Taking a history
Individual and collective histories

The ethnic minority population in the UK at any time reflects current and remote historical events, both local and global. Today this compels us to consider the impact of wars and genocide in parts of Europe and Africa on families and unaccompanied children seeking refuge in the UK. The immediate psychological and physical tasks focus on survival. However, our knowledge of past wars and immigrant groups informs us that the psychological fragmentation caused by these events may linger for generations, emerging in later seemingly acculturated generations as a desperate search for 'roots' that were torn away. While the impact of slavery and colonialism has been written about extensively, these events in the distant past continue to influence how the 'other' is viewed (Nandy 1983; Said 1978) – whether as white master or oppressor, as exotic black or inscrutable Oriental. When discussing minority groups it is necessary to be alert to the distinction between those who have migrated voluntarily and others. Ogbu (1990) names 'involuntary minority groups' who, like the black and Native American populations of the USA, exist within white cultures as a result of slavery, conquest or colonization.

We do not wish to suggest that therapists working with minority groups must equip themselves with all these stories; we do wish to draw attention to the need to explore these, and to how they influence the experience of ethnic minority children and their families in Britain. It is important to add that a focus on cultural history as a ground for understanding the personal present needs to include not only the tragic stories but also the heroic ones, and also to remember that 'history' itself is constructed and interpreted in each telling.

These stories about the past express themselves in how people see and think about themselves and others, in body language, range of permitted facial expressions and verbal styles, forms of address, manners, taste and personal dress; they also influence ways in which new experiences are received and interpreted. These behaviours, rich as they are in meaning, are often ignored in clinical encounters as 'soft' data, even interfering noise, that masks the 'true' and objective exchange of verbal information. The anthropological study of modes of communication and emotional expression in the west (e.g. Dreitzel 1981) restores a much needed sense of relativism to the western clinical sciences. Speaking of the Indian subcontinent and the influence of oral-based traditions, Kakar (1989) emphasizes the predominance of the narrative style, the tendency to think and reason about complex situations through the medium of stories. It must be borne in mind that a western professional preoccupation with abstract reasoning methods can, particularly in interaction with non-western groups (or indeed with non-professional groups in the west), veil one of the practices of professional power that places the patient at a disadvantage.

While gender appears to be a much simpler proposition, it is rarely so. How does a female therapist approach issues of authority, autonomy and sexuality, to name a few areas, with a boy or with his father, when they hold strongly patriarchal values? How do therapists' assumptions about gender influence the interaction with ethnic minority families who have different sets of beliefs about gender roles and hierarchies? Are we completely convinced about the separateness of the sexes (Phillips 1994), or agreed about the correct allocations of powers and roles between the sexes (Perelberg and Miller 1990); or are these thoughts about how we would like things to be rather than how they are? Williamson's (1976) review reveals that the preference for male children is not restricted to particular cultural or religious groups alone. Medical technology now permits the determination of the sex of the early foetus, and high rates of abortion of female foetuses are recorded in many parts of the world; in other countries such technology is unavailable but female infanticide, whether by exposure or more direct means, remains a concern. Where a preference for boys is not quite so strong, family practices may still treat girls unfavourably as compared with their brothers. These realities pose dilemmas in therapy that are not easily resolved by taking refuge in cultural relativism.

Public and private domains
Thinking about the setting
Many healing encounters in traditional Indian examples (Kakar 1982) are carried out in a public space and involve observers. However, the 'gaze' of the observers is not usually deemed to be hostile or unsympathetic, but rather a part of the social fabric of such encounters, and serv-

ing often as witness to the righting of a social order that has been disturbed by, and manifest in, the illness being healed. In western settings the gaze of the western professional may be more ambiguous, and perhaps feared as intrusive, hostile and potentially damaging.

Alternatively, and no less problematically, white professionals may be courted as the only contact which will be acceptable, and this can occur when children or adolescents seek support from adults who they believe will disempower their parents. It can also happen with families who feel that the gaze of the local community (of which the professional of the same cultural group is seen to be a part) will create an experience of shaming with the attendant problems that this would bring for the reputation of the family and the prospects of the children.

Case study: Nasima

Mr Khan came to the clinic with his 13-year-old daughter. They sat in the waiting room in a strained silence while Nasima glowered at her father, occasionally making spitting gestures in his direction. He was a slender Bangladeshi man in an ill-fitting suit, who sat hunched and helpless, face turned away from her. When the therapist walked into the waiting room she was horrified to discover that the girl's wrists were tightly tied together with her father's scarf. Her feet were bare. Professional concerns included fears of physical brutality and emotional abuse, and these persisted in reports on the family for several months. There were no other incidents on record of parental violence or abuse towards Nasima or the other children. Nasima was thought to be suffering from either a psychotic illness or a severe conduct disorder; the therapist's opinion was that Mr and Mrs Khan were both excessively controlling and ineffectual as suggested by their inability to keep Nasima 'under parental control'. The parents attended sessions erratically, mother did so only rarely, and further anxieties were aroused about their lack of cooperation with treatment that was essential for their daughter.

A referral was made to BM and she rang the family to arrange an appointment. The conversation began in English; Nasima's father spoke in rather stilted phrases that did not make clear whether he could attend on the day suggested. BM switched to Bengali, but uncomfortably aware of curious looks from colleagues in the office she struggled to keep her voice and intonation under some sort of 'colour control'. His voice rising in helpless frustration, Mr Khan insisted that he could not attend the clinic any more. His daughter shamed him in public, kicking and scratching passers-by as he had walked her to the clinic on the last visit. Failing to restrain her he had removed her shoes so as to protect anyone she kicked, also tying her hands for similar reasons. He and his wife were covered in bruises, but it was unthinkable that Nasima should be permitted to abuse others.

Mr Khan was very concerned about Nasima's rude and aggressive behaviour at home, but any display of this in public affected, in his mind, the family's standing in the community as well as casting a slur on Nasima herself. This, he feared, would have long-term implications in that Nasima would fail to learn behaviour considered appropriate for a Bangladeshi woman, and may even be seen by the community as 'mad', with inevitable consequences for her prospects of marriage and happiness. The ability to move clinical sessions into the home is a powerful strategic tool under such circumstances, as is access to the family's mother tongue. Both facilitate spontaneity of emotional expression and family interaction that is usually lost in the formality and 'public' nature of the clinic. Home visits also allow direct observation of the physical environment of the child, and clues about the emotional world the ethnic minority family live in (Maitra 1995) – photographs and objects from 'home', religious icons, attention to beauty and order, or the equally informative absence of these. Admittedly, the validity of such impressions is greatly dependent on the therapist's experience of homes within that culture. Such observations may guide the exploration of exactly those areas of feeling and experience that the family may otherwise find difficult to verbalize.

The family's mother tongue is another powerful means of entry into their 'inner' emotional lives, and not always because it eases the speed or volume of what is communicated. While Mr Khan was able to conduct day-to-day business in English his emotional expressions were stilted, and sometimes bizarrely exaggerated or distorted by his limited fluency, or his attempts to find literal translations for Bengali expressions. Nasima clearly enjoyed speaking to BM in English, and excluding her parents in this way. But she was also relieved that in sharing with BM this power (to speak English) she shared also her sense of unease and guilt at overthrowing parental power and authority, underscoring their powerlessness in white society.

Private space: the home

Case study: cleanliness

On a visit to a Bangladeshi home with an Asian colleague AM was surprised by the vehemence with which he commented on how 'dirty' the home was. AM, who had travelled and worked in the Indian subcontinent, had not been struck particularly by the levels of dust/grime.

BM and an English colleague visited an Indian home. The parents were middle-class Jains, members of a religious sect who live by a complex set of rules around purity and order. The meticulous attention to order and cleanliness in this home was obvious; lunch had just been served, but the kitchen was spotless and all evidence of cooking had been tidied away. The living room was bare of ornaments apart from two stone carvings of Hindu deities. In their young daughter's room dolls and soft toys were arranged in neat rows, bedroom slippers neatly parallel against the wall. The question arose of whether this was evidence of significantly obsessional traits, and a contributory factor in the child's feeding problems.

Observations of seemingly objective facts such as dirt, poverty and levels of hygiene are influenced by the position of the observer. Offended by stereotypes of 'Third World' poverty, and associations suggested between poverty, laziness, dishonesty and 'primitive cultures', more successful immigrants from these countries may seek to dissociate themselves from, or even pathologize, others who give apparent support to these stereotypes. The western observer may rate degrees of cleanliness or organization based on comparisons with western individual/group standards, on generalizations about practices in other groups that may be culturally remote, or on contemporary western cultural beliefs about physical environments and 'health'. On the other hand to avoid making any observation at all would mean the loss of valuable opportunities for enquiry into the meaning of what is observed.

    The idea of individual therapy for children has long been held by western-trained professionals as a special kind of private space, crossing the boundary of which is surrounded by careful negotiation. For some ethnic minority families this may seem strange in so far as it conflicts with their own idea of privacy, not as an exclusive space but as a space shared with the notional family. Even when children are accorded a right to be seen on their own, the fact that their privacy is not exclusive, but shared with the family, means that many parents expect to have complete access, without the necessity to seek permission, to any information imparted by the child to the professional. With the exception of teachers, who are viewed in many cultures as surrogate parental figures in their role in the socialization of the child, parents may view with distrust the idea that other professionals may have access to their child that they do not themselves have.

Family therapy on the other hand has been a much more public event, not only with more distant relatives being invited to therapy sessions but also, with the advent of teams, screens, cameras and video, with families being exposed to the gaze of a network of professionals (and 'viewing' machinery) who may not be in direct contact with the child and family, and may appear as disembodied voices commenting on the lives of those who have come to therapy. For some families a 'healthy cultural paranoia' (Grier and Cobbs 1986) will mean that they avoid such settings where they have the power to, or that they will want to check very carefully the safety of such a setting. There are still many black families, and others for that matter, who avoid statutory agencies on the basis that the risk of having their children 'taken away' is too high to chance.

Other private spaces: family relationships

Relationships within families are shaped by beliefs about the status of members, their duties, obligations and rights in relation to each other. The spaces between people, indicating closeness, formality and intimacy, are defined by rules that are shared by the cultural group though modified by personal experience and choice. The relationship between parent and child is based on a mesh of beliefs – about the nature of parents and parenting, the nature of children and childhood – which are transmuted by experiences such as immigration, economic mobility, exposure to white (British) culture, the nuclearization of family units that had been 'joint', the movement of women into the public sphere, or by marrying into another cultural group.

A recurrent theme (and an article of faith in some circles) that dominates western child psychology is the idea of the 'inner world of the child'. As sociologists and historians of western childhood have amply documented this is a fairly recent development that has followed industrialization and subsequent economic forces (Lijlestrom 1983). Freed from the labour market children were re-created in sentimentalized images of innocence; the need to occupy them within educational institutions became the child's 'right' to an education, and a progression of needs and rights were identified. In other words, modern 'childhood' was created. It is wise to remember that while this definition of the role of children may be eminently suitable as preparation for urban western society the ethnic minority family may continue to live, psychologically as well as in material terms (due to restricted employment choices), in a world that is somewhere between the country of origin and their new home. With little real understanding of western ideals, of self-realization and individual freedom, ethnic minority parents may continue to mould their children along traditional religious/cultural lines that value family and community connectedness and mutual responsibility. This is particularly relevant as the therapeutic goal of helping children (or helping families help their children) to develop in a manner appropriate to white British society may be in sharp conflict with the ethnic minority parent's wishes, and therapy may appear to be yet another attempt to 'colonize' the minds of their children.

That parents in other cultures hold very different views about what goes on inside children is revealed in their beliefs about the nature of childhood. Gil'adi (1992) discusses Islamic beliefs in the innocence of all children (as opposed to the Christian concept of original sin) and the need to teach them using sensory means of rewards and punishment (sweets and physical chastisement). With the development of *tamyiz* – the ability to discern between good and evil – around the age of 7, the child is now ready to be taught using reasoning. While the child's understanding is still limited her main responsibility is her obligation of obedience towards her parents.

Case study: Yusuf

Yusuf, age 12, was referred by the family doctor because he was completely out of the control of his Pakistani Muslim parents. They described themselves as very westernized and, for example, had stopped celebrating Eid and were now celebrating Christmas instead ('for the boy's sake'). Yusuf seemed obsessed with money and expensive gifts and his father thought he might be suffering from the same 'mental disorder' as his mother (she had a western psychiatric diagnosis). Yusuf's explanation was 'it's like half of me is a devil'. When asked if he knew anything about *jinns*, he said he had heard of them. He added that he was dissatisfied with the results of his behaviour because money and toys did not really make him happy.

AM (the therapist) hypothesized that the problems in this family could reflect the seeming opposition of western and eastern/Muslim beliefs, and also contained within them differing notions of individual responsibility. Thus Yusuf's rejection of his behaviour was based on an idea of its non-human/non-self source (the devil, or *jinns*) and a cure would need recourse to religious/spiritual interventions; to his mother it was unpleasantly materialist and westernized and in opposition to the family's Muslim spiritual heritage; to his father it was illness/disorder for which western medicine had a name, and therefore possible control over. Western professional beliefs may propose an explanation from the individual psychological domain, and describe Yusuf's behaviour as stimulated by psychological pain.

The concept of age-appropriate behaviour

Normative views of children's behaviour are not confined to psychologists or indeed to professionals. Parents and relatives themselves compare their children with various local norms and notice differences among their children. How they assign meaning to the differences governs parental expectation and anxiety about a particular child. For the professional, certain differences in child behaviour are assigned meanings which are quite different to those assigned by the parents, for example, rocking behaviour in a 6-year-old may be seen by a professional as a sign of underlying emotional deprivation, and by a parent simply as a habitual but otherwise unremarkable behaviour, or in some cultural groups it may be seen as the rehearsal of a learnt religious practice. Similarly, the history of child-rearing practices reveals an enormous range of what are seen as age- and gender-appropriate behaviours on the part of children.

Case study: Ali

Ali was 9 years old when his family fled from very traumatic experiences in the war in Iraq, finally arriving in Britain as refugees. On entering school, teachers noticed that Ali was extremely nervous, and appeared terrified each time an aeroplane flew overhead.

On referral Ali (now 10) was seen by AM and a bilingual worker with his parents and younger siblings. His father brought many documents with him as witness to the family's circumstances. They explained that Ali sometimes went to his room and screamed loudly. They had stopped remonstrating with him about it and his father explained apologetically, speaking for his wife and himself, 'We love our children but we are both so depressed, we can find no way to help them'. Ali sat silent and serious faced throughout the conversation and when he did speak, it was in the measured and serious tones of an adult.

In line with the family's request Ali was seen on his own, but before this interview the therapist sought the parents' clarification on what they, as Iraqis, expected of a 10-year-old boy. They explained, as did the bilingual worker, that the boy at this stage would be treated as a young adult and expected to behave responsibly, looking after his younger siblings.

In the interview, Ali disclosed his belief that the dictator of his country, Saddam Hussein, had sent someone to London to capture and probably kill his family. He had not discussed this idea with his parents but he believed they would confirm it. He watched the news every night with his father, so he and father 'both understood the situation'.

When she fed this interview back to the father, in the boy's presence, the therapist complimented the father on Ali's sensitivity and loyalty to his parents in attempting to take on responsibility for himself and his feelings. He had not wanted to worry his father any further, but the therapist felt that despite this courage on his part, he might have underestimated his parents' capacity to help him. She thought there were two ways in which his father in particular could help. First, it was to allow Ali for a short period to relinquish some of the responsibilities of a 10-year-old and to encourage him to act younger than his age, specifically in relation to his intellectual understanding of the complexities of the political situation in his country, and also in relation to the expression of his fears. With this in mind he should continue to watch the news with his father, but at the end of it his father should sit with him and carefully explain the meaning of everything on the news about his country and encourage Ali to ask questions about it. Ali's fears about Saddam Hussein were also explained to the father and he was asked if he thought this was likely. The father took Ali's fears seriously, but thought it highly unlikely that someone had been sent to kill him. He was again encouraged to explain this in detail to Ali and to answer his questions about it. Second, and after discussion between the therapist and the bilingual worker, it was suggested that he could call Ali to him at least twice a day and cuddle him for a few minutes, as he would a younger child.

Ali also had a problem with bed-wetting and this was worked on with his mother helping him keep a chart of wet and dry days and rewarding him with special time when he was dry. In working with both parents to effect change in their son's fearful and traumatized behaviour, Ali regained his confidence in his parents' capacity to help him and protect him, and his parents, with a growing sense of success in relation to him, experienced a lifting of their paralysing depression.

The idea that a child is treated as relatively adult at the age of 10 is not a universal. By accommodating it and respecting it, while at the same time suggesting a temporary 'regression' from part of it, a pathway was opened up for both the child and the parents to experience some degree of recovery from their highly traumatic experiences.

The positioning of the therapist

In the encounter between professionals, and child and parent from an ethnic minority, professionals can be seen either as members of the dominant culture, or linked to it by virtue of their position in a largely white organization. They will additionally be seen, potentially at least, as a repository of expert knowledge. For children still being inducted into cultural practices, the concept of a professional helper who is not a doctor or dentist is often either vague or non-existent. Permission from the family to talk to the stranger (when there are no examples of how to behave) is an important element in their readiness to do so. The child may be encouraged to adopt a 'fictive kin' position *vis-à-vis* the helper (Aziz 1979), and indeed families from some cultures may feel comfortable in talking about intimate matters only if they too can approach the therapist as kin or, at the very least, as a friend (Bang 1987). How this becomes enacted will vary from culture to culture, but important elements of it will include modes of address used by therapists and clients, tone of voice and body language – particularly proximity and touching.

Case study: Christopher

Christopher was an African Caribbean boy aged 10, the late child of his single mother who had two other grown-up children. He had been expelled twice from primary schools due, apparently, to his unruly and 'disruptive' behaviour. His mother made a self-referral, explaining that she was dissatisfied with what had happened in the previous clinic to which she had taken him. She said she had been asked questions of a personal nature by the male therapist in front of Christopher which she felt were insensitive. These were about her white boyfriend. Christopher appeared detached and fed up, but put his complaint into words: 'I have had to come here because nobody understands me'.

AM sympathized with Ms Johnson in the way in which she had been disrespectfully treated in the last clinic. She also raised a discussion with her about her experience of seeing white professionals and how this fed into her expectations about seeing another one. While Ms Johnson said she had no particular concern about the therapist being white, she did feel more comfortable with her being a woman. This discussion opened up the possibility of talking about how she perceived Christopher's treatment in his two previous schools particularly in the light of the fact that he is a black child. The presence of black teachers in his school and what they felt about it was explored. What eventually, though not immediately, became clear was that she actually felt very strongly that Christopher had been discriminated against in his last school. This emerged in the third session and would probably not have done so without the therapist's clearly signalled readiness to entertain this possibility.

It also led to a discussion between Christopher, his mother and the therapist about those ways in which his family had prepared him for coping with racism. What became obvious in the discussion was that this was an area he had not shared much with his mother, and that he felt quite strongly at times that he was attacked because he was black. He had not felt that his mother would discuss this with him. There was an important generational issue here, in so far as Ms Johnson had managed her life in white society by adapting herself to it and by attempting to submerge and ignore difference and discrimination. Christopher on the other hand, like his older siblings, lived in a subculture which talked about racism and confronted it daily. At this point there was still the possibility of negotiation between himself and his mother about developing a different 'survival kit', more suited now to his needs. At the same time Ms Johnson decided to appeal his exclusion and to take the previous school to the CRE.

For the white therapist, the experience of white racism can be understood only in so far as black people share it with her. In working with black children one possible position the white therapist can take is that of an explorer and facilitator of the child and family sharing with each other their different realities. So questions may be addressed to the parent: what do you teach the children about dealing with racism? Is it different from what you were taught? To the child: do you tell your mother when you've been upset by someone calling you racist names? What would your father think about the way you handle yourself in this situation? If your mother went to the CRE and complained that you had been treated unjustly in your previous school what do you think the result would be? Would the adults do anything about it as a result? How would you feel about her doing that for you? How would your grandmother think about it, would she agree it was a good idea? The white therapist can thus position herself as a person aware of the possible ramifications for a family living in a racist society. However, it seems likely that this can be done successfully only providing the therapist has gained the personal trust of the family members and providing also that she never loses sight of the paradox that she belongs to the dominant culture which is the source of the practices oppressing the family. In this way it sometimes becomes possible to open up a space in the therapy for the white therapist to be perceived either as 'neutral' in colour or alternatively as acknowledging (perhaps even challenging) racism in a way that the family and child can trust her to be sensitive to their ways of dealing with it without problematizing them.

Similarly, in working with white children, the white therapist can position herself as a questioner about racist or stereotypical attitudes in the child and family. When you say that all black people are the same, do you think your mother likes you to talk like that, do you think she approves of it? Do you have any black children in your class, what are their names? So if Delroy and Kwame are the same because they are black, in what way are they the same? I don't understand, are there any ways in which they are different? If your granddad heard the conversation we are having here, what would he say? What do you think your mum and dad will say about this conversation after they have left here? Do you think they will secretly agree with you talking in a racist way?

Sometimes the positioning of the therapist as a member of the dominant culture means that the family sees them, often rightly, as having more access to power in the organizations and institutions with which they deal. They can also be seen as a potential benefactor in helping the family gain access to services, goods or money. This view would fit well with the idea of the expectation of patronage. For example, within Bangladeshi society, entitlement

> operates both above and below the self. A man is entitled to subsistence from the big people he is dependent upon, but similarly there are people entitled to dependence upon him, including family members. (Maloney 1986, p.42)

In working with the 'Miah/Begum Family' (see case study below) AM wrote a letter to the Home Office supporting the application for a Bangladeshi mother's admission to Britain and also negotiated with the immigration lawyer on the family's behalf and at their request, as they had been unhappy with what they saw as his rather desultory attempts at processing their case. Although he treated the therapist with great courtesy when she called, he was obviously stung by what he saw as her implied criticism of his dealings with the family, and in fact he redoubled his obstructiveness in dealing with their case.

A well-documented stance of the therapist (Hoffman 1993) may be one in which professionals shed expertise by positioning themselves as ignorant of or seeking knowledge from the family, particularly about their cultural norms. While this position of itself can be of immense value in transcultural work (Krause and Miller 1995) it depends on the way in which the position is elaborated or enacted. If the therapist in adopting this position ignores hierarchies in the family, and treats children and adults in an egalitarian way then children from hierarchically organized families may themselves be placed in a curious position. They may feel that the 'expert' to whom their parents have brought them (or have been 'forced' to bring them) uses his or her authoritative position (as an adult and an 'expert') completely differently from the way in which their parents enact their own authoritative position. For the older child or adolescent from an ethnic minority who may be in a struggle for control with their parents and already challenging their parents' traditional values, the encounter with such a professional may fuel the child's scorn for the parents' authority. For others, who are already socialized into their cultural hierarchies of authority, the western therapist's 'democratic' stance may well appear insincere or dangerous. If the professional is from the dominant culture, there is considerable risk that the parents, in feeling disempowered by the therapist, may seek more rigid or extreme measures in their efforts to gain control in the battle with the child.

Case study: Soraya

Soraya, a 16-year-old Pakistani Muslim girl, was taken into care after her uncle and father had beaten her for attempting to go out with an Indian Hindu boy of whom they disapproved. The white professionals involved strongly disapproved of the father's views and had made little effort to mediate between the various relatives who might have allowed for some rapprochement to be found between Soraya and her father without either having to harden their positions. By the time health professionals were asked to consult on the case, Soraya had made secret arrangements to marry the boy, despite indications that neither of them was adequately ready for the marriage.

Case study: Rehana

Rehana was excluded from school for fighting with other children and for being abusive towards staff. BM wondered about the elderly Bangladeshi man seated with a young boy in the waiting room; the 'young boy' was Rehana. At 11 years age she was a stocky, bright-eyed child, hair cut very short and dressed in the contemporary 'uniform' of her British peers – the baggy trousers and shapeless jacket. She looked curiously at BM's sari, her expression a mixture of defiant bravado and shy smiles. She sneered openly at her father's discomfort as he struggled to find a way of responding to conflicting sets of stimuli – the setting of the clinic, and the encouragement to discuss (in Bengali) his thoughts and feelings about his daughter.

At the second meeting, at their home, BM heard from both parents how furious they were at Rehana's bad, unfeminine behaviour. Mother, full-term pregnant with their seventh child, was exhausted and tearful. The oldest daughter, a plump, pretty and light-skinned 19 year old, sat with her own infant, echoing her parents' complaints about how Rehana chose to dress in an immodest and revealing fashion 'like the English', refused to obey her parents, and chose to play football with boys. Rehana sat in a corner and hurled defiant responses at all of them. As the session wore on, the parents allowed that indeed girls in Bangladesh might play football though perhaps not quite as well as Rehana did, and they would be giving it up by Rehana's age, especially as she had just reached menarche. Her mother was sad about how quickly girls reached puberty nowadays, and that life in Britain was making Rehana grow up so much faster. She didn't really want Rehana to marry early but was very concerned that she might grow further and further away from Bangladeshi values and expectations. Perhaps marriage would help her to return to the order and stability of the Bangladeshi world; their eldest daughter, who had never taken to school since they arrived in Britain, seemed very contented with a traditional marriage and motherhood.

BM asked about the family's experiences since they had decided to join Rehana's father in Britain four years ago. They were non-committal until BM spoke about what she had heard other immigrant parents say, about racism, about fears of admitting unhappiness in their new lives because it sharpened the pain of all that had been left behind. They talked then of a daughter left behind in Bangladesh by a bizarre confusion around proof of paternity, about an ageing mother that they feared might die before they had saved up for the fare to visit Bangladesh. Rehana listened intently; she had heard this many times before, wept with her mother, and hated her father as her older sister did, for his ineffectual helplessness; but never when the story and its sadness had been shared with an 'outsider'. BM shifted the conversation back to experiences in Britain and soon they were all discussing the difficulties experienced, with shared animation and rueful humour. BM got Rehana's mother to talk about her childhood in Bangladesh. Rehana, now much less angry, turned her face away in embarrassment when asked to tell her mother how it was to be a child in Britain. We discussed how Bengali a child could really be in this environment, whether in fact Rehana would have to be a new sort of Bengali, and what a difficult task that was if one had no idea of the shape such an identity would assume.

These case studies reveal ways in which the therapist's self can be used in clinical encounters. For example, therapists may emphasize their own position in the political and social contexts within which treatment is being proposed; they may use their own racial/ethnic identity *vis-à-vis* the family to foster an exploration of the issues – of difference, of acquiring new, multicultural values or behaviours, of the temptation (or pressure) to acculturate or 'integrate'. Second, the therapist's use of tone of voice, body language, touching and direct emotional expression may permit and destigmatize alternative cultural ways of communicating or expressing feeling; culture being expanded here to include and explore professional and lay cultures as much as ethnic cultures.

Case study: the Patel Family

After strenuous attempts in half-a-dozen sessions to encourage Mr and Mrs Patel (both Hindu Indian but belonging to different regional and religious communities) to take 'parental responsibility' for their 1-year-old child, BM was exhausted and frustrated. They wished to spend every session angrily cataloguing each other's failings, citing events that had occurred between them and their families from the day they had married. In vain BM spoke of not wishing or being able to judge who was in the right; the couple just produced more evidence of how each had been let down or betrayed by the other. Eventually, with the uncomfortable task ahead of having to decide whether the child should be removed from their care because marital conflicts were interfering with childcare, BM abandoned all effort to maintain the stance of 'neutral' professional and with some impatience in her voice told the parents that they were behaving like children and not fulfilling their obligations to a child that had been given to them (by God). After a few moments of angry silence Mr Patel said that he 'didn't care', she (BM) could do as she wished. For the first time Mrs Patel allied herself with him, pleading with BM not to take him seriously or be offended, because her husband was only speaking from hurt. This appeared to electrify him and he spoke with much intensity, but now about his own family of origin, their past power and status, though currently much reduced. The session ended in this state of intense emotion; for the first time it was not one of unremitting hostility between the couple.

Subtle but significant change followed this session and, as suggested by Kakar (1982) and Roland (1988), we understand this as a response to the therapist's willingness to 'enter' the fray – as a family member or community elder who is visibly emotionally engaged; the neutral or dispassionate stance of the professional expert may be experienced as disengagement, or disinterest, and may wound or mystify the family that is desperately seeking help. To see the earlier endless locked argument as the couple's unwillingness to address their relationship (and their parental roles) would, indeed, be quite mistaken.

Cultural relativism in practice

Clinical work with other cultures frequently places the therapist in the uncomfortable position of not knowing how much 'cultural' information to gather, or how much is relevant. More difficult still is the emotional response aroused in the therapist by such information – whether of incomprehension, anxiety, disgust or admiration. One strategy is to take the stance that all cultural practices are equally valid and valuable – but this does not eliminate the need to act within British laws, nor does it eliminate the personal discomfort with beliefs that are dissonant with western cultural expectations of moral and psychological health.

Case study: the Miah/Begum Family

This Bangladeshi family with three children aged 11, 7 and 6 had recently arrived in London after being given permission to join their father and his first wife. When their father had gone to Bangladesh to collect them he had dropped dead with a heart attack but, knowing that the window allowing her children to emigrate would shortly close, their mother put them on the plane anyway. Their father's senior wife, Hasina, was looking after them very well but they were understandably very distressed, and the behaviour of the middle child, a girl, was so difficult that her second mother did not know what to do with her. The health visitor referred them to AM. The woman had five children of her own and was, of course, also in mourning for her husband. Nevertheless she was remarkable in her tenderness with these children and in her general care of them.

Having established that she saw no real possibility of returning the children to their mother, since their mother was now without support and would be unable to care for the children properly, it also became clear that she was overwhelmed with the demands of their behaviour. She felt that both she and her husband's junior wife wanted to carry out her husband's last wishes and keep the children in London and she wondered if the therapist could find a way to get the Home Office to agree to allowing their mother entrance.

In talking to the children about their opinions, an activity which Hasina found unusual particularly for the 5 year old, the therapist discovered that the middle girl, the index child, was the closest of the three children to their mother. Her older sister was showing few signs of missing her mother, and indeed felt that she was treated more kindly by her second mother than she was by her own. The change in her ordinal position in the family (from oldest to one of the middle children) had clearly released her from responsibilities that she had found onerous. In enjoying her new-found freedom, the 11 year old, instead of being protective to her 8-year-old sister, was annoyed with her because she felt that she may be jeopardizing their position in their new family. The youngest child was also clearly very upset, but he seemed to be able to attach himself to the new mother in a baby role and so was contained for the moment.

When these observations, and also the observations about how much the children appreciated her care, were fed back to Hasina she redoubled her energies in attempting to activate various professionals to support the junior wife's application for entry to England. In the mean time the children, bilingual worker and therapist, together with Hasina, composed a letter to be sent to the children's mother in Bangladesh giving her news of them and reassuring her that her co-wife was caring well for them. It also contained a request for the mother to send them some little object of hers (not a new purchase) for each child that they could have while they waited for the adults to sort things out.

AM's expression of a lively interest in discovering the relative positions of co-wives, the nature of their mutual responsibilities to the children of the other and the potential gains from family structures unfamiliar to western society, indicated an acceptance of this family's frame of reference with regard to family relationships. This attitude can be genuinely curious (rather than a passive and theoretical acceptance of all difference as 'cultural', or a predisposition to dramatize and exoticize non-western cultures) only after much exposure to non-western families, and to a wide range of family structures and beliefs. The danger of seeing the other as exotic, is that it is invariably accompanied by a view of them as regrettably primitive and therefore needing, however gently, to be Europeanized. Such negative assumptions may be visible in the tendency to translate 'co-wife' as 'stepmother'. The term stepmother, as evident in the fairy tales of many cultures, contains within it a value judgement of the negative sort, i.e. that they are less kindly disposed to the children of the earlier wife, and does not acknowledge the bonds that exist between women and co-wives in non-monogamous cultures. This is not to suggest that certain structures should be idealized, rather that the areas of both strength and conflict, such as in the hierarchical positions, roles and reciprocal obligations between the senior and junior wives, be explored with the family, community elders or bicultural professionals.

Conclusion

Psychological, psychiatric and psychotherapy training needs to look very carefully at models of, and values in, child development theory that are salient to ethnic minority children and families. In working with these families, professionals need to appreciate the ways in which culture is an evolving process, rather than a static one, and to be alert to ways in which the professionalization of discourse can be coercive.

References

Aziz, K.M.A. (1979) *Kinship in Bangladesh*. Dhaka: International Centre for Diarrhoeal Disease Research.

Bang, S. (1987) *We Come as a Friend*. Derby: Refugee Action.

Dreitzel, H.P. (1981) 'The socialization of Nature: Western attitudes towards body and emotions.' In P. Heelas and A. Lock (eds) *Indigenous Psychologies: The Anthropology of Self.* Berkeley, CA: University of California Press.

Gil'adi, A. (1992) *Children of Islam: Concepts of Children in Medieval Muslim Society.* London: Macmillan.

Grier, W. and Cobbs, P. (1986) *Black Rage.* New York: Basic Books.

Hoffman, L. (1993) *Exchanging Voices: A Collaborative Approach to Family Therapy.* London: Karnac.

Kakar, S. (1982) *Shamans, Mystics, and Doctors.* London: Unwin.

Kakar, S. (1989) *Intimate Relations: Exploring Indian Sexuality.* Delhi: Viking.

Krause, I.B. and Miller, A.C. (1995) 'Culture and family therapy.' In S. Fernando (ed) *Mental Health in a Multi-Ethnic Society.* London: Routledge.

Lijlestrom, R. (1983) 'The public child, the commercial child, and our child.' In F.S. Kessel and A.W. Siegel (eds) *The Child and Other Cultural Inventions.* New York: Praeger.

Maitra, B. (1995) 'Giving due consideration to families' racial and cultural backgrounds.' In P. Reder and C. Lucey (eds) *Assessment of Parenting: Psychiatric and Psychological Contributions.* London: Routledge.

Maloney, C. (1986) *Behaviour and Poverty in Bangladesh.* Dhaka: The University Press.

Nandy, A. (1983) *The Intimate Enemy.* Delhi: Oxford University Press.

Ogbu, J.U. (1990) 'Cultural mode, identity and literacy.' In J.W. Stigler, R.A. Shweder and G. Herdt (eds) *Cultural Psychology: Essays on Comparative Human Development.* Cambridge: Cambridge University Press.

Perelberg, R.J. and Miller, A.C. (eds) (1990) *Gender and Power in Families.* London: Routledge.

Phillips, A. (1994) 'Cross-dressing.' In his *On Flirtation.* London: Faber and Faber.

Roland, A. (1988) *In Search of Self in India and Japan: Toward a Cross-cultural Psychology.* Guildford: Princeton University Press.

Said, E. (1978) *Orientalism.* New York: Vintage.

Shweder, R.A. (1991) *Thinking through Cultures: Expeditions in Cultural Psychology.* Cambridge, MA: Harvard University Press.

Williamson, N.E. (1976) *Sons or Daughters: A Cross-cultural Survey of Parental Preferences.* Beverly Hills, CA: Sage.

Chapter 6

Can Talking About Culture be Therapeutic?

Work with Children and their Families

Tasneem Fateh, Nurun Islam, Farra Khan, Cecilia Ko,
Marigold Lee, Rabia Malik and Inga-Britt Krause

Introduction: the context and ourselves

During the 1990s clinicians, professionals and managers in the mental
health field increasingly began to talk about culture. With this also came
the recognition that meeting the needs of minority ethnic families,
adults as well as children, in a culturally sensitive way, is complex and requires a great deal of dedication. Because cultural differences are pervasive they also often become markers for inequality and discrimination as
well as for inequal access to health care. This can happen surreptitiously
or openly, but when such discrimination and racism are institutionalized
in organizations such as the police force or the health service, it may become extremely difficult to pin down and hazardous to address (Home
Office 1999). Under such circumstances the employment and understanding of the very notion of culture itself may become suspect and of
little clinical value. Can talking about culture be therapeutic? As with
other clinical issues it seems that mental health institutions should be organized around therapeutic efficacy rather than the other way around.
What, then, might a therapy which is sensitive to culture and free of institutionalized discrimination look like?

In this chapter we describe how talking and thinking about culture
entered into the clinical work which we as a team of systemic psychotherapists carried out in delivering services to a culturally and ethnically

mixed patient population of an outpatient mental health service situated in an inner city. Our service began as a project. This was initiated by two of our white colleagues, one of whom is a co-author here. The funding was limited and it was the aim to set up a service which could highlight and address cross-cultural and anti-discriminatory issues in mental health treatment as well as provide an impetus for managers and professionals in our mental health trust to take these issues seriously. As a team we had a unique identity in so far as we were known specifically as the Asian Service and from the point of view of the larger institution of which we were part, we represented 'ethnicity', 'culture' and 'otherness' to our more or less white British and other European colleagues. We thus shared some intimate knowledge of a language other than English as well as of a culture other than that which, despite local differences, might be described as mainstream. Yet, we also were, and are, different. Even if we can all be described as Asian, we come from different cultural and ethnic backgrounds (Chinese, Bangladeshi, Pakistani) and some of us even from societies which, in the fairly recent past, have waged war against each other (Bangladesh and Pakistan). We speak different languages (Cantonese, Sylheti, a dialect of Bengali, and Urdu) and some of us have been brought up and educated in the UK, while others have not. We adhere to different religions, although four of us are Muslim and our previous trainings, prior to becoming systemic psychotherapists, also vary. Finally, we have taken different routes to become systemic psychotherapists. Some of us have joined established training schemes and have battled with the inadequacy of the training provision in the area of race, culture and ethnicity, and others have attempted to find a less orthodox and for us more relevant training route. This has been, and continues to be, difficult for us and these difficulties highlight the complexity of trying to address discrimination and of developing culturally valid and sensitive treatments in mental health institutions.

From the beginning it seems we were employed to do something different from our mostly white European colleagues, and health service managers seemed in some way to have different expectations of us. Certainly employing staff from minority ethnic communities is an important way of addressing equal opportunities. However, the expectation has been that we were experts in particular languages as well as in culture (sometimes our own culture and sometimes in culture generally) and that clients from non-English, non-European, non-white communities especially need such expertise. Of course linguistic expertise is crucial in clinical encounters. However, language is not everything and although all of us have from time to time acted as interpreters, we were also specifically employed to address culture, to take the cultural angle on things, both for our clients and for the institution. Apparently our British and European colleagues were not able, or were not thought to be able, to do this. When we now think back about this, with the hindsight of what we have learnt through our clinical work with clients both from our own communities and from other minority ethnic groups, we realize that this was and still is an impossible thing to do. This is because talking about culture is talking about everything and in this sense every clinician does it all the time. That is to say he or she, like any one of us, cannot help but see the world though cultural lenses (Hoffman 1993; Krause 1998, 2001; Malik 2000). From this point of view it seems our British and European white colleagues, managers and employers abdicate responsibility and push on to us what really also belongs to them.

On the other hand, we have also learnt that when, for clinical reasons, we choose to address 'culture' directly in a clinical session, or when we do this indirectly either through our actions, through our questions or through the topics which we choose to address, then this may bring about conversations and interactions in the therapy around meanings which may enable our clients to address issues which they had not previously considered to be linked to their difficulties. So what happens when 'culture' is singled out for attention, when we name it with our clients, or when we notice it and it informs what we say and do? And what happens when culture is addressed with children? How can we use this ellusive concept called culture for therapeutic effect? This chapter describes our work with five families with whom talking about culture, either directly or indirectly, moved the therapy on. We first discuss culture and its relationship to emotions and the presentation of suffering. We then describe and discuss five cases with which we have worked and in conclusion we offer some views of what cultural expertise is and how such expertise can become more integral to systemic thinking.

Culture, Emotions and the Presentation of Suffering

Numerous definitions of culture abound. In general, they tend to place emphasis on culture as a shared system of meaning (Geertz 1993), which derives from 'common rituals, values, rules and laws and provides a common lens for perceiving and structuring reality for its members' (Goldeberger and Veroff 1995, pp.10–11). Whilst often it is assumed that one inherits or is born into one's culture, as if it is a top coat that we

don, it is cultivated (Mercer 1994) by the very performance of shared rituals, values, rules and laws. In the words of Unger (1999) it is not a noun
but a verb. On the one hand culture constructs us and our sense of who
we are, and on the other hand we construct it. Much of this, however,
seems invisible to us and remains unconscious. It pervades anything
from dress to the institutions that structure our society. It is often only
through the study of other cultures that we begin to gain a sense of culture as a 'system ' of meaning. However, cultures under scrutiny typically
tend to be non-western cultures and Euro-American cultures have
tended to remain untheorized as the neutral point of comparison, retain-
ing their claim to universality and in this way maintaining a position of
power. Cross-cultural work, then, should be used critically not only to
understand the meaning of suffering and emotions in other cultures but
also to recognize the particularity of our own cultural understanding of
suffering and emotions. Without this we cannot begin to develop a truly
cross-cultural approach to therapy. Furthermore, this rethinking of culture is all the more vital in a multicultural society where cultures are in
dynamic interaction (Parekh 2000).

The extent and invisibility of culture is apparent in the way we think
and talk about emotions. Ask any white English client how they feel and
they will describe a powerful feeling that arises within the body (Harré
1986; Rabinbach 1992). This highly internal conception is also mirrored in mainstream western psychological theories that construct emotions as natural essences. But this view of emotions is not universal, and
considerable cultural variation has been noted in the experience and
meaning of emotions (Lutz 1985; Schieffelin 1985; Shweder 1985).
Cultural influence is not merely a superficial external influence on the
expression of emotions, as is often assumed, but goes to the very core of
the person. Indeed it has been argued that concepts of emotions stem
from more general implicit assumptions about the culturally constructed
nature of the person (Lutz 1985; Schieffelin 1985).

In Euro-American cultures the 'self' tends to be constructed as an
'egocentric' (Shweder and Bourne 1991) or autonomous bounded individual self that is perceived as the locus of thoughts, actions and feelings.
So whilst emotions are acknowledged as being evoked in a social context, they are psychologized in terms of being seen as an index of a personal state. Moreover in this bounded self, emotions are seen as residing
within the body and ruled or interpreted and given meaning by cognitive processes residing in the mind. Such a view is also clearly evident in
theories of emotions, such as Schachter and Singer's, who argue that

emotions are subjective inner feelings which persons interpret (Schachter and Singer 1962). This model of emotions perpetuates a dualism between emotion and cognition (Crichton 2001) and between the individual and the social. As the 'feeling' and interpretation of emotions are all postulated to occur within the private space of the individual, the social and external influences on emotions are relegated to a secondary position.

However, this view is not universal. Persons in different cultures think of and experience emotions in different ways (Good, Good and Moradi 1985; Lutz 1985; Malik 2000). In so-called non-western cultures the 'self' tends to be constructed as 'sociocentric' (Shweder and Bourne 1991), unbounded and permeable, indexed in a particular set of social relationships. Behaviour, cognition and emotions are then seen as a function of relationships and are contextually located. In these cultures emotions are seen as the property of relationships and different relationships, such as the parent–child relationship, may be characterized by different kinds of culturally sanctioned emotions or themes (Krause 1998).

Across cultures, then, emotions are not only given differential meaning but may also be experienced and located differently. On the one hand, culture constructs and gives meaning to individual experiences of emotions and on the other is, at the same time, constructed by individual emotional experiences. What is to be considered suffering and what it constitutes in a British cultural context coalesces around and is validated by the medical system. Within the psychotherapeutic field we have numerous names and theories for emotional syndromes and suffering as well as ideas of how they are best treated. There is growing acknowledgement of the cross-cultural variation in notions of suffering and what constitutes an emotional disorder as well as treatment. This variation becomes all the more pertinent in the case of minority cultural groups. Within Britain research indicates variation in the rates of emotional disorder, such as depression (Cochrane 1977; Cochrane and Bal 1989), variation in the presentation of emotional suffering (Bal 1987; Wilson and MacCarthy 1994) and the lack of recognition of the suffering of minority ethnic groups by mainstream health services (Beliappa 1991; Bowes and Dmokos 1993; Currer 1986; Fenton and Sadiq 1993). Yet there is still little accompanying acknowledgement of the cultural particularism of the very notions of emotional suffering itself. As Bhugra (1999) points out, in the case of cultural minority clients, health practitioners attempt to fit them into diagnostic systems known to them, or where there is no fit, the causation is ascribed to cultural factors. Here again culture is seen as the property of 'others', namely ethnic minorities, and not the wider health care system.

Children

All this applies equally to children. In fact one could go as far as to say it applies especially to children. The infant's first interaction is with the mother or carer. But this mother/carer is not any mother or carer, it is a particular person in a particular space and time who interacts with, thinks about and feels according to the cultural conventions around her as well as according to how she herself was interacted with, which in turn was influenced by a particular cultural context. It is this person, herself a reflecting interacting being, who the infant experiences. Of course the infant knows little about how this could have or might have been different, but the infant may be able to have a glimpse of the way 'things hang together'. For example Toren (1990) showed that 8–10-year-old children on the island of Gau in central Fiji understand that chiefs and high-ranking people are of superior status because they sit in the area, which is referred to as 'above'. Adults do not see it like this. For them, where the high chief sits *is* above. The children thus experience something, albeit intuitively, which the adults tend to overlook, namely that the way people behave towards each other not only expresses, but also is constitutive of, their relationships (Toren 1990). Children are highly tuned into learning and also to what their parents, consciously and unconsciously, want them to learn. It is often in this space between adults and children and the accompanying cultural themes and patterns that our interventions can be most effective.

Case material

It follows that all talk about feelings, experiences, emotions, behaviour and thought may be culture talk and that children learn and experience the world and their relationships to their carers and others in culturally specific ways. While some feelings and sensations may be universally present and experienced by human beings, the way they are expressed and the meanings they communicate are culturally constructed. Culture pervades everything and in this sense we can never avoid addressing it. However, in different contexts and with different families we may choose to highlight one aspect rather than another and in some families one aspect of culture may be more salient than another. In the descriptions of cases which follow we made use of different facets of what we might broadly call culture and in each case we chose to highlight and work with one particular aspect because this seemed to fit with what the family needed. This does not mean that we could not have chosen other aspects. However, what we show is that whatever the intervention, cultural material must be addressed, not over and above other issues but as an integral part of the approach.

Case study: culture, language and familiar kinship

Children from non-white, non-European cultures who arrive in the UK face many difficulties. Children are quick to learn, but equally they do not face the world with the same kind of certainty and continuity with which healthy adults may successfully negotiate new problems. In school children may not understand their peers, they may see other children from minority ethnic communities being bullied, they may not know how to negotiate problems and difficulties, they may not be able to ask their parents' advice. Their parents too may be struggling with life stage issues in an unfamiliar social context. These experiences, in turn, may reflect and be reflected in a family situation in which children are at risk of physical and/or emotional abuse and neglect. Such was the case in a Bangladeshi family referred by social services to the Asian Service. This family consisted of Mr A (32) and Mrs B (29) and their four children (three boys and one girl, aged 10, 8, 6 and 5). Mr A came to live in England with his parents at the age of 16. He is the eldest of four siblings and the extended family used to live together until this became too cramped and Mr A and his wife moved to a flat nearby. Mr A used to work in a restaurant, but after his father's death a few years ago he began to drink excessively and take drugs. He also began to be violent to his wife in front of the children. On one such occasion the eldest boy called the police and Mr A was removed. The children were then placed on the social services' At Risk Register and a referral was made to the service in which we work. After a while Mr A saw a psychiatrist who prescribed antidepressants and he was allowed to join his family on a trial basis. At this point we offered family therapy and we saw this family intermittently over three and half years.

Our first session was a home visit and one of us, who is Bangladeshi speaking the same dialect (Sylheti) as the family, took the lead. We consciously aimed for this session to concentrate on the parents and their suffering. This was in accordance with the family's own expectations, namely that unless specifically asked to do so, children should not join in when parents or elders are talking to visitors. The next session took the same course, except that halfway through we asked for permission to speak to the children. The parents both granted this and the children joined the meeting. The next few meetings took place at home with the whole family and the children increasingly related to us as members of their extended family. The youngest climbed on our laps and all of them were eager to use our pens and paper.

After some time the father began to drink again and after a violent incident had to leave the family. We continued to work with the children as if we were members of the extended family, supporting Mrs B, encouraging the children to do well at school and giving advice both about school work and about life in the UK generally. Eventually, all the children did well at school and Mrs B became able to manage independently. Throughout, contact with the father remained supervised.

Although we had hoped that we would be able to address the issues faced by Mr A (his childhood experiences, his mourning of his father, the difficulty of being the eldest surviving son in an immigrant setting) we felt compelled to focus on the predicament of the children. In this we consider that we were successful first because sessions could take place in Sylheti and second because we approached our connections to the children in ways which were isomorphic with general principles of Bangladeshi kinship (Gardner 1995). We did not begin by talking to the children, but spoke first to their parents, whose permission we sought before talking to the children directly. This showed to the children that we were of their parents' generation and that we respected their parents. We also allowed the children to interact with us as if we were kin. In many kinship systems this is a common way of incorporating strangers (Holy 1996). Thus they sat on our laps, asked us questions etc. and Mrs B came to see us more as relatives than professionals.

Case study: addressing culture as a general theme

In Cantonese the term for culture is a combination of two words: *wen*, the meaning of which is encapsulated by the opposite of 'force', and *hua*, which means to teach, to inspire and to influence. Together these meanings point to a different and perhaps more pervasive notion than is commonly understood in English. To influence, inspire and teach without the application of force is clearly integral to life generally and involves moral as well as technical domains. In the following family the therapist addressed culture in this general way, referring to tradition, practices, morality and how things generally 'used to be done'. There were three children in this Chinese family from Hong Kong: Kong (15), Yee (12) and a baby girl aged 2. The parents Mr and Mrs Chan were in their early forties and they had arrived in England four years before. Mrs Chan appeared upset and nervous and Mr Chan spoke for her saying that she needed help with her emotional problems. Mrs Chan herself said that she thought that she was not being a good mother. After some conversations it emerged that Kong found it difficult to control his temper. He hit his sisters and he had also thrown and broken things at home. Kong managed to convey that he felt unhappy and that sometimes it felt as if he was about to explode. He had few friends at school and he was embarrassed about his own English and about Chinese people speaking English. The therapist encouraged Kong to talk more about his difficulties and also asked how these difficulties compared with Mr and Mrs Chan's own experiences when they were at school. This led to a comparison between the different traditions, the different expectations and the different 'teachings' in Hong Kong and in England. For example the parents were able to see Kong's quest for independence in a new light and in this way understand the issues not as a result of a defiant son, but as a result of the new social context in which they all found themselves. Collectively this allowed the family to move from feeling divided by different unexplained emotional experiences to being united in recognizing their predicament.

Case study: kinship roles and social contexts

In this case Mrs M, a Bangladeshi woman, was referred to our service by a community mental health team. Mrs M had been prescribed antidepressant drugs and her psychiatrist was seeking to understand more about the family dynamics so that the family could be given appropriate support. The family consisted of Mrs M (50), her eldest son Sohail (27), who was suffering from a mental illness and who was in care, Muhammad (22), who was a student and worked part-time, the only person in the family who worked, Begum (18), Mrs M's only daughter, who also was a student and her two youngest sons Ali (16) and Ahmed (8), both still at school. Mrs M's husband had lived in England for 25 years and had intermittently visited his wife in Bangladesh. There the family had lived in his parents' house under the domination of their paternal grandmother, Mrs M's mother-in-law. Muhammad had taken the decision four years ago that the whole family should move to England in order to improve their lives. Once the family arrived their father refused any contact with them and they did not in fact know his whereabouts. The first meeting was attended by Mrs M, Begum and her two youngest sons. Muhammad was not there and later it became clear that collectively the family held the view that a man should not have to talk about personal matters such as his mother's mental state. Mrs M was unable to dress and bathe without help, she had a very slow gait and she said herself that she was 'stuck to the ground'. Throughout this first session she sat almost motionless in a chair relying on her daughter to answer all the questions put to her.

The therapist, a Bangladeshi Sylheti speaker, worked slowly over several sessions introducing herself and talking to the family about their difficulties. She listened to the daughter's request that no one speaks about her father in front of Mrs M and also heard Begum express her worries that her mother might refuse to take the prescribed medication regularly. Indeed Begum was, as were all the children in the family, a competent child. She fetched her youngest brother from school and she generally cooked and carried out the household work. Her eldest brother was the breadwinner and the younger sons also contributed to the running of the household. The therapist acknowledged their efficiency openly, but also talked about how this competency paradoxically helped make their mother 'incompetent'. If they mothered her then she could do less mothering of them. In effect this deprived their mother of one of the roles about which she must have had much expectation as a new bride and a young mother. Sadly in this area her expectation had not been realized because she had been under the domination of her mother-in-law. The therapist stressed that Mrs M was still a mother and that each of her children must also have expectations of her in relation to them, even though these expectation would be different for, say, Begum and the 8-year-old Ahmed. At the same time the therapist shared with Mrs M her own experiences of having different roles. She spoke to Mrs M about being a mother herself and also about being a daughter-in-law. They drank tea and chewed betel leaf together. This opened up a conversation between the therapist and Mrs M which addressed what the therapist felt to be issues that had never been talked about. Mrs M told the therapist about her role as a daughter-in-law in a home where the husband/son was absent and suspected of having married again abroad. She had been ostracized and in many ways blamed for these events. When she once had tried to escape from the household with Muhammad when he was a baby, her in-laws had considered her to be mad. Since then, for 22 years, she had never been allowed to mother her own children. She never fed them or bathed them and was never allowed to spend much time in their company.

This, then, revealed a different story. Mrs M had been deprived of the one role in which her competency could have flourished. Further, now in a different context this old 'system' was maintained by different circumstances. She was diagnosed as mentally ill and her children had taken the parenting roles upon themselves. The children wanted their mother to be independent, but still it was not clear what kind of and how much independence was acceptable to the family and possible for Mrs M. Conversations about these issues became the focus for subsequent sessions and after a while Mrs M became able to shop, to cook and to grow a vegetable garden. She also managed to socialize with some of her Bangladeshi neighbours. By focusing on the cultural content of kinship roles the therapist was able to open up a conversation about an area in which Mrs M, despite her sadness and suffering, could develop some competency. This could not be addressed without also addressing both the overt and covert cultural dimensions of Mrs M's role as a mother.

Case study: symbols and their meaning

So far we have written about our work with clients where these clients are more or less like ourselves in the sense that they broadly come from our own cultural backgrounds and/or have some connection to the same geographical locations. However, as we have suggested in the beginning of this chapter, no match can be complete. In the work with Mrs M the cultural and language similarities concealed class differences between the therapist's own family and that of the client's. The next case is an example of work which was clearly cross-cultural. This family came from Tunisia and they were seen by two therapists: one, a British Pakistani woman, who like the family is also a Muslim, and the other, a white French man, who spoke to the family in French. The family consisted of a mother, a father and Ali, who was 5. However, both parents also very often referred to their own families in Tunisia right from the beginning of the therapy. In this the family of the mother was considered more traditional than the family of the father and this family was also more connected to our clients perhaps because the mother had been in England for a shorter time (less than ten years) than the father.

The referral was made by a health visitor, who was concerned about Ali's diet. Ali had had physical problems with his reflux and had received surgery in order to have this put right. Consequently eating often resulted in him vomiting and in him not wanting to eat. The therapists quickly felt that there were some issues which somehow seemed to belong to the parents, but which also did not seem easy to talk about. The therapists did not know enough to be certain what these issues were and also felt that keen interest or curiosity about the couple might involve the crossing of boundaries which the family had not invited them to do. Instead the therapists explored with the family their idea of 'a good life' of how they wanted to live as well as their hopes and fears for the future. As Muslims these questions entailed a preoccupation with faith in Allah and a commitment to something bigger than oneself or the family. They also allowed recognition of the importance and meaning of 'Insah Allah' (God willing), an utterance which can be heard in Muslim cultures and which very often accompanies statements of hopes and wishes for the future. The gist of this is not that individual motivation and agency are denied. Rather it implies that a more realistic picture of the world, social as well as physical, as one in which persons are part of an ecology, which incorporates not only relationships between persons but also some notions about the meaning of their existence.

This provided a way of connecting the worldview or general outlook of this family with their current predicament. Food plays an important role in Islam, in rituals as well as in family life and in the economy of a family. Indeed in many ways food can be seen as a point where these different spheres intersect. The following are examples of this intersection, which were discussed with the family:

1. Ramadan, a period of fasting and abstinence.[1]

2. Feeding a baby is in many cultures not only a symbol of nourishment and attachment, but also of the passing on of vital physical characteristics.

3. The family were experiencing financial difficulties and the father found it difficult to 'feed three mouths'.

4. Traditional food was sent from Tunisia by relatives, thus providing not only nourishment and connection but also a cultural reminder.

Through these discussions some of the issues, which the therapists had felt, but could not pin down, in the beginning of the therapy, emerged. For example, while the mother considered it a man's primary duty to feed his family, the father felt that he had worked hard at this for many years and that he was not succeeding. This difference expressed a difference in orientation. While the father played football and socialized with English friends or wanted to take the family out, the mother preferred to stay at home referring to parenting skills such as protecting a child from the cold or from the gaze of strangers. These skills she had learnt from her mother. The therapists continued to frame all these issues around feeding and to connect these to the difficulties of feeding Ali. In this way they stuck to their concern about Ali but also addressed the underlying issues in a culturally appropriate manner using the agenda set by the family itself.

Case study: addressing culturally constructed background material

Our last case takes the idea of working towards addressing something which the therapist feels needs addressing but about which he or she is not certain and may not know how to begin. The option of asking the family may not be there, either because the very act of asking may offend the family or because the family is not itself aware of this material. In the previous case the therapists felt that the parents were aware of their disagreements, but they were not able to know or see that these disagreements expressed something bigger than their predicament. The task of the therapist is to help bring such background understanding to the fore (Krause 1998) and in the last case we offer an example of how a therapist used such culturally constructed background understanding in her work with a boy from a similar background to herself.

Tom, who is a 10-year-old Chinese boy from Hong Kong, was referred with his father, Mr C, his 26-year-old stepmother and his 3-year-old stepsister. The whole family said that they felt very unhappy but also emphasized that they were homeless. It is not unusual for non-western families to emphasize the practical problems in the same vein as or instead of disclosing psychological and emotional problems. This was a reconstituted family. Tom's mother had died in childbirth and Tom had been cared for by different carers before his father had remarried. He had lived with his aunt, the elder sister of his mother, for five years, but apart from this there had been no continuity of attachment to a mother-figure during Tom's childhood so far. Mr C was working long hours in a restaurant and was also involved in other business and the care of Tom and his stepsister was therefore mostly left to Mrs C. Mrs C found this difficult and she discussed this in individual sessions with the therapist, herself Chinese. Mrs C said that she knew that in Chinese culture a son was far more important than a daughter and there was also the fact that Mr C's first wife had risked her life in giving birth to his son. Mrs C said that sometimes she doubted whether Mr C loved his daughter as much as his son and she suspected that he had married her because he wished her to care for Tom. When Mrs C and her daughter went to China for two months over Christmas in order to visit her mother, the therapist decided to meet with

Tom on his own in order to explore how Tom himself experienced people in the world around him. Foremost in her mind was the distance between Tom and his father (Tseng, Qui-Yun and Yin 1995). The therapist herself had a distant relationship with her father and remembered how he also never verbalized his affection and care for his children.

When the therapist collected Tom from his classroom, Tom began to talk on the way to the therapy room about how he had been scolded by his father in the afternoon. Mrs C had also told the therapist about how, in fact, Mr C was a passionate and caring father. Although he might speak to his son in a rough way often with a tone of blame, he had admitted to his wife that he missed Tom when he was away. When the therapist asked Tom about the reason for his father's scolding, Tom told her that he had been scolded because he coughed. This again reminded the therapist of her own father and she said: 'Whenever I had a cold or when I coughed, my father always complained that I did not take good care of myself. He said I did not wear enough clothes, so I got a cold. But when you are sick, you are sick. It might not be because I did not wear enough clothes as he said.' Tom agreed by fervently nodding his head. The therapist then said 'And he never bought me clothes'. Tom responded enthusiastically by saying 'Exactly'.

In this sequence the therapist used her own childhood experience in order to show her empathy towards Tom and in order to be able to set a better context for communication (Wilson 1998). She used her own cultural knowledge, some of which had only become conscious and integrated into her emotional outlook and understanding during her therapeutic training. Since Mr C came from rural Hong Kong she assumed some similarity between his background and that of her own father, who was born towards the end of the nineteenth century. Both fathers were of Hakka cultural origin.[2] Tom, on the other hand, was born in the UK and educated during a different era in Hong Kong and the UK by people who had different beliefs and worldviews. It was therefore possible that Tom did not recognize his father's style and his ways of showing affection and care. With this in mind the therapist had the following conversation with Tom.

Therapist: You told me that your father was very fierce this morning. Can you guess what made him like that?

Tom: Because he was angry and upset.

Therapist: What made him upset?

Tom: He was upset that I swallowed phlegm.

Therapist: I remember my son did the same thing when he was young. What did your father tell you about the phlegm?

Tom: He said it was no good. I should spit it out...

Therapist: Did he tell you why you have to spit?

Tom: He said that I was hot and the phlegm made me cough.

> Here Tom is referring to a traditional Chinese medical model (Hsu 1999) that yin, which is cool, and yang, which is heat, together construct the physical processes in the human body. A good balance between yin (cool energy) and yang (heat energy) around different organs of the body will maintain good physical health. Tom did not explain this, but the therapist decided to check it out and use this for further conversation to explore whether Tom understood why his father acted and talked the way he did. Her aim was to explore Tom's relationship to his father further.

Therapist: Do you know what is hot?

Tom: I always coughed and felt sick when I was hot.

Therapist: Have you heard of white and yellow phlegm?

Tom: No...

Therapist: Some people say that when you have white phlegm that means that your body is cool and when you have yellow phlegm that means that you are too hot. And they also say that the Lo-Han-Kuo can take away the heat. Do you think that your father thinks these things too?

Tom: Probably...

Therapist: But it sounds interesting to me. Just then we talked about those Chinese fathers who did not buy clothes for us. It seemed they left the mothers to do this job. Talking about the same thing...boiling herbal medicine, making drinks like Lo-Han-Kuo or caring for children. Usually they left these things to the mothers. But your father bothered to do

that this morning and care about your phlegm... Did it
mean that he cared for you...do you think?

Tom: I...don't know.

Tom then proceeded to tell the therapist how his father used to
make an extra effort to please him when he was younger. He
would buy him toys so that he would drink his herbal tea, eat his
rice and pass the 'pooh' in the toilet. He said that his father did
not try to please him any more, but that he tried to please Tom's
3-year-old stepsister because she was still young. He was clearly
upset about experiencing this loss of affection. The therapist was
aiming to connect to this experience of a child who wished for
affection instead of being blamed for being sick. In the
beginning she joined Tom by challenging and blaming the
Chinese cultural practice of scolding children and by letting him
know that she also knew that a Chinese child could not disagree
with his or her parent. With this she was sharing something with
Tom about the differences between an English father and a
Chinese father. Tom had clearly also described a Chinese father
who cared for his son, a father who wanted him to drink herb tea,
who wanted him to wrap up warm and who showed an interest in
his health. The therapist's own understanding and experience of
yin and yang and hot and cool was vital in her tuning into Tom
and the way in which his father cared for him. This provided a
chance to ask Tom to reflect on his ideas and feelings about why
his father had been fierce towards him in the morning. In this
way the therapist was able to help access and elucidate the
cultural background understanding which in part formed the
context of the life of this family and in this way provide a place
for reflection for Tom both about the similarities and the
differences between him and his father. This was addressed later
in sessions with the whole family.

Conclusion: Talking about Culture

There is thus a sense in which talking about culture is like talking about
everything else too. Talking about culture is talking about being a human being connected to other human beings. Children connect to their
carers and the adults around them in culturally specific and sanctioned
ways. What they all share is that they connect, but they do not share how
they connect. This is why our work always moves from the knowledge

of the former to an exploration of the latter. This latter part cannot be left out because this is not only about how we connect but also about how therapists communicate with their clients. This implicates technique and general approach as well as training. Sometimes the 'how' is obvious and we know it either consciously or unconsciously, but equally often even when we work with clients who broadly come from similar cultural and language backgrounds to our own, we cannot assume the 'how'. This means that we must use similarities as well as differences to do our work and although some information and experiences are useful, we cannot apply such knowledge directly without first checking out whether it is relevant to particular clients in particular contexts. It is true that *we* might be better than our white British and European colleagues at making therapeutic use of culture in our work because of our own experiences of more than one culture and language, and our experiences of cultures that are dissimilar in fundamental respects. In relation to this we argue that attention to culture enhances systemic paradigms and systemic psychotherapeutic interventions. Indeed without attention to culture systemic thinking is not properly systemic. We therefore consider that the work of family therapists from minority ethnic communities like ourselves adds particular value to mainstream mental health services. We do not therefore see ourselves primarily as cultural experts, but as systemic experts with cultural knowledge. Fundamentally, then, the issues about culture and discrimination are issues for everyone, for all clinicians and trainers as well as trainees. Why, then, do these issues get pushed onto us as if we should own them? Two answers come to mind. It could be because our extra value has been recognized. However as we have argued above this is not how it feels and judging by the reluctance with which cultural diversity is addressed generally in the NHS currently, there is not good evidence to support this. As the Macpherson Report acknowledges (Home Office 1999), it is therefore more likely to be because cultural differences have joined race, skin colour and ethnicities as vehicles for discrimination and power politics.

Acknowledgement
We wish to thank our colleagues Sue Fyvel and Philippe Mandin for giving permission to write about work in which they, too, have been involved.

Notes

1. Ramadan happens once a year and persons are expected to abstain from food, water, sexual intercourse, impure thoughts and smoking from sunrise to sunset. Symbolically this highlights the 200-mile journey the Prophet made from Medina to Mecca, because on this journey he did not have access to food or water. The aim of Ramadan is to refresh and to review the soul and to bring you closer to Allah. It is a test of the will of persons to perform this duty and successful observance brings with it raised motivation, hope and pride.

2. Hakka: Ha = guest, Ka = home. The early Hakka people were groups of Chinese migrating from Kwantung Province (South) of China to Hong Kong. They always regarded themselves as Ha (the guests in Hong Kong). Since they fancied to return to China when they retired, they treated Hong Kong as their 'guest-home'. Another view is that those Chinese who migrated from Southern Kwantung in China had been discriminated against by local residents of Hong Kong as Ha (guests). That is to say they were living where they did not belong.

References

Bal, S. (1987) 'Psychological symptomatology and health beliefs of Asian patients.' In H. Dent (ed) *Clinical Psychology: Research and Development.* London: Croom Helm.

Beliappa, J. (1991) *Illness or Distress? Alternative Models of Mental Health.* London: Confederation of Indian organizations.

Bhugra, D. (1999) 'Cross-cultural psychiatry revisited.' *International Review of Psychiatry 11*, 91.

Bowes, A.M. and Dmokos, T.M. (1993) 'South Asian women and health services: a study in Glasgow.' *New Community 19*, 4, 611–626.

Cochrane, R. (1977) 'Mental illness in immigrants to England and Wales: an analysis of mental hospital admissions.' *Social Psychiatry 12*, 25–35.

Cochrane, R. and Bal, S. (1989) 'Mental hospital admission rates of immigrants to England: a comparison of 1971 and 1981.' *Social Psychology and Psychiatric Epidemiology 24*, 2–12.

Crichton, P. (2001) 'Mind over mood? The paradoxical triumph of Beck's cognitive therapy.' *Times Literary Supplement* 27 April, 14–15.

Currer, C. (1986) 'Concepts of mental well- and ill-being: the case of Pathan mothers in Britain.' In C. Currer and M. Stacey (eds) *Concepts of Health, Illness and Disease: A Comparative Perspective.* Leamington Spa: Berg.

Fenton, S. and Sadiq, A. (1993) *The Sorrow in my Heart: Sixteen Asian Women Speak out about Depression.* Bristol: Commission for Racial Equality.

Gardner, K. (1995) *Global Immigrants: Local Lives, Travel and Transformation in Rural Bangladesh.* Oxford: Clarendon.

Geertz, C. (1993) *The Interpretation of Cultures.* London: Fontana.

Goldeberger, N. and Veroff, J. (1995) *The Culture and Psychology Reader.* New York: New York University Press.

Good, B.J., Good, M.J.D. and Moradi, R. (1985) 'The interpretation of Iranian depressive illness and dysphonic affect.' In A. Kleinman and D. Good (eds) *Culture and Depression.* Berkeley, CA: University of California Press.

Harré, R. (1986) *The Social Construction of Emotions.* Oxford: Basil Blackwell.

Hoffman, L. (1993) *Exchanging Voices: A Collaborative Approach to Family Therapy.* London: Karnac.

Holy, L. (1996) *Anthropological Perspectives on Kinship.* London: Pluto.

Home Office (1999) *The Stephen Lawrence Inquiry: Report of an Inquiry by Sir William Macpherson of Cluny.* London: Stationery Office.

Hsu, E. (1999) *The Transmission of Chinese Medicine.* Cambridge: Cambridge University Press.

Krause, I-B. (1998) *Therapy across Culture.* London: Sage.

Krause, I-B. (2002) *Culture and System in Family Therapy.* London: Karnac.

Lutz, C. (1985) 'Depression and the translation of emotional worlds.' In A. Kleinman and B. Good (eds) *Culture and Depression.* Berkeley, CA: University of California Press.

Malik, R. (2000) 'Culture and emotions.' In C. Squire (ed) *Culture in Psychology.* London: Routledge.

Mercer, K. (1994) *Welcome to the Jungle.* London: Routledge.

Parekh, B. (2000) *Rethinking Multiculturalism: Cultural Diversity and Political Theory.* London: Macmillan.

Rabinbach, A. (1992) *The Human Motor: Energy, Fatigue and the Origins of Modernity.* Berkeley, CA: University of California Press.

Schachter, S. and Singer, J.E. (1962) 'Cognitive, social and psychological determinants of emotional states.' *Psychological Review 69,* 379–399.

Schieffelin, E.L. (1985) 'Cultural analysis of depression effect: an example from New Guinea.' In A. Kleinman and B. Good (eds) *Culture and Depression.* Berkeley, CA: University of California Press.

Shweder, R.A. (1985) 'Menstrual pollution, soul loss and the comparative study of emotions.' In A. Kleinman and B. Good (eds) *Culture and Depression.* Berkeley, CA: University of California Press.

Shweder, R.A. and Bourne, E.J. (1991) 'Does the concept of the person vary cross-culturally?' In R.A. Shweder (ed) *Thinking through Cultures: Expeditions in Cultural Psychology.* Cambridge, MA: Harvard University Press.

Toren, C. (1990) *Making Sense of Hierarchy: Cognition as Social Process in Fiji.* London: Athlone.

Tseng, W-S., Qui-Yun, Lu and Yin, P.Y. (1995) 'Psychotherapy for the Chinese: cultural considerations.' In T-Y. Lin, W-S Tseng and E-K. Yeh (eds) *Chinese Society and Mental Health.* Hong Kong: Oxford University Press.

Unger, R. (1999) 'Some musings on paradigm shifts: feminist psychology and the psychology of women.' *Psychology of Women Section Review 1,* 2, 58–62.

Wilson, M. and MacCarthy, B. (1994) 'GP consultation as a factor in the low rate of mental health service use by Asians'. *Psychological Medicine 24,* 111–113.

Wilson, P. (1998) *Child Focused Practice: A Collaborative Systemic Approach.* London: Karnac.

Chapter 7

What is a Positive Black Identity?

Nick Banks

Introduction

Historically psychologists have categorized 'identity' as two 'components' – one of 'personal identity' and one of 'social identity'. Social identity is a concept that was developed in the early 1970s by Tajfel (1972). He defined this as 'the individual's knowledge that he/she belongs to certain social groups with some emotional and value significance to him or her of the group membership' (Tajfel 1972, p.31). Social identity was seen as relating to the individual's view of self as a group member. Social identity comes about through membership of particular social groups, e.g. being black, a woman or a teacher. Social identity was seen as important in that one could derive a sense of involvement and pride from one's experience of sharing a social category membership with others, without having close personal relationships and 'knowing' the group members by knowing of their achievements. It was believed that individuals developed a psychological connection to their group (whether culturally, nationality, gender or sexuality based) through their self-definitions as members of that group. It is important to be aware that in this context, 'self-definition' may relate to the introjections or internalized views of others. This may be either negative or positive in effect. The second component of identity, 'personal identity', relates to the way that an individual defines her or himself as different from others.

Personal identity relates to an individual's particular qualities, both psychological and physical, that are seen as unique to that person, as an interaction of both genetic and environmental influences. This covers a wide range of factors such as sexuality, ethnicity, culture, gender, disability etc. It may be that personal identity can be best seen as the outcome of a socialization process.

In this chapter the term 'racial identity' will be used to mean how individuals conceive of themselves in relation to their ethnic group (however they define this group membership) and how they perceive their 'goodness of fit' within their ethnic group.

Abrams and Hogg (1990) argue that when personal identity predominates over social (group) identity, one does not feel as though one has to identify or act as a group member. When social identity predominates, the group is represented in the individual's self-concept, and this allows the structure and coordination of collective group behaviour. Individuals are therefore seen as psychologically connected to social groups through their self-definitions as members of these social groups.

While the distinction between social and personal identity may be theoretically interesting, it may be seen as essentially an artificial and abstract separation. In real-life terms, it would be difficult to separate the two concepts particularly when considering the development of children. Richard (1994) suggests that a more accurate conceptualization would be to speak of 'psychological' and 'sociological' identities. His argument is

> This would make it clear that we have a personal identity which is not something outside of society and the social (in a broad and deep sense including history), but which is something different from the sociological description of the individual as belonging to certain social groups in the here-and-now class, ethnic group, religion and so on. It has a psychological inner reality which has an existence apart from these on-going group memberships in the external world. (Richard 1994, p.83)

While this may seem initially seductive the difficulty may be that in the case of considering the black child living in a white society, Richard's conceptualization appears to require the black child to separate (black) 'self' from (black) 'group' and the external pressures of (white) society. Seen from another point of view this relegates the black child to what could be seen as a disenfranchised group membership or disrupted social belonging with all of the ensuing psychological conflicts and dilemmas.

Tizard and Phoenix (1994) pose the question of the problematic nature of defining exactly what a 'positive black identity' is. Tizard and Phoenix suggest that the use of the term 'positive' suggests that it is not acceptable for any black child to feel anything other than proud of being black. From my point of view this would appear a quite reasonable and justified expectation. However, they make the suggestion which draws on a view of Jackson *et al.* (1981) that a more relevant question is one of 'what is the balance of their positive and negative feelings towards their group, and to what extent do they identify with the positive rather than the negative images they have of the group?' Given this reconstruction of the notion of 'positive identity', the question still remains whether it is unacceptable for any child to feel other than positive about being black.

Tizard and Phoenix (1994, p.94) go on to suggest that 'Young black people can have negative feelings about their racial identity, and yet have a positive self-concept'. Such a notion that black children can experience negative views about their racial identity and have a positive self-concept appears to attempt to abstract them from a social and psychological reality. The difficulty may be in the application of Eurocentric psychological concepts to non-European groups (Parham 1993). For example, Baumeister (1986, p.4) states that 'An identity is a definition, an interpretation, of the self'. He also provides what can be seen as an ethnocentric view when he disregards the search for one's historical roots. He discusses the book *Roots* by Alex Haley and dismisses this by saying that

> Unfortunately, one's ancestry is no longer a vital part of one's identity. It now usually makes very little difference who your great grandfather was. The roots obsession can be seen as a misguided attempt to gain self-knowledge by reviving an obsolete feature of identity. (Baumeister 1986, pp.8–9)

What Baumeister fails to recognize is that for most black people of African Caribbean and African origin, their historic roots have been denied them and they seek out the little-known 'black positive' to replace the often asserted negative image of black contributions and ways of being in order to orientate self and group historically and culturally.

Aboud (1988) argues that ethnic self-identification relates to a recognition that one is a member of a particular ethnic group possessing particular attributes common to that ethnic group. She also indicates that some researchers use the term 'ethnic identity' in a broader sense to include the self as an 'active agent' rather than solely a 'conceptual entity', and measure ethnic identity in terms of the child's adoption of feelings and behaviours that are seen as characteristic of their group. Aboud (1988) suggests that this may be difficult to measure and too inclusive to be of much use. Aboud's definition relates ethnic self-identification to the 'perceptually and cognitively based knowledge that one is a member of a particular ethnic group'. This however does not take into account the possible emotional component associated with ethnic self-identification. I have offered a definition of a positive black identity and this is modified (Banks 1992) for this chapter as where children display strong ethnic group worth without being dismissive of other cultural groups, are able to engage with their cultural group's behaviours without shame and can accept their colour difference without feelings or beliefs of self-devaluation. When operationalized in this way, the conception of a 'positive black identity' becomes more accessible. One may still be left wondering what a positive black identity contributes to an individual's development.

Cross (1995) outlines three functions of what he sees the benefits of a positive black identity to be:

1. An ability to defend and protect a person from psychological insults that stem from having to live in a racist society.

2. Providing a sense of belonging and social anchorage.

3. Providing a foundation or point of departure for carrying out transactions with people, cultures and human situations beyond the world of blackness. (Cross 1995, p.113)

It is Cross's argument that a positive black identity, i.e. where one has reached a habituated and internalized sense of 'blackness', is a foundation for all of life's transactions. Once one's view of 'black self' is internalized he argues one is free to concentrate on issues that:

> presuppose a basic definition with blackness. One is black; thus one is free to ponder matters beyond the parameters of one's personal sense of blackness (organizational development, community development, problem solving, conflict resolution, institution building, etc.). One of the most important consequences of this inner peace is that the person's conception of blackness tends to become more open, expansive and sophisticated. As general defensiveness fades, simplistic thinking and simple solutions become transparently inadequate and the full complexity and inherent texture of the black condition mark the point of departure for serious analysis. (Cross 1995, pp.113–114)

Cross (1995) argues that one of the initial functional modes to come about is a defensive or protective function which operates as a protective psychological buffer when an individual encounters racist experience, particularly that of a psychological nature. The defensive function becomes an intact filter that allows the person to process and reduce, to engage with information without distortion so that this does not present a threat. Here the process would appear to be one of the development of:

> (a) an awareness that racism is part of the (black) experience; (b) an anticipatory set recognizing that regardless of one's station in society, one could well be the target of racism; (c) well developed ego defences that the person can employ when confronted with racism; (d) a system blame and personal efficacy orientation in which the person is pre-disposed to find fault in the circumstances and not in the self, and (e) a religious orientation that prevents the development of a sense of bitterness and a need to demonise whites. (Cross 1995, pp.117–118)

Children confronting Racist Experience

Pinderhughes (1995) has seen the ability to learn how to handle racism without feeling personally stigmatized as one which facilitated a protected sense of personal worth and a 'unified identity'. In her view, this enabled an active coping with the racist incidents that a child is likely to experience. The more flexible and stronger one's ego defences are, the greater the ability to cope with a variety of racist incidents. When one is able to 'depersonalize' and 'destigmatize' the effects of racism, this acts as a self-protective strategy. Cross saw the spiritual factor as a way of avoiding bitterness and anger and destabilizing resentment that may arise if one began to hate whites. Hatred or resentment was seen as inevitably self-destructive. Cross also points out that there can be two extremes to this protective function and these are where a person becomes hypersensitive, seeing racism where it does not exist, or emotionally 'anaesthetized' to racism as a defence mechanism similar to denial and unable/refusing to see its presence. For children, the ability to engage with a spiritual function would depend on their level of cognitive development and family socialization values.

Black adult identity development

Adult black identity development is important to consider in the family and life-span developmental context. Cross is seen as developing the term 'nigrescence', which is defined as the process of 'becoming black'.

As a consequence, models of black identity are often termed 'models of psychological nigrescence' (Cross 1980). Typically there are four or five stages to these models of black identity change. First, a stage which typically describes an 'encounter' stage or the individual before he or she has considered and acknowledged the personal and social implications of being black. Here, the individual may deny the social relevance or personal significance of issues such as racism and cultural oppression. The next stage usually describes the outcome that results from the individual's experience of racism that he or she can no longer deny. Here, the person is required at both an emotional and cognitive level to review their previous position. This stage is usually seen as the motivational trigger for review and change. The third stage typically consists of a period of emotional, cognitive and behavioural 'activism' where the person attempts to remove all traces of any previous passive 'non-black identity'. The fourth stage typically describes a person who has successfully integrated aspects of his or her old ways of being with aspects of their new black identity. A person at this stage is seen to have successfully consolidated issues of conflict and progressed in personal growth and, as a result, is able to establish positive relationships with both black and white people. Cross (1995) gives a full account of the revised model of nigrescence.

In revising his model, Cross (1995) suggests that the self-hatred dynamics, which he initially believed characterized people at the pre-encounter stage, were exaggerated. He takes this view as research now suggests that a person's low salience or connectivity with racial awareness does not necessarily impact on their mental health. It appears that black people can achieve personal happiness within a variety of differing group identities, and therefore, as Cross (1987, p.126) indicated, 'black identity is not predictive of personal happiness, but is predictive of a particular cultural-political propensity or world view'. Cross believed that it was 'personal identity, although not predictive of a person's reference group orientation, that was predictive of ego-strength, mental health and inter-personal competence' (Cross 1987, p.126). However, in his revision of his nigrescence model, Cross does indicate that although a 'pre-encounter' stage is not necessarily a position of confusion, self-hatred and mental illness, 'some pre-encounter types, albeit a minority, do show classic signs of self-hatred' (Cross 1987, p.97). Cross also notes in the revision of his model that very little personal or self-esteem change may accompany the development of a black identity. Cross cautions against believing that a high measure of racial group orientation will necessarily lead to a sociocultural or politico-economic consensus and believes there will still exist a great deal of ideological diversity with black people who move into the higher stages.

Children's Racial Identity Development

Cross (1995) notes:

> nigrescence is not a process for mapping the socialisation of children, it is a model that explains how assimilated as well as deracinated, deculturalised or mis-educated adolescents or black adults are transformed by a series of circumstances and events, into persons who are more black or Afro-centrically aligned. (Cross 1995, p.98)

All children regardless of their ethnic origins have a 'racial identity'. Having characteristics which allow one to be seen as being in a majority and powerful ethnic group may, to a large degree, 'cushion' one from the need to consider in any depth the questions of 'Who am I?' and 'Where and how do I fit in?' This is likely to be as long as one does not feel threatened in one's powerful position by the development and assertion of the identity of previously unconsidered groups. When such minority groups begin to define themselves independently of the imposed definitions of more powerful groups and assert a common view of self and identify, this may act as a threat to the implicit non-articulated identity of more powerful groups. A shift in mutual self-perception then starts to emerge as each group is forced, in their mutual social transactions, to take account of the other's new view of 'self' and other.

Supporting processes

Although all children have an identity development need, for some children, from some groups, there may be a greater likelihood that additional help, in the form of overt intervention, is necessary to counter the negative images that may be encountered. For example, for black children, 'you are inferior', 'you will not succeed', 'your features are unattractive' may be both explicit and implicit messages.

Such messages are delivered in a number of ways, often subtle and covert, sometimes through verbal means, sometimes through non-verbal means. Whatever mechanism is used, the effect will be the same; a message which communicates to the child that they, and often those the child cares about, have little social value to those who see themselves as 'mainstream' and others as 'marginal'. When black children 'judge' or evaluate their own group attributes using the racist notions of others, they enter a process of internalizing racism and, in effect, devalue themselves in devaluing their racial group. Notions of 'self' and 'group' need to be consolidated and coexist in a harmonious relationship for positive racial identity.

A secure individual identity and positive social identity are necessary to allow children to feel good about themselves and thus develop a positive self-image. With all children, whatever their family position, individual characteristics or group membership, research has shown that an awareness and understanding of one's origins is likely to be important in developing a positive sense of personal identity and self-esteem (Triseliotis 1973). The development of a positive view of one's self allows children to become sufficiently secure to come to terms with their life situation. For example, with adopted children it appears that a self-awareness of a child's origins helps to lessen the impact of stigmatization when others highlight the child's 'difference' or the 'failure' of their birth families.

Ethnic identity

I would suggest that black children can be helped to overcome the negative images that impact on them by specific techniques (Banks 1992).

Research has shown that the development of a child's 'racial identity' can be measured as young as 2.5 years of age (Clark and Clark 1939). 'Colour-blind' notions do not appear to exist in the nursery. It appears that some childcare workers/professionals may see the overt recognition of 'ethnic difference' as a potential source of prejudice. However, as Aboud (1988) argues, the reality of ethnic difference exists and denying differences may create more problems that accepting differences. One must also consider that if difference is to be denied, which particular group's difference will be the difference chosen to deny? It is likely that the more powerful, dominant group's difference will be the one to prevail.

Aboud (1988), in her review of racial consciousness, notes that white children, as young as 3 years of age, have been shown to consistently express negative attitudes towards black people, and that prejudice becomes much more observable with increasing age, particularly among 4-year-olds. Furthermore, researchers have compared the responses of children of different ages and found that prejudice actually increases between the ages of 4 and 7 years (Clark, Hocevar and Dembo 1980). Most of the research evidence does suggest that white children consistently, between the ages of 3 and 5, perceive black people as looking 'bad', having more negative qualities and being a least preferred playmate. Katz (1987) makes the observation that although the interpretation of children's attitudinal responses may vary, findings tend to be quite consistent. She notes that white children never show a desire to be anything else but white, whereas black children frequently express fewer own-group preferences at early ages, and appear to be less prejudiced towards white children than white children are towards black children. However, some exceptions to these responses appear in the literature. For example, when white British children who had a black foster sibling were tested (Marsh 1970) there was a marked preference for the choice of a black child over a white child, and Clark *et al.* (1980) found that white children, when tested by a black examiner, tended to give neutral rather than white-biased responses. Except for these few exceptions, white children consistently show a strong preference for their own ethnic group from an early age continuing through all age groups tested.

'Racial identity' does not develop overnight and needs to be nurtured carefully as a developmental process. Some childcare professionals appear to show concern that young black children do not refer to themselves as 'black'. This can reflect an adult politicized perspective that does not recognize that a black child may be operating at a concrete cognitive level and see themselves in literal colour terms of 'brown'. 'Blackness' is an adult perspective that will take some time to achieve through a process of experience, reflection and interpretation of one's experience. It may actually be confusing to a black child's developing identity and self-image to coerce them to think in terms of them being black if they are not yet ready to do so. A racial identity cannot be forced, it must be socially viable and psychologically satisfying. The other issue to be considered is that, like it or not, a child's 'culture' is essentially what they have lived and known and not what a childcare worker with an abstract political ideal would wish for the child. Children behave in the way they have been socialized, and to take on board another's sociopolitical 'script' will bring difficulties if children are not helped to discover their own character and explore and develop their own identity.

Biracial Identity Development?

Johnson (1983) found that one needed to be careful when analysing the difference in obtained choices on racial preference measures between black and white children. She found that white children tended to select white but black children on the other hand tended to show a preference for both black and white. Johnson may have been uncovering a bicultural identity. She suggested that the black child's dual preference was not a function of same-race rejection but resulted from an attraction to both choices.

One must consider that if the black child with two black parents has some difficulty in orientating his or her personal and reference group orientation appropriately, how are children in a mixed white–black relationship placed to develop their identity? It would appear that children's subjective socialization experiences are the primary factors affecting their subjective feelings and cognitions of themselves and others (Holmes 1995; Spencer 1983). Pinderhughes (1995) makes the point when discussing mixed-race identity development that identity development is 'complicated for bi-racial persons' (p.75). She asserts that this is because the developmental mastery of the task occurs in the context of negative social influences that work against the recognition of their dual heritage origins and denigrate the positive recognition of their dual heritage. How this is different from any black dynamic identity development process is not made clear, unless she is suggesting that this is a two-way process from both black and white society. It is commonly asserted both in Britain and in the USA that a child of mixed-race background will be perceived as black regardless of their physical characteristics, once their origins are known. Root (1992) and Johnson (1992) believe that the recognition of both black and white self-origin is necessary for the development of a healthy positive biracial identity.

Phinney and Rotherham (1987) note that the term 'bi-cultural identity' is used in different ways in the literature. It is sometimes used in reference to children of one particular culture and ethnic group who find themselves having to operate and be competent in another cultural context, e.g. South Asian children in a mainly white English school, or in the context of children who are of mixed race having to operate within a family unit which has different cultural influences within. Phinney and Rotherham (1987, p.24) argue that 'Children can not have a bi-cultural self definition; that is, they cannot simultaneously label themselves as belonging to two different groups (except perhaps children from mixed marriages'. Phinney and Rotherham (1987) note that in the literature there is some conflict of view as to whether biculturalism has a positive or negative effect on development. My view would be that this 'duality' distinction may be artificial and that rather than being seen as either a positive or negative effect, it may be simply that the effect is simply one of 'difference'.

Some writers have assumed that conflict is the inevitable result of being 'different' from the white majority and that choices must be made in order to obtain a consolidated ethnic and personal identity. As long as a child is 'in between' two ethnic groups or cultures, it has been argued that this will be connected with insecurity, anxiety and increased lack of self-surety and confidence. Other writers have argued that children raised within a two-culture context show greater flexibility both in cognitive style and creativity (Wilson 1987), and a child socialized within this environment is seen as accruing additional social benefits, leading to higher self-esteem and greater social and personal awareness than children raised within a monocultural context (Ramirez 1983).

Poston (1990) suggests a separate theory is needed to explain how mixed-race people begin to develop an ethnic identity. Poston suggests a 'five-stage mixed-race identity' process of:

1.   Personal identity: where the individual has little or no awareness of self as a mixed-race person. Poston indicates that this stage is likely to occur during young childhood when children are influenced by issues other than race.

2.   'Choice' of group categorization: here the individual is seen as having a forced choice as to which racial group to identify with. This stage is seen as being a time of crisis and alienation where social pressures force choices to be made. Individuals can either reject such a choice by declaring a 'multicultural' identity or they can identify with one of their racial group origins. The 'choice' is seen as being influenced by the relative social status of the groups of origin as well as the social neighbourhood in which the individual resides, as well as family and peer influence. In addition the 'choice' that people make is seen as being affected by their own individual physical and psychological attributes. No real 'choice' may exist as a person obviously having mixed-race physical features 'choosing' to be white may not be

grounded in social reality, no matter how psychologically 'satisfying'.

3. Enmeshment/denial: this stage is one where an individual may show confusion and guilt at having to make a 'choice' that does not reflect his or her identity at a psychologically satisfying level. Poston (1990) suggests that this lack of psychological satisfaction may be due to a person not experiencing a sense of group acceptance or affiliation with resultant low self-esteem. The forced choice has the effect of making individuals feel disloyal to one or the other of their parents. Furthermore, there are concerns about how their peer group may behave if contact is made with parents. Poston (1990) suggested that the child attempts to resolve the anxiety by identifying with both racial groups. Spencer, Cunningham and Swanson (1995) noted that typically during the adolescent period adolescents look to their peers for social acceptance and popularity. Generally the adolescent peer group works to act as a buffer to social paradoxes and inconsistencies and helps to influence coping styles. The paradox of mixed-race identity may be that adolescent peer groups serve, at least where a satisfactory identity has not been developed, to create dissonant anxiety in the development of a mixed-race identity. This would appear to impose an additional task to be mastered for children or adolescents of mixed-race origin.

4. Appreciation: here, while still psychologically connected to one racial group, the mixed-race person is enabled to explore and develop knowledge about the other side of his or her dual heritage. It would seem that this stage serves to act as a buffer, safety net, or secure landing station, from which to view the individual's total environment and connectedness to both parents as well as the more abstract notion of connectedness to racial groups.

5. Integration: here, the mixed-race individual is able to acknowledge and value both their 'ethnic identities' (Poston 1990, p.154).

Herring (1995) argued that although Poston's model has some use, it also has limitations in that Poston consistently confuses the concepts of 'race', 'ethnicity' and 'culture'. This critique may be seen as more of academic interest than having 'real world' implications as if one substitutes 'ethnicity' or 'culture' in Poston's model for 'race' the model still has meaning and therefore utility. Furthermore, Poston does suggest in his second or 'choice of group categorization stage' that physical features and sociocultural issues as well as family issues have influence in the development of a mixed-race identity. Carter (1991) poses a further criticism of the model in that even if a mixed-race person makes a 'choice' of a reference group, as was previously suggested, they may not have a guaranteed acceptance by that or any other racial group. He cites Root (1992) as suggesting that the continuing search for 'acceptance' from others has the effect of placing the mixed-race person in a dichotomous racial classification which may function to keep them marginal to achieving 'acceptance' from any ethnic reference group. Carter suggests that in order for the mixed-race person to achieve a psychologically grounded identity the mixed-race person must first accept both sides of his or her dual racial heritage and, second, declare how he or she wishes to identify himself or herself and with this develop strategies for coping with any encountered resistance or probing about his or her racial identity origin. Carter cites Root (1992) as indicating that 'the central conflict for the bi-racial person is the tendency to compartmentalise and separate the racial components of their parents' (p.117).

What psychosocial meaning the phrase 'racial components' will have to an individual may be a moot point. The important issue appears to be one of mixed-race children seeing themselves as having personal and social worth regardless of social stigma and being comfortable with 'difference' as marked by them having a black and white parent. Where both parents are available and present positive role models and the parents are able to discuss issues of 'difference' openly, the child's development of a positive racial identity is likely to be facilitated.

Direct 'racial' identity work

There are several main principles for doing direct identity work. By the term direct identity work I mean direct engagement whereby an attempt is made to support and develop a child's knowledge, understanding, acceptance and positive regard of self in the context of his or her 'racial' group. The means by which this is undertaken may be based on educational, therapeutic and psychological techniques as is required to meet the needs of the individual child. In the space allowed I cannot give a full exposition of the methods and tasks that could be carried out. Other sources give further information (Banks 1992, 1999). There are several basic principles to be considered.

Direct 'racial' identity work principles

1. The worker must be knowledgeable of child development principles to engage at the appropriate developmental level and pace. For the child to be able to make sense of the material, content and level of engagement the worker must be able to plan their work at the appropriate level of a child's understanding (Siegler 1983). This includes an understanding of the language level used by the child.

2. The worker must strive to meet the needs of the child, not the worker's own 'politicized' agenda which may be 'anti-child'. An example of a scenario to avoid would be that of a worker who had difficulties with mixed-race relationships working with a mixed-race child and attempting to deny the child's white family heritage and, by implication, denying an important part of the child's background identity. This would create conflict and confusion and undermine the basic reason for approaching the task – that of facilitating the child to feel good about him or herself and those they have family links with. Also, the child must be a willing participant and cannot be 'dragged' to a position they are not ready to experience.

3. The worker must make a needs-based assessment to consider the starting point of the child and not take a cookbook-based approach. The work should be process driven not 'item led'. All work should be planned around the needs of the individual child. Not all children will have the same needs, experience and starting point. Get to know the child by developing rapport with the child. Build trust and confidence before exploring themes which may be painful for the child to consider with an unknown person.

4. In any direct work, the core principles of humanistic counselling models must be the basis for engagement. Without these the basis for the necessary relationship between worker, child and carer is unlikely to be established.

5. The worker should always attempt, where possible, to involve the child's parents or carers as this is the context of the child's daily living. The child lives in the context of the family. The worker should not be so arrogant as to believe that what he or she might do in a half-hour session cannot be undone by the child's carers as soon as the child arrives home. When possible, supporting the child's carers to support the child is a more efficient way of engagement with the child's needs. This will equip the carers to work long term with the child when you can no longer offer input. It may be that separate sessions are needed with the child and carer depending on specific need. For example, a white parent may be threatened by not knowing the content of the work, believing this may undermine his or her importance to the child and disturb existing attachments.

Assessing the child's starting point

For the purposes of illustrating a piece of work to be done, let us consider the following case study.

Case study: James

James, a 6-year-old boy of African Caribbean origin, tells his father during a conversation about going on holiday to a hot country, that he does not want to get tanned (as suggested by his father as a possibility). James says that he wants to stay white. The father becomes upset and then cross with James for believing that he is white. The father disagrees with James in an angry manner and tells him: 'You will never be white' and 'Don't say stupid things like that again. You'll always be black.' James disagrees and says that he won't get darker than 'brown'. Father becomes more angry and tells James: 'You are not brown, you are black.' There are several issues of interest that arise in this scenario. First, the high emotion that is felt by father, unless it can be controlled, is likely to be a block to positive working. A professional worker would need to explain this to father. Father would appear to see his son's perception as a personal threat, perhaps because he feels he has failed as a black father in his 'teachings'. The worker would also need to explain to father that it is not that uncommon for black children to make such statements as James as, even at this age, the privilege that comes from white skin is perceived by children. Thus, it is likely not to be worthwhile to look for a specific 'trigger' to James's wish to be white. Father's resistance to James's preference of the term 'brown' may be related to his lack of developmental understanding that a child thinks in literal concrete terms (Piaget 1926) and thus is likely to perceive themselves by their actual colour i.e. 'brown' and not by a politicized inclusive label of 'black.'

It may be that father approaches a black local voluntary education project for support. There are several ways the workers could engage with James e.g. asking James to draw himself, giving him five felt-tip crayons of brown, blue, green, yellow and pink. The worker should observe the colour that James draws his skin. The worker could then ask James to draw the worker. (This raises the question of how a white worker should proceed which will be discussed later.) Discrepancies between the worker's colour and James's depiction should be discussed. For example, a narrative might be: 'You have drawn me blue but I am brown' (staying with the child's understanding and not 'politicking'). 'I like being brown. You have drawn yourself green. You look brown. Can you tell me what colour you are?' (asking for the child's opinion but staying with reality as expressed in the previous sentence). This is an initial approach and further discussion will depend on the child's self-description. It is likely that as this discussion proceeds the worker will notice the child becoming increasingly anxious. If, and when so, the worker should stop focusing on the child. The worker can discuss his or her own perceptions of self or can begin to talk about a 'third party' to remove the pressure from the child. This may need to take place in a further session with further planning. Some sessions may last only ten minutes and this may be sufficient. An example of the next session's starting point may be that of providing a vocabulary of self-descriptors for the child by looking at pictures of other children. The use of other children may help the child to distance themselves from discomfort and engage in more depth before being able to consider self further.

The use of pictures of a black child to provide the child with positive self-descriptors may be a technique that white workers may use with the child. There is no evidence that a white worker will be less satisfactory in identity work with a black child (for example white workers who are advanced in their own racial identity development (see Chapter 10 'Mixed-race Children and Families' dealing with white racial identity development) are likely to be more effective than a black worker who is at the encounter stage. However, the ethnicity of the worker is likely to mean that comparisons of 'self' with the child will be different and that the child cannot identify with the worker's positive view of his or her black self where the worker is white. The ethnicity of the worker will, at times, place a different emphasis on the work to be carried out but white workers should not absent themselves from supporting the racial identity needs of black children. White workers and black workers have positive contributions to make to black children's needs. In work with mixed-race children in particular white and black workers may have specific contributions to make where children require 'validation' of their 'ethnic mix' from both ethnic groups.

Conclusion

With some children the use of black people in a historical context to show the contributions black people have made to art, music and science may be valuable. However, this is likely to be a technique further along the process after the child begins to develop an acceptance of self before being able to identify with another. Workers should have some knowledge of psychological defence mechanisms and resistance which may often appear during psychotherapy and counselling. The process that is important is one where the child can begin to show comfort in discussing their views on colour and gain a self-acceptance and positive regard as well as begin to identify with others from the child's own group. The father in the scenario discussed earlier will need to be involved to become less anxious about his son's exploration. He may also have work to do in the area of exploring the depth of his own identity and what emotions from previous experience his son triggers in him.

References

Aboud, F.E. (1988) *Children and Prejudice*. Oxford: Basil Blackwell.

Abrams, D. and Hogg, M.A. (eds) (1990) *Social Identity Theory: Constuctive and Critical Advances*. Hemel Hempstead: Harvester Wheatsheaf.

Banks, N. (1992a) 'Techniques for direct identity work with Black children.' *Adoption and Fostering 16*, 3, 19–24.

Banks, N. (1992b) 'Some considerations of racial identification and self esteem when working with mixed ethnicity children and their mothers as social services clients.' *Social Services Research 3*, 32–41.

Banks, N. (1999) 'Direct identity work.' In B. Ravinder (ed) *Working with Black Children and Adolescents in Need.* London: British Agencies for Adoption and Fostering.

Baumeister, R.F. (1986) *Identity, Cultural Change and the Struggle for Self.* Oxford: Oxford University Press.

Carter, R.T. (1991) 'Racial identity attitudes and psychological functioning.' *Journal of Multi-Cultural Counselling and Development 19*, 105–115.

Clark, A., Hocevar, D. and Dembo, M. (1980) 'The role of cognitive development in children's preferences for skin colour.' *Development Psychology 16*.

Clark, K. and Clark, M. (1939) 'The development of consciousness of self and the emergence of racial identification in Negro pre-school children.' *Journal of Social Psychology 10*, 591–599.

Cross, W.E. (1978) 'The Thomas and Cross Models of psychological nigrescence: a review.' *Journal of Black Psychology 5*, 13–31.

Cross, W.E. (1980) 'Models of psychological nigrescence: a literature review.' In R.L. Jones (ed) *Black Psychology.* London: Harper and Row.

Cross, W.E. (1987) 'A two-factor theory of Black identity: implications for the study of development in minority children.' In J.S. Phinney and M.J. Rotherham (eds) *Children's Ethnic Socialisation: Pluralism and Development.* London: Sage.

Cross, W.E. (1995) 'The psychology of nigrescence: revising the Cross Model.' In J.G. Ponterotto, J.M. Casas, L.A. Suzuki and C.M. Alexander (eds) *Handbook of Multicultural Counselling.* London: Sage.

Herring, R.D. (1995) 'Development of bi-racial ethnic identity: a review of the increasing dilemma.' *Journal of Multi-Cultural Counselling and Development 23*, 29–38.

Holmes, R.M. (1995) *How Young Children Perceive Race.* Series on Race and Ethnic Relations, vol.12. London: Sage.

Johnson, D. (1983) 'Racial attitudes and bi-culturality in inter-racial pre-schoolers.' Unpublished master's thesis, Cornell University.

Johnson, D. (1992) 'Developmental pathways: towards an ecological theoretical formulation of race identity in black–white bi-racial children in racially mixed people in America.'

Katz, P.A. (1987) 'Developmental and social processes in ethnic attitudes and self-identification.' In J.S. Phinney and M.J. Rotherham (eds) *Children's Ethnic Socialisation: Pluralism and Development.* London: Sage.

Marsh, A. (1970) 'Awareness of racial differences in West African and British children.' *Race 11*, 289–302.

Parham, T.A. (1993) *Psychological Storms: The African-American Struggle for Identity.* Chicago: African American Images.

Phinney, J.S. and Rotherham, M.J. (eds) (1987) *Children's Ethnic Socialisation: Pluralism and Development.* London: Sage.

Piaget, J. (1926) *The Language and Thought of the Child.* New York: Routledge and Kegan Paul.

Pinderhughes, E. (1995) 'Bi-racial identity: asset or handicap?' In H.C. Blew and E.H. Griffiths (eds) *Racial and Ethnic Identity: Psychological Development and Creative Expression.* London: Routledge.

Poston, C.W.S. (1990) 'The bi-racial identity developmental model: a need edition.' *Journal of Counselling and Development 69*, 153–155.

Ramirez, M. (1983) *Psychology of the Americas: Mestizo Perspectives on Personality and Mental Health.* New York: Academic Press.

Richard, B. (1994) 'What is identity?' In I. Gaber and J. Aldridge (eds) *Culture, Identity and Transracial Adoption: In the Best Interests of the Child.* London: Free Association Books.

Root, M. (1992) *From Short Cuts to Solutions in Racially Mixed People in America.* New York: Sage.

Siegler, R.S. (1983) 'Five generalisations about cognitive development.' *American Psychologist 38*, 263–277.

Spencer, M.B. (1983) 'Children's cultural values and parental child rearing strategies.' *Development Review 4*, 351–370.

Spencer, M.B., Cunningham, M. and Swanson, D.P. (1995) 'Identity as coping: adolescent African American males' adaptive responses to high risk environments.' In H.W. Harris, H.C. Blew and E.E. Griffith (eds) *Racial and Ethnic Identity: Psychological Development and Creative Expression.* London: Routledge.

Tajfel, H. (1972) 'Experiments in a vacuum.' In J. Israel and H. Tajfel (eds) *The Context of Social Psychology: A Critical Assessment.* London: Academic Press.

Tizard, A. and Phoenix, B. (1994) 'Black identity and transracial adoption.' In I. Gaber and J. Aldridge (eds) *Culture, Identity and Transracial Adoption: In the Best Interests of the Child.* London: Free Association Books.

Triseliotis, J. (1973) *In Search of Origins.* London: Routledge and Kegan Paul.

Wilson, A. (1987) *Mixed Race Children: A Study of Identity.* London: Allen and Unwin.

Chapter 8

Emerging Ethnicity

A Tale of Three Cultures

John Burnham and Queenie Harris

Introduction

One of the main effects on us of writing this chapter together has been to enhance our belief that it is useful to think of our practice as always developing, always 'emergent'. Each time we have reached a position with which we felt 'satisfied' another experience would lead us to question, modify, elaborate or radically change our position. Our realization was that we are always adopting a position of changing position, not only because of our therapeutic curiosity (Cecchin 1987) but also due to the fact that ethnicity and culture are constantly emerging and we cannot hope that it will conveniently stay still so that we can count, categorize and describe in an absolute sense the characteristics of 'The Black Family' or 'The Irish Family' or 'The White Family'. Hence we will always be positioning rather than be loyal to any particular position (Langhove and Harré 1994).

One position that seems of enduring value is the view that meeting the needs of children from ethnic minorities can be construed as *creating a context in which those needs can be expressed to the services that aim to meet those needs.* Otherwise the needs that are being met are likely to be those that professionals hypothesize need to be met. Common ways of meeting the needs of children from ethnic minority family backgrounds include engaging interpreters; matching therapist to child/family; matching ethnicity in fostering or adoption; creating equal opportunities policies; race relations training; creating a welcoming environment and the training of therapists from ethnic minorities. All of these measures create possibilities and constraints to achieving respectful and resourceful services. It is important to bear in mind the limitations of each practice so that services can continue to evolve in response to feedback from clients. For example, to maintain a general policy of matching clients and therapists in relation to ethnicity may not meet particular desires of individual clients. An Indian teenager expressed her fury at being 'matched' (without her consent) to an Indian social worker. She eventually chose to work (successfully) with a white, male medical doctor, arguing that nobody else would have allocated her to such a person! General policies and practices are to be promoted and admired for the tremendous political profile that they introduce into the community at large. Professionals also require particular resources and practices that allow them to co-create ethnically sensitive practices with the families and individuals with whom they are working. In developing this it is useful to have working definitions of ethnicity in relation to culture and race. Joel Phillips (personal communication, October 1990) has suggested a useful distinction between race, ethnicity and culture. He describes race as a person's biological inheritance, ethnicity as the way a person thinks about that biological inheritance and culture as the social network within which conversations about race and ethnicity evolve. We would propose that ethnicity refers to a client's 'definition of self' in relation to his or her race and culture at a particular point in time. As such it cannot be defined by 'another' and can be created only in a conversation between therapist and client. It may well include and reflect 'cosmopolitan ethnicity'. It may not be sufficient to define ethnicity as the colour of skin or the nationality of the person. It might be important to include particular national or regional affiliations expressed by the client, for example 'white/northern English', 'black/south Birmingham', 'Welsh valley/white'. The terms used and the ordering of those terms may be used to reflect how, *at this particular point in time*, the person constructs his or her ethnicity. A conversation about ethnicity may take place at one or more times in a therapy. It may assume different levels of importance within a particular therapy when compared with other clients. Therefore it cannot be prescribed when or how to have a conversation about ethnicity. It is desirable for such a conversation to be aesthetically useful in therapy rather than a research or monitoring question.

Interpersonal team process

The issue of how to become more culturally and racially sensitive in our practice and training courses formed the basis of many discussions between us. An interesting aspect of these discussions and emerging practice was the realization that, as in the development of our practice as systemic therapists, we did not have to be experts in order to make a start. We learnt that it was better to be 'clumsy' than not do anything, to be prepared to learn from our clients and from our mistakes. This was very liberating for both of us, and enabled the application of many of the concepts and ideas from our existing practice, instead of waiting to be properly trained or searching for an ideal way of intervening and 'doing therapy' in order to provide a better service to children from different ethnic or minority family backgrounds. All that we have been able to achieve has required working in teams and/or meeting with groups of people who have been prepared to create facilitative interpersonal processes, allowing mistakes to become contexts for curiosity rather than criticism. In this way team and group members have been able to be transparent about their prejudices, ideas and practices so that these ideas and biases may become more open and available for refreshment and reconstruction and learning from other people.

Theory for practice

Since we began our work together in 1978 (see Harris 1994) there have been a number of theories that have been useful to us in developing our practice. Here we will highlight some of the ideas that have been most useful to us and refer readers to the source material for their further exploration.

Observed and observing systems

The shift from studying problems in an individual to understanding them in the context of the family seemed to promote a view that the family is in some way 'dysfunctional' or the cause of the problems. This view guided therapists to work in ways to change the 'observed family' through direct and indirect ways.

The idea of the 'significant system' (Boscolo *et al.* 1987) or the 'meaningful system' – that configuration of relationships and beliefs in which the family's problems and issues make sense – was an influential and important development in the Milan-based practice of systemic therapy. This thinking invited systemic therapists to avoid construing persons, families or cultures as dysfunctional and could be regarded as 'news of a difference that made a difference' (Bateson 1973, p.315) to how therapy and the relationship between families and therapists came to be viewed.

Other influential ideas throughout the 1980s came from second-order cyberneticians like Heinz von Foerster, Humberto Maturana, Francisco Varela and Ernst von Glasersfeld. These constructivists proposed that one could never know what is really 'out there' independently of one's own constructions. The idea that we can acquire objective knowledge about others and the world is being seriously and convincingly challenged by scientists. Mendez, Coddou and Maturana (1988) proposed the term *multiverse* to emphasize that there are many equally valid ways of perceiving the world, though one might add not all equally desirable. Von Foerster (1981) offered the idea of the *observing system*, emphasizing that the observer is always 'in' what is observed. This concept invites us to step aside from the notion that an observer can describe something or somebody as separate from themselves. Each time we act as an observer, or group of observers, to describe we *inscribe* something of ourselves in the so-called description.

Lyn Hoffman (1993), a well-known chronicler of developments in the field of systemic therapy, draws our attention to the social nature of reality creation:

> Varela emphasizes that the observing system for him always means an observer community, never a single person, since we build up our perceptions of the world not only through our individual nervous systems but through the linguistic and cultural filters by which we learn. (Hoffman 1993, p.41)

This conceptual distinction between observed and observing systems becomes important when it helps a professional or team to recognize their descriptions as inscriptions and to see how their approach, methods and techniques (Burnham 1992) help to co-create what kinds of families they meet, see and work with.

Nevertheless, respect for the observed system position can have tremendous advantages when an observer rigorously devotes time and effort to the apparently 'selfless' study of subjects. Knowledge is constructed which acts as general guidelines for practitioners who are contemplating working with families who are from a different ethnic group than themselves. For example, knowledge of resources needed for work with these families would include learning about different cultures, the employment of interpreters rather than using family members as interpreters, and drawing on the experience of other families sharing the same cultural background. Knowledge and familiarity with the work of voluntary agencies working with families from ethnic minorities with particular problems e.g. domestic violence, the care of elderly people, can help the therapist to enable particular families to connect with them.

This 'observed system' position has generated much useful information: see Boyd-Franklin (1989), Lau (1984, 1986, 1988), McGoldrick and Rohrbbaugh (1987) and McGoldrick *et al.* (1982, 1991). It has also enhanced awareness of differences between people from different ethnic groupings so that professionals have become more prepared to step aside from the comfortable assumption that 'we are all human beings' and therefore we treat everybody the same. This position tends to inhibit a therapist's ability to adopt a posture of contextual curiosity which we regard as an essential ability if therapeutic conversations are to be created. It is important to bear in mind that gaining more knowledge of the culture can tempt the creation of a grand narrative about cultures, tempting and promoting a static view of culture. One needs to guard against the development of a myth that more knowledge necessarily means less racism, or that more knowledge necessarily means more understanding.

Adopting an observing systems position invites single or groups of observers to examine reflexively how their own prejudices, values, passions and theories are situated within their own ethnicity and culture. Deconstructing their practice in these ways can help a practitioner to gain a more useful appreciation of their position in a particular network of clients, colleagues, agency and society. On the other hand the ideas of observing systems can lead one to think that the therapeutic system is created only between you and the client and so it is important to remember that these conversations are situated within broader political conversations that include immigration policies, racism and other oppressive practices of the ethnic majority (dominant) culture. Therapists who become preoccupied with the effect that they have on the family can become superficial in the sense that they fail to explore rigorously the client's situation for fear of being offensive and doing something that would be culturally insensitive. Wishing not to be the all-knowing expert can lead one to adopt the 'not-knowing position' (Anderson and

Goolishian 1992). This can lead to a swing from the 'knowing every-thing' position to a 'not-knowing anything' position. Either of these po-sitions can become disingenuous and unhelpful.

For instance, in an early attempt to ensure that he was being respect-ful to the cultural rules of one particular family the author (JB) repeat-edly asked them if it was alright to interview in the way that he did. Each time he noticed signs of discomfort on the part of family members he re-doubled his efforts to be sensitive and this pattern escalated until the father in the family said: 'We came here because the GP said that you might know something about how to deal with childhood problems, would you please continue and we will tell you if you ask us to do some-thing that is difficult for us!'

Ascribing all that one sees to cultural or ethnic factors may lead one to overlook important personal difficulties experienced by one or more members of the family.

Inhabiting a second-order world in which social realities are per-ceived to be socially constructed in many different ways offers much scope for professionals working with people from different cultures. The worker is freed from the idea of fitting everyone into the same set of be-liefs and practices and therefore is less likely to commit 'cultural vio-lence' by imposing the values and practices of the dominant (majority) culture upon persons from a minority culture. This freedom can also be experienced as a practical constraint since it can be difficult to know how to proceed in the absence of clear frameworks. In this situation it is useful to have a theoretical framework which is sufficiently clear to fol-low at a general level yet is sufficiently flexible to respond at a local level with each family that is being seen. Such a model for us continues to be the Coordinated Management of Meaning (CMM) developed by Pearce and Cronen (1980) with many further developments (e.g. see Cronen and Lang 1994; Pearce 1994). Most specifically in relation to culture see Hannah (1994).

A communication perspective

Social constructionism proposes that social realities are constructed lo-cally, between people in communication over time (for reviews see Gergen 1992; Pearce 1992, 1994). In this perspective communication is regarded as the primary process rather than a tool that can be picked up, used and put down.

Multiple levels of meaning

Bateson's (1973) dictum that there is 'no meaning without context' has been elegantly elaborated and clarified by Pearce and Cronen (1980) and Cronen, Johnson and Lannaman (1982) in their CMM model, which has been further developed into a working tool for therapists in published works by such practitioners as Burnham (1986), Burnham and Harris (1988), Cronen and Pearce (1985), Hannah (1994), Hannah and McAdam (1991), McAdam and Hannah (1991), Oliver (1992), Pearce and Cronen (1980) and Tomm (1987a, b) and Roper-Hall (1993). Cronen and Pearce (1985) propose a hypothetical hierarchy of levels of context in which the meaning of any level can be understood by reference to a higher level. The contexts that give meaning can be arranged as follows in ascending order: *content* (of a statement); *the speech act* (the utterance as a whole); *episode* (the particular social encounter); *interpersonal relationship* (the definition of the relationship between the people creating the episode); *life story* (stories people have about themselves); *family narratives* (family mottos and ways of behaving in the world); *social mores* (laws, regulations and social prescription for the citizens of a particular society) and *cultural patterns* (the beliefs, values and practices that distinguish a culture as unique and different from other cultures). Although the higher levels exert a stronger (contextual) force downwards, the lower levels also exert a weaker (implicative) force upwards. *It is proposed that the relationship between levels is circular and reflexive over time* (Boscolo and Bertrando 1993) *rather than vertical and linear.* Cronen and Lang (1994) repeated the message that this arrangement should be viewed as fluid, where any level of context can be privileged in discerning the meaning of a given episode. Scaife (1993) proposed using the term *heterarchy* to replace the word hierarchy, with the same intention of accentuating the 'living' qualities of the relationship between the levels. It is unlikely that any two cultures will have corresponding details in the levels but likely that each culture will 'have something to say' in relation to each of these levels.

The impression of a 'regular' hierarchy is easy to understand since the levels are usually presented in the form of a ladder as in Figure 8.1, in which the loops indicate the reflexive connections between the levels. Alternatively, Figure 8.2 maps these aspects of experience in a way which may seem to many readers as closer to how they experience their day-to-day living. The map in Figure 8.2 intends to convey that the aspects of experience are not separate and distinct but are more likely be lived as 'tapestry' (Peter Lang, personal communication, July 1993), 'kaleidoscope' (Pearce 1992) or 'seascape' (Shotter 1994). Figure 8.2 is a much more difficult text to read and this difficulty is intended to convey the difference between 'lived experience' and 'told experience'. It is this kind of 'lived experience' which can be 'read' only in conversation with the persons concerned. Both maps can be useful when talking with a particular family or child. A therapist would explore each of the aspects of experience as shown in Figure 8.2 but would intend to interview so as to bring forth the particular map (of the persons seeking help) organized like Figure 8.1. In this way the therapist is clear about what he or she is doing and the clients' experience of their own experience is privileged. The therapist will endeavour to use the terms, descriptions and orderings that the clients think are important, which may change during the course of a session, therapy or lifetime. For example: an Indian teenager said that mapping out her family tree with her *and then* inviting her to connect her personal and family experience to the broader level of culture was the best way round as it ensured that discussion about culture was always related to a person's particular family situation rather than culture as an abstract generalization.

Children moving between home, school and different peer groups are likely to organize their map of experience differently depending on the particular context they are in at any particular time in the day. For instance they will participate in several different cultures during the day, each with different 'language games' (Wittgenstein 1953), requiring different grammatical abilities (Cronen and Lang 1994) and ways of behaving. Thus their life story is not likely to be a 'singular' internal entity and 'self' may emerge in the coordination between these different contextual demands and resources.

CMM can be useful in many ways. Here we are emphasizing its potential for helping practitioners:

- to be constantly aware of the complexity of experience

- have a way of visually mapping experience

- have ways of organizing and reorganizing the coherence of different aspects of experience

- exploring the 'seascape' of consciousness and action (after Bruner 1986).

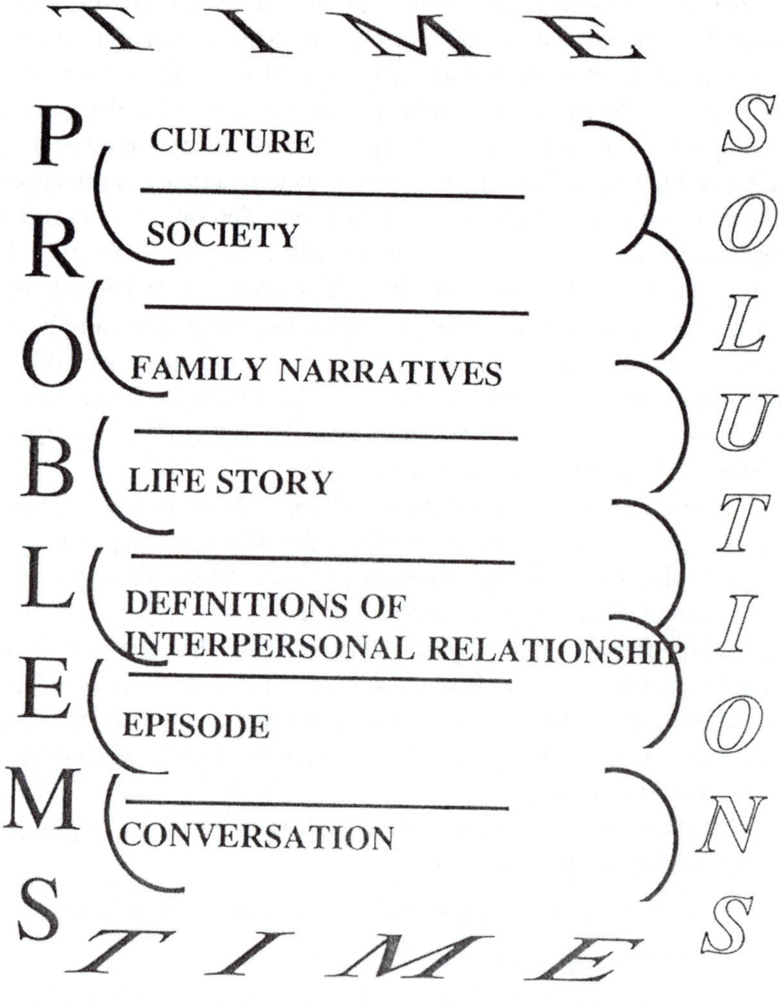

TIME

P (CULTURE
R   SOCIETY
O (FAMILY NARRATIVES
B (LIFE STORY
L (DEFINITIONS OF
    INTERPERSONAL RELATIONSHIP
E (EPISODE
M (CONVERSATION
S

TIME

PROBLEMS

SOLUTIONS

Figure 8.1

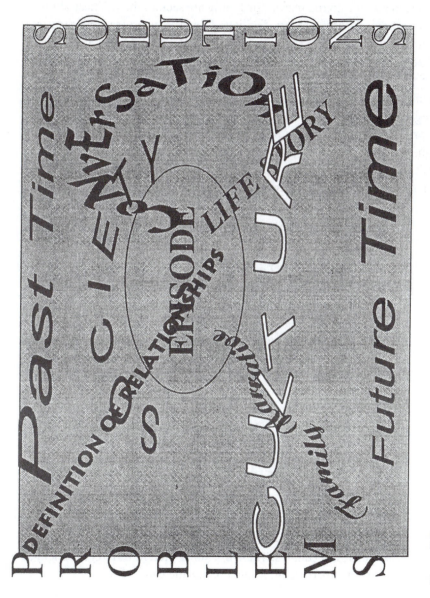

Figure 8.2

To use this structure effectively therapists will need to develop several abilities including to explore within each level; to orient themselves to the local arrangement of the levels; to elicit the patterned connections between the levels; to bring forth which levels are most influential and how, in relation to the reason the family are seeking help. These abilities are coherent with and are facilitated by the postures and practices known as circular interviewing (Burnham 1986; Cecchin 1987; Penn 1983, 1985; Selvini Palazzoli *et al.* 1980; Tomm 1987a, b, 1988). Some of these are demonstrated in the following case example, which is intended to illustrate some of these ideas in action. The examples are best regarded as a series of snapshots from a therapy that covered other important aspects of the families life that are not re-presented here. Vignettes from the therapy have been chosen in relation to the themes of ethnicity, culture, CMM and circular questioning. Details have been changed to protect the identity of the family members.

Case study: therapeutic interview

This therapeutic interview was conducted by the therapy team of the authors with QH as therapist. The family consisted of a family of four: mother, father, son 1, son 2. The social services department was contacted by the headmistress of the school that son 1 attended, following Mr X's request for help because of son 1's difficult and outrageous behaviour at home. The family doctor who was consulted later described son 1 as having a very controlling role in the family. The problems presented by son 1 were set in the context of a family where Mrs X suffered a mental health problem requiring hospitalization and follow-up. Mr X came alone at first to discuss his problems with son 1. He described how he would replace expensive items that son 1 had destroyed when in a temper. As he talked he began to realize he was not helping his son by giving in to him.

From this therapy we have extracted several episodes in which we directly work with the dilemmas faced by children, parents and therapists in co-creating new forms of coherence within emerging cultures. These dilemmas present different challenges to each participant in the therapeutic endeavour.

Section 1: assumptions and curiosity

The therapist enters the conversation with the intention of being aware of her own assumptions and trying to maintain her curiosity in the context of those assumptions. Part of the pre-session preparation is often to declare and look at the team members' own maps of their cultural, personal and professional values in relation to the dilemmas presented by the family members. These assumptions, once publicly declared as hypotheses, hunches or musings, then become more available for deconstruction and exploration as to their usefulness in this particular situation. These assumptions are often reconstructed into questions intended to explore the relational theme connected to the assumption without being restrained by the cultural content which is particular to the therapist or team.

The text has been arranged with a transcript of the interview on the left-hand side and a *deconstruction* of the therapist's/team's thinking about the interview on the right-hand side. The transcript begins with an exploration of the sleeping arrangements of the family as they are related to the difficulties experienced within the family.

Therapist: In your setting, in Chinese families, what age would you, let me put this in a different way. In different cultures it varies as to whether children sleep with their parents. For you, in Chinese families, what is the sort of rule, the norm?

Here, the therapist reflexively 'catches herself' and opens a more neutral space through recontextualizing her question and re-presents herself as a therapist who accepts that different cultures may think differently and that there is no 'universal' way of handling this situation.

Father: We are quite liberal in the sense that the children normally sleep with the parent until they themselves decide to go. They decide to; when son 1 decided he wanted his own room it was just out of the blue. Son 1 was a mature age, his voice started to change and he said, 'I want my own room.' You know the rules are all there but for us we have never made a conscious effort to tell them.

Therapist: Yes, that's what I wanted to know because it's important you see.

Validates answer and the inherent difference..

Father: But with son 2 it wasn't so much I did not want to sleep with him but because his impositions were too rigid. I mean, I couldn't read my paper, he would take my papers out, my things out, my books out and he even wanted to empty my top drawer where I put all my little private things. I found that too much, I mean [*laughing*] if I can't read in my own bed.

Therapist: So in your family you [father] are deciding when to leave [the bed].

Father: Yes, I have been, you know, eased out. I have been made to do more or less all the donkey work.

Therapist: So generally the norm is that children leave the bed, your bed, when *they* are ready.

Therapist reconstructs the problem as dilemma about the relationship between following traditional cultural rules and personal experience.

Father: Yes, yes, when they are ready themselves.

Therapist: And that is a practice that would be adhered to in your brother's family, your sister's family?

Therapist's questions place discussion in the context of others who are likely to be significant in the process of making 'cultural stories told' into 'family stories lived'.

Father: Well, not so much with my sister's family because they have been here longer than us and they have adopted the western style, you know, to put the children in their own beds when they are young so that they get used to that.

Therapist: So do they give you advice? Do they kind of say…?

How do cultural rules become mediated within particular extended family narratives?

Father: Well they tend to look at us and tell us.

Therapist: So they kind of put the pressure on you, do you think?

Father: They used to mention it but I never used to take much notice. Because I thought that if they'd be happy [*pointing to his two sons*]…because we all liked to sleep in one big room [*pointing to the whole family group*] it's like one big room, it used to be two rooms, now it's joined together. I think it was quite good in a way.

What are the contextual influences? This sequence of conversation juxtaposes several contexts which are influential in creating the dilemma about which the father speaks. The therapist's attitude of cultural curiosity from a multi-versal posture brings forth a richer story than might have been created by adherence to the dominant cultural values relating to the issue of sleeping arrangements for parents and children.

Therapist (*to the mother*): So you don't feel under pressure from his relatives to do something different?

Mother[*quietly*]: No.

Therapist: It's quite OK by you?

Mother [*hesitantly*]: OK.

The therapist notes the 'quiet' voice of the mother both literally and metaphorically.

Section 2: Inter-intra generational conflicts: between cultures, between people

The therapist picks up the father's cue: '*my sister's family because they have been here longer than us and they have adopted the western style, you know, to put the children in their own beds*' and spends some time asking the two sons which of their parents has adapted more to the western culture. Both children have some difficulty answering the question even though they say they understand what the therapist is talking about. This may indicate a rule 'not in front of the parents'. Finally the younger (and bolder?) says it is his mother.

Therapist [*to son 2*]: We were hearing just now, your mum and dad come from a way of life that's different from here, it isn't like what they had in Malaysia?

Tone of voice creates a speech act of 'interested curiosity' (tell me more) rather than 'interrogative curiosity' (what is the problem here?).

Son 2: Oh yes, actually she speaks this funny accent. [*He looks at son 1 and mother, laughing.*]

The content and manner of what is said indicates a speech act of 'mockery' and gives another understanding of mother's 'quiet voice'.

[*Mother looks at therapist.*]

The therapist notes the mother's 'appeal' to her but decides not to openly 'challenge this challenge' by the children to the mother but quietly resolves to make sure that she persists in including the mother in the conversation and openly demonstrates respect for her.

Therapist: Yes, OK. You have to follow certain rules like your dad said just now to show respect to older brothers and mums and dads and all the rest of it, OK? Which of them is having difficulty in having to settle down here with things the way they are here?

Son 2: Mmm, my mum, my mum.

Therapist: Do you think your mother…[*to the children and then switches to the parents*] In your opinion, which of you two have had most difficulty in keeping to Chinese traditions and the way of life in a Chinese family since coming here?

The therapist decides not to amplify the children's criticism and instead accepts/places the parents' life script stories in the context of the parental relationship and the movement between cultures.

Mother: He [*pointing to her husband*], he tries to keep to the Chinese ways of life, to the customs and all that but me, I am in between, sometimes I follow, sometimes I don't, but he, [*continuing to point to her husband*] at Chinese New Year he will get all those Chinese crackers but I wanted to follow the English custom by having a Christmas tree do you see, but he follows Chinese custom like with the respect for his older brother, do you see?

The mother seems to feel encouraged and 'finds' her voice in the session.

Therapist: So you are more half and half but he, your husband, is more Chinese if I can put it that way.

Mother: He is very Chinese but also he is quite western.

Differences between parents are brought forth within a broader context that gives meaning to 'parental incosistency'.

Therapist: Yes, but suppose say Chinese and western, he is 60 per cent Chinese, 40 per cent western and you [*mother*]?

Distinction creating questions brings forth different personal realities.

Mother: I am 60 per cent western, no 70 per cent western and 30 per cent Chinese.

Therapist: 70 per cent western and 30 per cent Chinese, I see. So has this come about recently, what do you think?

Therapist introduces time into these changing relationships between parents and between loyalty to 'old' culture and engagement with 'new' culture.

Mother: No, it has always been like that.

Therapist: Even from the first time you came would you say that you are more western than Chinese and he was more Chinese than western.

Mother: Yes, yes, that's right.

Therapist: Do you think he would agree?

Mother: I don't know, why don't you ask him [*laughing*]?

Therapist accepts mother's question as a 'teasing challenge'.

[*Therapist asks husband*]

Father: I don't know about the percentage but from my own personal experience there are some types of behaviour that I have always been brought up to.

Therapist: But would you say you are more Chinese than western?

The questioning brings forth through the eyes of the parents the issues of movement between cultures and the contextual influence of this movement on the emerging autobiographies and daily episodes between family members. There are no simple differences between two cultures but an emerging seascape of culture within a 'single family unit'. Each individual is relating to multiple cultural contexts simultaneously. The influence of these different cultures mediated through the autobiographies of each of the individuals as they together create the family story. The next section shows how these multiple influences create a definition of relationship between the couple in relation to the problem they brought to the clinic.

Father: Depending on the type of situation, I mean I would try to maintain some form of, you know, our own culture and tradition but I don't expect them [*gestures towards the children*], you know, to be against western culture, the British culture but I do expect them to understand our own.

Therapist: So how does your lifetime's experience influence your relationships?

Father: Well, my wife doesn't know very much about our Chinese culture because her parents lived in Malaysia for the past 30 to 40 years, but I was born in China, I emigrated to Malaysia although I was only 7 but my family always lived in Chinese culture. That's why she, in fact she doesn't understand the culture that's why she doesn't appreciate it but now sometimes when I explain to her why I am doing something she is now beginning to understand. [*Mother is nodding*]

Therapist [*to mother*]: Do you agree, would you go along with that?

Section 3: multiple levels of relationship

The seascape of cultural contextual influences has real and practical effects in creating the 'local' relationships between the members of a family. The effects on parenting of the parental preferences for different blends between western and eastern cultures is vividly illustrated in the next section which is from the next session three weeks later.

Father: Well, it [*the problems at home*] is much less. My concern is now that when he [*son 1*] comes back [*from school*] he behaves towards him [*son 2*] in a way that belittles him, I don't like that.

Therapist: So he doesn't act like a Chinese brother?

Therapist places child's actions in a context of father's cultural expectations of how to do 'brotherhood'.

Father: Well, he is so much younger, he is no competitor. He [*son 1*] doesn't have to prove to me...he should be protective toward him [*son 2*] like last week, he [*son 2*]...

Therapist: So if he was to listen to you he would be more like how you would like Chinese brothers to be?

Father: Yes, there are only two of them and if they are not going to have a good relationship, well...

Mother [*to father*]: They will have it [*a good relationship*] when they are older now they are still young and this fighting it is sibling rivalry, [*to therapist*] that is quite normal in most families.

Mother appears more able even with her 'funny voice' to express her views.

Therapist [*to mother*]: Do you see that as normal in most families? Do you see that as normal in Chinese families too?

Mother: Yes, it's umm, in all families it's bound to, all children have sibling rivalry.

Therapist: So your idea is whether it's western or whether it's Chinese this kind of thing takes place?

Therapist: Yes, whatever culture it might be... So what kind of solution do you think needs to be applied, a Malaysian solution to this problem, a Chinese solution to this problem or a western solution?

The therapist avoids the temptation of constructing the influence of three cultures as a problem or offering a solution from a position of expert as to which culture should be chosen (i.e. The 'When in Rome' posture). Instead she moves the conversation from problem formation to soulution creation while still remaining within the intercultural framework and thus brings equal privilege to the three strands of culture that may be resources to this family now.

Mother: Solution? I think... [*pauses in a thoughtful- looking way*]

Therapist [*to father*]: OK, let me ask you this question because your wife doesn't see this as a problem, she sees it as a kind of temporary sibling rivalry common in all cultures, right, but you see it differently. So what solution do you think needs to be applied, Malaysian, Chinese, western?

The father tells a long and interesting story about how he wants his children to feel free to express their views and that he respects their views. If they experience respect they will behave well.

Therapist: When you respect them [*children*], will that be a kind of Chinese way?

The therapist highlights through her question the emergent nature of culture when the context for relationships is cosmopolitan rather than ethnocentric. In struggling to achieve a both–and position there will (inevitably) be difficult moments when it will appear that to do something (for example brotherhood, respect, father–son relationships) within the rules, of one culture will compromise a person's ability to do it in another.

Father: No, traditional Chinese will never let very young children express their views, they wouldn't let them talk.

Therapist: So when you are doing that you are being more western than Chinese?

Father: Yes, I keep my children as friends, I hear what they want to tell me.

Therapist: So that would not be acting within your strict... [*Chinese culture*]

Father: No, not in that strict... [*looking very thoughtful*]

Therapist: Not like it was for you?

Father: Not like in Chinese tradition.

Therapist: Would you see that being more western?

Father: Yes, more western.

Therapist: You would see that as being more on 'this side' [*western*], so you try to listen to them to be on 'this side'.

Father: Yes, to find out what upsets them and what they want, But you see this disrespectfulness to each other, no matter what culture, if you don't respect each other you are going to have this. The problem comes from continual fighting.

Therapist [*to father*]: Can I ask you your view on this because I know your view [*to the mother*] that it's sibling rivalry and that it will all come all right in the end and at the moment it's sibling rivalry because you see it in that way. I want to come to you, the father, because you see it differently. If you were to somehow think like your wife that this is sibling rivalry and this kind of fighting is something that lots of brothers in western cultures do, what difference would that make to you? Would you come to consider as healthy development or not healthy development if you were to kind of push yourself to think 'this is western, this is a way of adapting to this culture and this was no more than what for most families takes place between brothers'. Would that make you regard that as a kind of healthy development or not?

The therapist constructs a reflexive (Tomm 1987b) question inviting the father to imagine that he agrees with the mother's view and to speculate what effect that would have on how he construes his sons' behaviour. It may be important for the mother and sons to hear the therapist begin this way instead of inviting the mother to take the father's position. Simultaneously, it also fits with the father's expressed wish to have a more 'western' father–son relationship

Father: I don't mind so long as they don't eventually become a physical battle.

Section 4: explanations for change

The therapist through using distinction-clarifying questions, facilitates the family members to struggle towards a more 'cosmopolitan' form of communication.

Like all other forms of communication, 'cosmopolitan' is a means of achieving coordination, coherence, and mystery within the constraints imposed by the 'facts of life' and in response to particular social and material conditions. Its distinctive features derive from giving primacy to coordination rather than coherence, and from its unusual means of achieving mystery. (Pearce 1989) Thus while the therapist endevours to respect the family's wish to be coherent with being Chinese she is also facilitating the parents to achieve coordination between their different adaptations to what they see as western culture. This may make it easier for the children to know which cultural rules thay are supposed to be following in different social contexts and what kinds of behaviours those rules require of them.

At the next session the mother and father attended without the two children. The parents agree that things have been much improved with the boys at home.

Section 5: Which culture? both–and (the therapist's personal position)

Father: Well I think that during the last two months, to me anyway he has made quite a lot of improvement from the last time when we saw you. He still once in a while reverts back to his old ways, his old character, but that could be just because by his own personality he has got a very strong, very determined kind of personality and that comes through and his unwillingness to submit to his older brother. If you have got a situation where the youngest child accepts the authority of the oldest child they will play well and the older child will fit in but because before I was playing the wrong role with him (son 2), this overprotection and he sees me as the person that fights on his behalf, he yells and I go but now I don't.

The father tells a story in which he both remains loyal to the Chinese idea of how to 'do brotherhood' and introduces the idea of 'strong personality' which he had previously seen as more of a western idea. He also recognizes his former position in the interaction between brothers as not helping the rules of brotherhood to operate successfully.

Therapist: How did you stop doing that?

Father: Since when you asked us to 'imagine what would happen if I said no.' and we tried to introduce 'no', e.g. he has been keen on collecting all those stickers for those *Beanos* and *Dandy*, last year he was collecting football cards, he wanted the cards every day, he would go to the shop and not just buy one packed he would buy as many as he thinks he can get, but now I don't

Cites the influence of hypothetical questions in generating change and speaks of a shift from 'I' to 'we', indicating a greater coordination between parents. He refers to particular episodes that have been generated in the context of this different definition of parental relationship.

Two months later there was a final session arranged as a follow-up attended by father and mother and young son. The episodes of success were repeated and confirmed with a much happier story emerging among all family members. The therapist invites the family members to look forward to the future. The therapist's own experience of immigration and evolving family and personal values are evident in the interview and provide much food for reflection.

Therapist [*to father*]: What about eight years' time, how do you imagine your family will be?

Future-oriented questions (Penn 1985) invite family members to escape current difficulties and create a preferred story for the future which can recursively re-generate the present.

Father: Well I imagine that they, as time goes on, we will eventually emerge as, for me anyway, as a reasonably average family.

Therapist: Do you think your children will be more like your wife in her views and attitudes or more like you in your views and attitudes?

A question which explores the coordination between the parents' influence on their childrens' emerging ethnic iden-tity.

Father: I think they will have adopted both [*mother and father look at each other nodding in agree-ment*].

A new story emerges both ver-bally and non-verbally which indicates the parents are privi-leging coordination between rather than coherence within their different ethnic heritages.

Therapist: So they will have half and half whereas you, the mother, are 80 per cent western and 20 per cent Chinese and you, the father, have 20 per cent western, 80 per cent Chinese. They (the children) will have half and half.

Therapist confirms a multi-versal position through further questioning within the metaphor of per cent which was used earlier in the therapy.

Father: Probably they will have less of mine because it is easier to be western here. I take them to ancestral worship and they go through the rituals but they don't understand the whole concept, not that I'm Buddhist, I am more Chris-tian in my outlook but I carry on in traditions because I was able to understand these things ...

An apparent support and con-firmation of the contextual in-fluence of the mother's cultural (more western) position in the current context as well as the father's ability to continue to enjoin the children with connec-tion with his heritage in the present

Therapist [*to mother*]: In eight years' time, do you think the children are more likely to be western?

Tone of voice and non-verbal posture is of curiosity rather than predictive or advisory.

[*Both mother and father nod indicating that the children will be more western.*]

Father [*continuing*]: Yes, it's a trend with immigrants to any country the minority will be absorbed, you know, if their parents come from traditional values then some of the tradition will be kept on or you segregate them like the Jew does.

Therapist [*to mother*]: What do you think, are you in agreement?

Therapist persists in hearing mother's voice in the session.

Mother: Yes, they are in this country, my children, and they came very young. They are more likely to adopt the English way, they mix with English boys, they are less likely to be Chinese than us.

The mother seems more confident to express her opinions than previously and the father and son are both listening to her compared to previous episodes when their attitude was to discount her contribution.

Therapist: Do you think it is a good idea that they have some Chinese?

Therapist takes a complementary position to explore the continuity of culture

Mother: Umm, I don't know if I can really say that [*she sounds very uncertain*].

Therapist [*to son 2*]: What do you think in eight years' time, your parents say that they think you will be more westernized, do you think it will be very sad if you don't have a little bit of Chinese?

Future hypothetical questions explore some of the potential disadvantages for individuals and family groups of disconnecting from cultural heritage for children raised in a different culture from their parents.

Son 2 [*nodding*]: Yes, very sad.

Therapist: Who do you think will be more sad?

Exploring emotion as socially constructed in the context of significant family relationships.

Son 2 Both of them.

Therapist: Both of them? What do you think about yourself, how will it be for you, will you want to give up everything, every bit of Chinese in you or what?

Drawing out the distinction of individual experience the therapist explores further the idea of the child's future ethnicity.

Son 2 [*answers immediately in a definite tone of voice*]: Probably.

Therapist: Probably? Why is that? There must be some attractive bits you want to keep.

The therapist expresses surprised curiosity at the definite tone of the boy's answer and he becomes a little less certain in his response. The therapist re-cognizes her position and attempts to keep the topic open by acknowledging the uncertainty of what the future might hold so as to avoid pushing the boy into a definite 'anti-chinese' position.

Son 2: I don't know.

Therapist: It's a hard question, I know. It's kind of guessing about the future.

Reflections

This session and the therapy drew to a close shortly after this episode and in the post-session discussion the therapeutic team reflected on how complex and exciting the issue of ethnicity is when one comes to regard it in a postmodern sense as *always emerging*. Therapists who wish to participate knowingly in this emergence can adopt an observing-systems position through developing reflexive abilities. In this last vignette it may be seen how therapists from different cultural positions may have responded differently. A therapist from the 'host' country might have inscribed the expediency of adapting to the 'western' culture, whereas a therapist with personal experience of immigration might be inclined to inscribe the advantages of maintaining connections with the parents' cultural heritage. And yet the positions could also have been reversed. A reflexive therapist is likely to monitor their participation in the creation of conversations so that many possibilities are considered for the present without closing down future possibilities.

Readers of these vignettes might say 'But this is just like any two parents disagreeing' (this is a comment often made when a 'local' similarity is inscribed in such a way that a larger difference is disguised). The difference between the parents is set within a multilayered discourse which is more likely to degenerate into cultural confusion than generate choice. In this situation silencing the voice of the mother might be seen as an attempt to create an acceptable universe. This kind of situation might invite therapists to say which is best, to instruct the parents to choose one way (to be consistent). We prefer to ask reflexive questions or create rituals (Imber-Black, Roberts and Whiting 1988; Selvini Palazzoli *et al.* 1978) which invite people in such dilemmas to 'step out' of their current position and 'step into' the position of another person, time, relationship etc. and consider the dilemma from that position. When they take up their 'own position' again they may well have more options than they had previously imagined. An important part of the work *for the children* was to bring forth the discounted voice of the mother who was categorized as: female 'mental' patient with a 'funny' voice (the kind of voice which is so often caricatured by comedians in the British culture in which the boys were engaging). To silence the voice of the mother could in a way be construed as silencing the voice of the culture which the mother represents when she is talking to/for the children.

Meeting the needs of children from ethnic minorities requires the therapist or professional to examine their own needs first. By this we mean the professional might usefully ask themselves the question 'In order to work effectively for this child what do I need to know, what do I need to be able to do?' In our working together in this area we have found that our differences and similarities have both been immensely useful in developing practice. To put it a different way, it is how we use the relationship between our differences and similarities that is most likely to help us in developing practice in this and other areas. Our differences relate to our race, gender, spiritual beliefs and original training. Since we began working together in 1978 we have developed similarities in how to coordinate the relationship between our differences so that 'news of these differences become a difference that makes a difference in our practice'.

Conclusion

Professionals wishing to explore, confirm and amplify their abilities in meeting the needs of children from ethnic minorities are assisted in this mission by theoretical postures and practices which are both reliable and flexible. We do not see ethnicity as a static entity but as a narrative which is constantly emerging through the relationships between people, groups of people and nations. Professionals may find practical theories such as CMM valuable in this emerging field of work. Perhaps we can end with ten guidelines on culture and ethnicity that we use to guide our practice:

1. Culture and ethnicity are always important but not always obvious: explore issues such as culture and ethnicity even when professional and client 'look' the same.

2. People who are different (from you) are not necessarily the same (as each other): avoid assuming that all people from the 'same' country, family, or local culture follow the same rules of behaviour, preferences and so on.

3. Ethnicity and culture are socially constructed: as well as asking 'what is?' ask 'how do you do…sadness, joy, saying hello, saying goodbye, being the eldest daughter, leaving home?

4. Hypothesizing: through the process of hypothesizing make your ideas, assumptions, values and prejudices open to colleagues and clients so they can be examined as to their usefulness and relevance.

5. Suspend your belief: step outside your own cultural rules that are often 'taken for granted'.

6. Suspend your disbelief: step into other people's ideas, customs and patterns.

7. Be 'clumsy' rather than 'clever': the value of 'not knowing' and the potential of curiosity.

8. Not an education lesson for the professional: curiosity of the professional is most useful to the family when it is related to the reason that the family are consulting you.

9. Be sensitive not superficial: you have a job to do. How to take risks safely?

10. This list is always emerging and so what would you add to this list?

References

Anderson, H. and Goolishian, H. (1992) 'The client is the expert: a not-knowing approach to therapy.' In S. Mcnamee and K.J. Gergen (eds) *Therapy as Social Construction.* London: Sage.

Bateson, G. (1973) *Steps to an Ecology of Mind.* London: Paladin Granada.

Boscolo, L. and Bertrando, P. (1993) *The Times of Time: A New Perspective in Systemic Therapy and Consultation.* New York: Norton.

Boscolo, L., Cecchin, G., Hoffman, L. and Penn, P. (1987) *Milan Systemic Family Therapy: Conversations in Theory and Practice.* New York: Basic Books.

Boyd-Franklin, N. (1989) *Black Families in Therapy: A Multisystems Approach.* New York: Guilford.

Bruner, J. (1986) *Actual Minds, Possible Worlds.* Cambridge, MA: Harvard University Press.

Burnham, J. (1986) *Family Therapy: First Steps towards a Systemic Approach.* London: Tavistock.

Burnham, J. (1992) 'Approach – method – technique: making distinctions and creating connections.' *Human Systems 3,* 1, 3–26.

Burnham, J. and Harris, Q. (1988) 'Systemic family therapy: the Milan approach.' In E. Street and W. Dryden (eds) *Family Therapy in Britain.* Milton Keynes: Open University Press.

Cecchin, G. (1987) 'Hypothesizing – circularity – neutrality revisited: an invitation to curiosity.' *Family Process 26,* 405–413.

Cronen, V. and Lang, W.P. (1994) 'Language and action: Wittgenstein and Dewey in the practice of therapy and consultation.' *Human Systems 5,* 1–2, 5–44.

Cronen, V.E. and Pearce, W.B. (1985) 'Toward an explanation of how the Milan method works: an invitation to a systemic epistemology and the evolution of family systems.' In D. Campbell and R. Draper (eds) *Applications of Systemic Therapy: The Milan Approach.* London: Grune and Stratton.

Cronen, V., Johnson, K. and Lannaman, J. (1982) 'Paradoxes, double binds and reflexive loops: an alternative theoretical perspective.' *Family Process 21,* 1, 91–112.

Gergen, K. (1992) 'Social constructionism in question.' In B. Pearce (ed) *Social Constructionism,* a special edition of *Human Systems 3,* 3–4.

Hannah, Chris. (1994) 'The context of culture in systemic therapy: an application of CMM.' *Human Systems 5,* 1–2, 69–82.

Hannah, Clare and McAdam, E. (1991) 'Violence – Part 1.' *Human Systems 2,* 3–4, 201–226.

Harris, Q. (1994) 'A systemic approach to working with families from ethnic minority backgrounds.' *Context 20*, autumn.

Hoffman, L. (1993) *A Cooperative Model for Therapy*. In Systemic Thinking and Practice Series, edited by David Campbell and Ros Draper. London: Karnac.

Imber-Black, E., Roberts, J. and Whiting, R. (eds) (1988) *Rituals in Families and Family Therapy*. London: Norton Press. Chapters 1 and 2.

Langhove, L. and Harré, R. (1994) 'Positioning and autobiography: telling your life.' In N. Coupland and A. Nussbaum (eds) *Discourse and Lifespan Identity*. London: Sage.

Lau, A. (1984) 'Transcultural issues in family therapy.' *Journal of Family Therapy 6*, 2.

Lau, A. (1986) 'Family therapy across cultures.' In *Transcultural Psychiatry*. London: Croom Helm.

Lau, A. (1988) 'Family therapy and ethnic minorities.' In E. Street and W. Dryden (eds) *Family Therapy in Britain*. Milton Keynes: Open University Press.

McAdam, E. and Hannah, C. (1991) 'Violence – Part 2: creating the best context to work with clients who have found themselves in violent situations.' *Human Systems 2*, 3–4, 217–226.

McGoldrick, M. and Rohrbbaugh, M. (1987) 'Researching ethnic family stereotypes.' *Family Process 26*, 89–99.

McGoldrick, M., Pearce, J.K. and Giordano, J. (1982) *Ethnicity and Family Therapy*. New York: Guilford.

McGoldrick, M., Almeida, R., Moore-Hines, P., Rosen, E., Garcia-Preto, N. and Lee, E. (1991) 'Mourning in different cultures.' In F. Walsh and M. McGoldrick (eds) *Living beyond Loss*. New York: Norton.

Mendez, C., Coddou, F. and Maturana, H. (1988) 'The bringing forth of pathology.' *Irish Journal of Psychology* special issue *9*, 1.

Oliver, C. (1992) 'A focus on moral story making in therapy using coordinated management of meaning (CMM).' *Human Systems 3*, 3–4.

Pearce, W.B. (1989) *Communication and the Human Condition*. Carbondale, IL: Southern Illinois University Press.

Pearce, W.B. (1992) 'A camper's guide to constructionisms in social constructionism.' Special edition of *Human Systems: The Journal of Systematice Consultation and Management 2*, 139–162. Leeds Family Therapy and Research Centre and Kensington Consultation Centre.

Pearce, W.B. (1994) *Interpersonal Communication*. London: HarperCollins.

Pearce, W.B. and Cronen, V. (1980) *Communication, Action and Meaning: The Creation of Social Realities*. New York: Praeger.

Penn, P. (1983) 'Circular questioning.' *Family Process 21*, 3.

Penn, P. (1985) 'Feedforward: future questions, future maps.' *Family Process 24*, 3, 299–310.

Roper-Hall, A. (1993) 'Developing family therapy services with older adults.' In J. Carpenter and A. Treacher (eds) *Using Family Therapy in the 90s*. Oxford: Blackwell.

Scaife, J. (1993) 'From hierarchy to heterarchy.' Unpublished dissertation, University of Birmingham/Charles Burns Clinic Diploma in Systemic Therapy.

Selvini Palazzoli, M., Boscolo, L., Cecchin, G. and Prata, G. (1978) 'A ritualised prescription: odd days and even days.' *Journal of Marriage and Family Counselling 3*, 3–8.

Selvini Palazolli, M., Boscolo, L., Cecchin, G. and Prata, G. (1980) 'Hypothesizing – circularity – neutrality: three guidelines for the conductor of the session.' *Family Process 19*, 3–12.

Shotter, J. (1994) 'Becoming someone: identity and belonging.' In N. Coupland and A. Nussbaum (eds) *Discourse and Lifespan Identity*. London: Sage.

Tomm, K. (1987a) 'Interventive interviewing Part I: Strategizing as a fourth guideline for the therapist.' *Family Process 26*, 3–13.

Tomm, K. (1987b) 'Interventive interviewing Part II: Reflexive questioning as a means to enable self healing.' *Family Process 26*, 167–183.

Tomm, K. (1988) 'Interventive interviewing Part III: Intending to ask lineal, circular, strategic or reflexive questions.' *Family Process 27*, 1–15.

von Forster, H. (1981) 'On constructing a reality.' Republished in *Observing Systems*. Seaside, CA: Intersystems.

Wittgenstein, L. (1953) *Philosophical Investigations*. Oxford: Basil Blackwell.

Chapter 9

Antiracist Strategies for Educational Performance

Facilitating Successful Learning for all Children

Gerry German

Introduction

> In what ways are your programmes going to benefit the
> oppressed – working class pupils and their communities the
> world over; girls the world over; black pupils in white societies;
> children with disabilities and learning difficulties the world over;
> ethnic and cultural minorities the world over? In what ways, that
> is to say, are your programmes going to close gaps, reduce
> inequalities, remove discriminations, in particular
> discriminations which are covertly, indeed invisibly
> institutionalised? And how are you going to win the trust of the
> oppressed? Which is to say, what risks – real risks to your material
> well-being, your career prospects, your reputation, your
> livelihood – are you taking? What boundaries of convention and
> courtesy are you prepared to transgress, what conferences,
> forums and arenas are you prepared to subvert, what comforts
> and friends are you prepared to lose? (Richardson 1990, p.53)

All children, black and white, want to succeed at whatever they do. They
want to work, play and make friends to the best of their ability. Parents,
too, black and white, have the highest hopes for their children. They
want them to succeed at school. They want them to get a good job. And
they want them to lead happy lives as responsible citizens worthy of re-

spect on the one hand and capable of respecting others and cooperating with them on the other.

Teachers, too, would like the children in their schools to succeed, and they have obvious reasons for aiming at a high success rate. In the current climate of league tables, it would enhance public relations as well as job satisfaction and status. It would redound to the credit of the school, and there would be a growing and gratifying demand for appointment as teacher or governor and admission as pupil. Some people might deny that such an interest exists but they would be hard pressed to produce children, parents or teachers who would express a greater concern with failure than with success. On the other hand, one needs to recognize that there are children and parents, as well as teachers, whose experiences have made them cynical about the future.

Why Ethnic Minority Young People are Failing

If there is such an apparent general unanimity of outlook with regard to academic success, why is it that so many children fail and why is it that so many of the failures come from identifiable groups such as the working class, or travellers, or certain black communities?

The quotation at the beginning of this chapter is aimed at the transformation of individuals and structures in order to make society less unequal and less unjust and to ensure that individuals have the energy and skill to develop structures and procedures that are a permanent guarantee of justice (Richardson 1990, p.45).

The problem is that schools and other educational institutions as they now exist are so structured and organized that they seem inherently incapable of ensuring the success of all the children and young people in their care. One recalls the response of the then Secretary of State for Education, John Patten, at the announcement of the record-breaking number of GCSE passes in the summer of 1993 when he expressed the opinion that it must have been due to easier marking and lower standards than in the past (*Education Guardian*, 7 September 1993).

If academic performance is related to a particular view of intelligence, and if intelligence is hierarchically distributed along a success–failure continuum, the so-called bell curve of the distribution of ability, we should not be surprised that examinations, tests and standard assessment tests produce failures as well as successes. Nor should we be surprised by the obsession of some people in authority with the need for the education process to identify failures!

It can be no surprise, therefore, that the system of selection and rank-ing seems to favour certain groups rather than others. In a system charac-terized by perceptions and practices based on concepts of social class status – male superiority and white supremacy, for example – it is inevi-table that those who are seen to attain the highest academic standards are generally white, male and middle class. The exceptions only serve to pro-vide the rule, and those who emerge from the ranks of the otherwise dis-advantaged very often do so as a result of embracing establishment values. This serves in turn to confirm the validity of those values.

Value-added-benefit to Ethnic Minority Young People

With the introduction of league tables to identify institutional excellence or otherwise, teachers in poor-performing schools have been calling for the inclusion of value-added criteria to indicate the nature of the prob-lems of social deprivation in their schools; for example, to show how much they have managed to achieve with such disadvantaged children compared with other schools enjoying social privilege, parental support and pupil motivation.

Children and their parents – and possibly teachers – are hardly likely to be encouraged by a finely tuned statistical account of unem-ployment, poor housing, ill-health, crime and delinquency, and one-parent families to rationalize and explain away low standards of lit-eracy and numeracy as well as the absence of success in external exami-nations. If career prospects and life chances are so closely tied to examination success, it is no consolation for people to be told that while they have no academic qualifications to take them up the next rung of the ladder, they have done very well bearing in mind social background and family circumstances. Such a record is unlikely to impress either the college admissions tutor or the employer when it comes to seeking a place in further of higher education or something better than casual, low paid jobs.

What happens, however, if the value-added exercise shows a down-ward spiral – as well it might – rather than progress of one sort or an-other? A study of 6000 children aged 5 years by the Birmingham local education authority (Birmingham Metropolitan Council 1994) shat-tered the conventional belief that African Caribbean children are trapped by underachievement and low aspirations almost from birth. On the contrary, the study shows that they start school with the best grasp of the basic skills and that they maintain their lead until at least 7 years of age. African Caribbean children were shown to be almost twice as likely as 5-year-olds from other ethnic groups to be classed as above average, against national norms, in numeracy tests that included tasks such as counting up to 20 and identifying shapes. White and Indian pupils came next, followed by Bangladeshis and Pakistanis.

Highs and Lows

Almost 1 in 20 (4.6%) black pupils were about a year or more ahead of what would be expected of 5-year-olds in the English National Curriculum, compared with 1 in 28 (3.6%) white pupils. About one-third (32.1%) of the African Caribbean pupils were average or above for their age, against 30 per cent for all Birmingham pupils. Similar results were revealed in National Curriculum tests for 7-year-olds in English and mathematics.

By the time they reach 16 years of age, African Caribbean pupils are among the least successful ethnic groups. They are four times more likely to be excluded from secondary school and considerably less likely to get five or more GCSE passes at grades A to C. What happens to deny their early promise of academic success?

This is a question that many black parents have been asking for a long time. Why were their children unhappy at school? Why were they punished, apparently frequently and unfairly? Whey were they suspended from class or from school? Why were they underachieving? These were matters that they were at first reluctant to take up with teachers because of an initial combination of faith in schooling and respect for the authority of teachers. When at last they felt compelled to make representations on behalf of their children, they felt that they were not getting the answers they sought, and in addition many of them became alienated by their humiliating treatment when they visited the school. They felt even more humiliated when they had to attend the school in response to a summons for them to discuss their children's alleged misdemeanours.

In 1971 Bernard Coard's book *How the West Indian Child is made Educationally Sub-normal in the British School System* articulated what many African Caribbean parents felt about the inferior education their children were receiving and the threat of the white establishment to their children's identity. He urged parents to cooperate in creating a black educational environment with a curriculum of black studies taught by people who could provide black professional role models (Coard 1971, pp.38–39).

The role of Supplementary Schools

This gave a further fillip to the black voluntary school movement where weekend teaching attended not only to the basic skills but also to other aspects of the curriculum that children and parents felt were being neglected in the mainstream schools. However, it is still only a small number of children who attend these schools, and it is unfortunate that mainstream teachers fail to avail themselves of the opportunity to learn from their experiences in enhancing both self-discipline and academic progress even among otherwise disillusioned and disaffected black children. The enrolment record shows keen, well-motivated children for the most part, strongly supported by their parents (Chevannes and Reeves 1987, pp.147–169).

Such schools exist also for children from other black communities. There are language classes for children of African, Chinese and Asian origin. Many are initiated into their culture through dance and festivals, for example. Children whose parents originate from Muslim countries are brought together to study the Koran and learn Arabic as well as practise their mother tongue.

These are interesting examples of vigorous self-help on the part of communities whose parents are often criticized by teachers as either lacking any interest in their children's education or being over-ambitious for them and therefore impractical. What greater practical commitment to children can there be than long-term efforts to raise funds, hire premises, provide equipment, books and other resources, recruit teachers on a voluntary basis, arrange a timetable and encourage children to attend in their own time?

In addition to the black voluntary schools' implicit criticisms of racist attitudes and practices in mainstream schools, they are also affirming the arguments of the advocates of alternative educational provision and community education. They want curriculum relevance, service to and participation by the community, and democratic accountability within and outside the learning community. In alternative education, the emphasis is on schools as communities rather than institutions.

As Clark (1971, pp.122–123) states, it is counter-productive to pursue policies and practices that fail to develop the vast potential of human beings while at the same time criticizing children and parents – and even teachers – who are the product of such an inefficient system. On the other hand, his demand for alternatives to what he terms the state monopoly is hardly likely to be satisfied by the growth of grant-maintained schools and city technology colleges, for example, which give an illusion of parental choice but still deny democratic participation in terms of governance, pupil participation and real accountability.

It would be wrong to conclude from the discussion about identity that black underachievement is the result of a widespread problem of poor self-image or low self-esteem. There is no doubt that a positive sense of identity is enhanced by the presence of role models, relevant curriculum content and resources that provide positive images of black children, but one needs to remember that racial violence and discrimination do not avoid choosing as their victims black children and adults who are self-aware, self-confident and assertive. The trigger to racial violence and discrimination is skin colour, not one's ranking on a quickly applied, primitive ready reckoner of self-esteem.

Milner's (1983) work on the black–white orientation of black children led him to assert that

> Black consciousness has grown. Black social and political organizations have flourished, and Black culture has evolved a specifically British variant, all of which has given Black children and youth an alternative acceptable image of their group with which to identify. (Milner 1983, p.161)

People cannot have it both ways. On the one hand, poor academic performance may be attributed to a poor sense of identity, among other things. But then self-assertive, articulate black children may be punished for expressing their reservations and criticisms and even challenging curriculum content, resources and teacher–pupil relationships.

Understanding the Ethnic Minority Young Person

A 13-year-old African Caribbean girl was excluded from a London school after a series of carefully logged allegations of misbehaviour. One of the charges against her was that she had refused to collect the books from her class when asked to do so by her teacher, a white woman of Australian origin. She added 'slavery finish'. The confrontation continued and the girl challenged her teacher about the mistreatment of the aboriginal peoples of Australia. She was told to go to the year head and the incident was logged as another example of her rudeness and indiscipline (Working Group Against Racism in Children's Resources (WGARCR) 1994a).

How much better it would have been if the teacher had put her pupil's sense of self and history to good account in getting her to present her views as part of the process of developing debating skills, for example. Instead, an opportunity was lost because of a stereotypical knee-jerk reaction to a situation perceived as a challenge to constituted authority rather than the occasion for dialogue and exploring relationships. In the end, the school lost a good human resource which could have added to its fund of wisdom. It may well be that both the teacher and pupil were reacting to each other on the basis of stereotypes. Here was a good opportunity to examine the issue within the curriculum in a way that would have enhanced understanding and relationships as well as the function of schooling.

But what happens even when such open confrontations do not occur? Wright (1992) carried out an ethnographic study in a small number of inner-city nursery, first and middle schools in the north of England which had equal opportunities policies and training programmes and support structure for staff.

African Caribbean and Asian young people: school approach and attitudes

Despite the schools' policies, training programmes and support structures, both Asian and African Caribbean children experienced negative but different interactions with the teachers in the classrooms. Asian children were seen as weak in the English language, social skills generally and their ability to socialize with other groups in the classroom. On the other hand, they were also perceived as tractable, hard-working and eager to learn, with stable and supportive family backgrounds where educational success was highly valued.

African Caribbean children, on the other hand, especially boys, were regarded as disruptive and in need of frequent reprimanding. Wright (1992) observed that they were singled out even when other children from different ethnic groups were engaged in the same behaviour. While African Caribbean children experienced conflict with auxiliary staff outside the classroom, Asian pupils suffered from peer-group racial harassment in the playground which was a further extension of the racist name-calling initiated by white pupils in the classroom. Staff were observed as unwilling to intervene despite the self-evident intimidation of and fear in the Asian pupils.

While Asian parents were generally satisfied with the quality of teaching, they were critical of the schools' tokenistic approach to cultural diversity and their failure to tackle the racial harassment of their children. Muslim parents were concerned about the failure of the schools to accommodate religious and cultural demands and the frequent occasions when teaching the curriculum caused conflict between school and family values. African Caribbean parents were among the most dissatisfied, especially with what they felt was the unjust treatment of their children by teachers. White parents were generally satisfied, although some had reservations about teaching methods and discipline while others objected to a curriculum they saw as favouring black children.

But despite conflict and dissatisfaction, an analysis of standardized test scores showed African Caribbean children to be performing better, especially in reading, than other groups. Asian children's performance in the tests was marginally lower. The latter were evidently not helped by the teacher's perceptions of them as tractable and hard-working. Obviously, one of the key problems was how the teachers viewed their language skills: bilingual strengths were overshadowed by English language weaknesses, and the former was not used as an opportunity to enhance the latter by paying tribute at least to the ability to speak more than one language.

Wright's findings in 1992 echoed the findings of a previous ethnographic study by her at secondary level between 1982 and 1984 (Wright 1987). Teachers were generally seen to hold adverse attitudes and expectations regarding African Caribbean pupils. The pupils described how unfortunate encounters with teachers they perceived as hostile were fixed in their minds and the extent to which these then influenced their perceptions of schooling. African Caribbean boys and girls were often perceived as trouble-makers and reprimanded and punished accordingly. A higher proportion of them were suspended and even excluded permanently without alternative educational provision. Little wonder that they became academic failures as a result of their experiences.

The influence of stereotyping and the breakdown in relationships was so strong, however, that behaviour criteria outweighed cognitive criteria in assessing African Caribbean pupils. Consequently, they were likely to be placed in ability bands and examination sets below their actual academic ability, even as demonstrated in tests devised and conducted by the teachers who, in the event, failed to exercise objective, professional judgements in their allocation to bands and sets.

Why underachievement and stereotyping?

Underachievement is not a neutral term. It is particularly loaded as far as black pupils are concerned. For them schools are not a purely meritocratic arena where they are assured of equal opportunities in teaching and assessment in order to develop their potential to the full. On the contrary, the generally lowly outcome is the result of a complexity of school processes involving a combination of prejudice, destructive stereotyping and low expectations.

Take, for example, the treatment of four 9-year-old black children at a largely white rural primary school in eastern England. They were children of mixed parentage whose parents wanted them to be fully aware of their black identity. Their parents were members of the same support group who had originally come together to share their concerns about the harassment of their children and the absence of curriculum content and play and learning resources that presented positive images of black children. Parents and children had much in common and they had personal experiences of the workings of racism in relation to everyday treatment of themselves as black and white spouses and their offspring. The children drew strength and inspiration from their solidarity, as a group where they could share experiences and work out coping and survival strategies. Some of the teachers saw this as a threat and wanted to separate them. The parents sought advice from a national organization, courteously but firmly stood their ground, advised against such a negative response and diplomatically offered in-service training to the staff by the national group to which they belonged. The advice and the offer were accepted. The children, the parents and the teachers have all learned a valuable lesson from the experience. From all accounts, there has been some improvement already in school relationships and in the position and performance of the black children whom the parents see as potential high achievers anyway (WGARCR 1994b).

But still opportunities are missed. In one of the London boroughs, the mother of a 5-year-old child asked the head of his new school to change his name from Kieron, under which he had been registered for admission some months previously, to his African name. The head refused on the grounds that the labels had already been prepared for the school's opening the next day. The mother offered to prepare the new ones on her word processor. The head still refused. The mother sought advice from the national children's organization to which she belonged. Her rights with regard to name changes were explained and tactics for a new approach discussed, especially since, as she explained, she had been so humiliated by her encounter with the head in a matter of such significance for her and her child. In the event, she wrote a carefully worded letter to the head, with a copy to her child's teacher, firmly reiterating her request and enclosing a number of new labels to replace those prepared by the school. She succeeded and she believes that her child now has the opportunity to learn in congenial circumstances, which she has helped to create (WGARCR 1994c).

The point to be made is that *nothing succeeds like success.* It is not only the parents and children at the rural school who have gained but also the school itself. Similarly, the London infant school has made progress. Significantly, it is the children's confidence that has developed while witnessing their parents' struggle on their behalf resulting in the school's acceptance of their position on their terms. What both sides have learned is that there is no need for conflict. Agreement can be negotiated, and through acceptance the performance of both individuals and community can be enhanced.

Unfortunately, despite the work of the past, despite the inquiries that have been initiated, despite the recommendations, despite the adoption of policies, the provision of training and the availability of positive learning resources, the same struggle is being waged and the same battles fought by countless black families who feel that their children are being disadvantaged by the schools they attend and by teacher attitudes and classroom practices.

This means that much of the energy that should be available for learning has to be expended on overcoming and compensating for the racial discrimination that threatens the welfare and progress of black and ethnic minority children, even those who emerge with a clutch of examination successes guaranteeing a place in higher education. If circumstances are uncongenial for learning, they are also bad for effective teaching and teacher self-fulfilment and the promotion of mutual respect and cooperation among pupils and teachers.

Bilingual teaching and multilingual provision

What about the absence of effective bilingual teaching and progress towards multilingual provision in schools? There are obvious situations where such a provision is desirable in order to facilitate the effective learning of skills and concepts as well as to promote the ability of ethnic minority children to identify more closely with their school as offically recognized speakers of other languages. White monolingual children will also benefit by the opportunities to recognize and appreciate linguistic diversity, not only on a continental but a global scale – and through that the richness and variety of spoken English by themselves and others, nationally, regionally and locally.

Gurnah (1989) sees multilingual studies as the natural and necessary development of bilingual support for black pupils with first languages other than English. He describes multilingual studies as 'a new subject for a new generation' (Gurnah 1989, pp.176–198). His priorities are ethnic minority children's community language and the various forms of English and Creole because of the obvious neglect of those children's potential as well as their special needs. To be meaningful and relevant, European languages can eventually or even simultaneously be included in the same framework.

Gurnah envisages a holistic dynamic approach for black and white children that will include providing not only an induction to linguistic rules and conventions but also the range of issues, concerns and aspirations expressed in those languages through literature, philosophy and religion as well as through social and political organization and economic and cultural choices. 'An important aspect of that curriculum must follow up the historical and political relationship between the said languages and cultures and their resolution in contemporary society' (Gurnah 1989, pp.191–192). Bilingual provision, for example, would enable children to inhabit the two worlds where English and their first language were spoken. It would promote an understanding by *all* children that 'British culture is now more multifaceted' (Gurnah 1989, p.192, original emphasis).

Gurnah says that such a framework is essential to eradicate the impoverishment of most bilingual support, the low status of bilingual teachers and the marginalization of working-class ethnic minority children. He is talking not just about an adjustment of the curriculum but its fundamental reorientation, and he concludes with a challenge to providers and practitioners:

> Language is a symbolic expression of individual and community life. If that life reflects a multiplicity of backgrounds, experiences and languages, our education system must learn to recognise their worth, create ways of absorbing them in the curriculum, and promote sharing them with everybody else. (Gurnah 1989, p.197)

It is that kind of recognition of individuals as valued and respected that enhances self-esteem along with feelings of security and well-being as well as a range of good social and working relationships within which children and young people will feel encouraged both to learn and be themselves. It is in such circumstances that they can make optimum use of their energy to develop all aspects of their lives freely without having to struggle against attitudes and practices that constantly question their presence and threaten the space that they occupy.

The importance of early years provision: equality of opportunity

Jane Lane (1989, pp.75–101) stresses the importance of understanding that attention must be paid to early years provision in the lives of children if they are to develop their full range of intellectual, emotional, physical and social skills. She deals with the low priority accorded to meeting the needs of young children and their carers as well as with the myths about childhood innocence and minimal social influences in the early years. While adults pay lip-service to equality, she says, they fail to appreciate that their commitment has implications for organizations, management and practice in early years play and learning provision. She states that:

> The struggle for equality starts in the earliest years and is about breaking down practices, customs and procedures that result in some people having poorer life chances, poorer job opportunities, poorer housing and poorer education than others and having little influence on the political and economic decisions that affect their lives. (Lane 1989, p.78)

Lane deals with the muddle and inadequacy of national provision, and she exposes the labelling and stereotyping that can follow allocation to particular types of provision. For example, children in social services day nurseries may be stigmatized as having (or being) a problem because of the admission criteria based on 'social and physical need'. This in turn can lead to the pathologizing of families and communities, with unfortunate effects on future educational progress.

In addition to exposing inadequacy and myth, she stresses the importance of recognizing both the diversity and value of the range of different practices of child-rearing, for example, and in making provision for the children and parents accordingly. She looks critically at language and how it is used about and in relation to the children. She deals with resources as a means of conveying positive messages about children, and she details the activities that might be pursued in the quest for genuine equality of opportunity. She makes practical suggestions about how adults can deal with ignorance, prejudice, harassment and inequality in discussion with children. Her conclusion is clear:

> If children in their earliest years are not given a chance to be equally valued, there is even less hope that they will be accorded equal treatment as they grow up. Providing a framework where young children can think for themselves, evaluate information and respect and value difference may give them a chance of justice and equality that is the fundamental right of all children. It is a right that adults (under-fives workers and families) must support. (Lane 1989, p.100)

Lane's exhortations are strongly supported by the Working Group Against Racism in Children's Resources who urge not only the provision of good antiracist resources in domestic, caring and learning situations but also their use by properly trained adults who are equally convinced about equal respect and provision for *all* children who benefit from the ready availability of resources that present positive images of black children. White children must also be enabled to correct the distorted vision of the world imposed by adults choosing to restrict their experiences to things that flow from the myth of white supremacy (WGARCR 1990, p.6).

Importance of Quality Teaching: Assessment and the Environment

Successful academic performance depends on good teaching and honest assessment. In a paper delivered by Dreyden (1989) to the National Foundation for Educational Research, there is a thought-provoking examination of the effect on assessment procedures of a body of knowledge arising out of a particular worldview held by white people. People from groups that have been excluded from contributing to that worldview are therefore likely to have their talents under-measured by the assessment procedures. To counter the anachronisms of such a view, Dreyden suggests infusing curricula with the 'histories and cultures of under-represented groups' in largely white as well as multi-ethnic areas. The so-called subcultures should be presented, she says, in ways illustrating their importance as 'ballast' to the predominant culture, thus enhancing its chances of survival in facing the increasingly complex challenges of the modern world. As far as test results are concerned, she says they should be used with 'a healthy dash of professional scepticism', especially since 'they have a limited validity in predicting real world success'. In support of her last claim, she quotes the findings of the US Office of Employment in relation to the equally good performance of black employees appointed under the positive discrimination quota system.

She also deals with the stresses and strains imposed on ethnic minority pupils by hostile learning environments. She contrasts them with the way in which members of majority groups can use their reservoirs of energy simply for playing the game of life by the rules enunciated to ensure their participation in the first place and ultimately their success or victory. She says 'A normal intelligence may be said to have at its disposal limited resources to expend for self-preservation, than more disinterested motives'. She adds:

> Members of the society devalued by the tradition are in the position of...having to spend limited resources on a hierarchy of priorities beginning with diffusing hostility to obtain physical security; to transforming the environment to one that is sympathetic to non-traditional experience; to establishing and extending one's own traditions. (Dreyden 1989, p.12)

Learning opportunities for teachers

Mac an Ghaill (1992) describes a two-year ethnographic study which illustrates further how young black Asian and African Caribbean people in Britain have, in response to their alienating experiences of schooling, 'collectively and individually, creatively developed coping and survival strategies.' The young people are placed at the centre of the research. And it is their experiences of school, teachers and friends that enable Mac an Ghaill to conclude that:

> Their adoption of a variety of coping and survival strategies that are linked to the wider black community illustrates that, more than any other fraction of the working class, they are consciously creating their own material culture. (Mac an Ghaill 1988, p.56)

In so doing, they are rejecting the model of white society presented by teachers and are resisting institutional incorporation into white cultural identities (Hall *et al.* 1978, p.341).

One of the important things to come out of this research and one of the things that needs to be repeated for teachers and other people in authority who often pontificate on the problem of inter-generational conflict in the black communities – between the parents' 'traditional rural culture' and the young people's 'modern urban lifestyle' – is the fact that without exception all these students explicitly identified with their parents and saw them as their main support and source of inspiration.

Here is yet another important resource as yet inadequately recognized by teachers. There is a tendency for the professionals to disregard the experiences and views of parents because they see them as unqualified and amateur instead of being prepared to learn from their knowledge of their children, gained in the closest encounters over many years in a variety of settings. Likewise, their classroom organization limits the opportunities that could supply them with honest feedback about the effectiveness of teaching, relationships, discipline and extracurricular activities in their schools, insights just as valuable, if indeed not more valuable, than the views exchanged in staff meetings. Their work could be enhanced if their protestations of an interest in community outreach were matched by an interest in how individuals, families and communities actually lived in their catchment area.

Racism versus Equality

As far as black and ethnic minority people in Britain are concerned, one of the biggest obstacles to their children's success and security is racism. What they would like to see is teachers and schools availing themselves of every opportunity to eradicate the effects of racist attitudes and practices in all aspects of school life so that they can enjoy their full share of equality with regard to education access, treatment and outcome.

Inclusivity, Integration and Integrity: Promoting education and racial justice

The agenda for education virtually ignores the existence of institutionalized racism identified by Sir William Macpherson in the Stephen Lawrence Inquiry Report (Home Office 1999). Unless there is a willingness to acknowledge its existence, school exclusions, one of the key issues identified in that report, will continue to bear down disproportionately on children and young people from black communities, especially those of African Caribbean origin.

Exclusions are wasteful, destructive and discriminatory. They are the tip of the iceberg. Exclusions are costly in terms of time and financial resources. They stifle good practice aimed at the development of self-discipline and good relationships. They are demonstrably discriminatory on the grounds of 'race' and class. They provide too convenient a culling system that further oppresses and victimizes identifiable groups who are already part of a downward spiral of dislocation and failure.

For example, the Commission for Racial Equality (1985) Investigation Report found that in Birmingham, African Caribbean pupils were shown to be:

- four times more likely to be excluded from school
- at a younger age
- for fewer offences and for less serious offences than white pupils
- less likely to re-enter the mainstream.

Monitoring in Birmingham schools showed that between 1980 and 1990 there was 20 per cent improvement in the direction of parity. This is an average rate of 2 per cent per year. At that rate it could take half a century to achieve equality! Can we call that progress?

African Caribbean pupils are still between four and six times more likely to be excluded than pupils from other ethnic groups. In some parts of some boroughs they are up to 15 or 16 times more likely to be excluded. In short, discrimination is still very much a fact of life for identifiable different groups.

The fundamental reason for this lack of real progress is institutionalized racism based on unquestioned assumptions and unexamined practices. This racism includes a crippling combination of negative prejudice, destructive stereotyping and low expectations.

For many years, research in Birmingham has shown 5 and 6-year-old African Caribbean children to be more advanced in their basic skills of literacy and numeracy than children from other ethnic groups. This reflects ability, achievement and parental support, qualities often stereotypically denied by schools. We need to question what happens to such children over the next ten to eleven years of compulsory schooling to cause failure and disaffection.

The government set targets to reduce exclusions (and truancies) by one-third by 2002. This would still leave us with 9600 permanent exclusions, 67,000 fixed-term exclusions and 667,000 truancies per year. In short, a lot of time, money and effort will be expended for relatively insignificant returns. In addition, the present disadvantaged groups will continue to be disadvantaged by an inherently unjust and discriminatory system.

Exclusions procedures became nationally systematized by the Education (Number 2) Act in 1986. This resulted in an increase in reported exclusions. Formal procedures were refined be DfEE Circular 10/94 and local education authorities (LEAs) appointed exclusions officers, many of whom regarded it as their duty to assist schools in excluding pupils. Exclusions increased.

Circular 10/99 was intended to formalize the principles of natural justice and reduce exclusions and truancies. The circular's good intention were later thwarted by the Secretary of State's letters in January and August 2001 about excluding for first-time or for one-off acts of violence etc. Schools, unions, authorities and adjudicating bodies have tended to misinterpret the advice. There has been a leap in exclusion since.

Conclusion: Congenial secure teaching and teaching conditions

The Community Empowerment Network (CEN) is founded by the Community Fund and provides advice, support, counselling and representation for children, young people and their families experiencing problems in education, particularly school exclusions. CEN would like to see schools adopt the three 'I's, namely:

- *I for inclusivity*: schools should be genuinely comprehensive, community based, accessible and accountable to teachers and taught alike.
- *I for integration*: education should be holistic and concerned equally with mind, body and spirit.
- *I for integrity*: school provision should be values-based and both individually and institutionally accountable.

Similarly the following safeguards are recommended to achieve a nil-exclusion policy:

- Adjudicating bodies should have at least one member from the same ethnic group as the excluded pupil.

- All members of discipline committees and independent appeal panels should be trained in exclusion procedures and antiracist strategies.

- Every excluded pupil should be represented by a completely independent trained advocate.

- Every exclusion should be reviewed by governors and the LEA, even when accepted and not challenged by parents.

- Exclusions should be honestly and accurately featured in local/national inspection reports.

- For every pupil excluded, schools must accept an excluded pupil from another school.

- Immediate alternative full-time education provision should be provided for every excluded pupil.

- The 'two strikes and you're out' clause should be abolished.

Acknowledgement

I am extremely grateful to Morcea Walker from Northampton for her help in revising this chapter.

References

Birmingham Metropolitan Council (1994) *Report to the Birmingham Education Services and Special Needs Sub-Committee 28 June 1994 – Baseline Assessment for the Primary Phase Autumn 1993 Analysis of Results.* Birmingham: Birmingham Metropolitan Council.

Chevannes, M. and Reeves, F. (1987) 'The black voluntary school movement'. In B. Troyan (ed) *Racial Equality in Education.* London: Tavistock.

Clark, K. (1971) 'Alternative public school systems.' In B. Gross and R. Gross (eds) *Radical School Reform.* London: Victor Gollancz.

Coard, B. (1971) *How the West Indian Child is Made Educationally Sub-normal in the British School System.* London: New Beacon.

Commision for Racial Equality (1985) *Report of a Formal Investigation into School Exclusions in Birmingham.* Birmingham: CRE.

Dreyden, J. (1989) 'Multiculuralism and the structure of knowledge: a discussion of standardised tests.' A paper given at the National Foundation for Educational Research.

Gurnah, A. (1989) 'After bilingual support?' In M. Cole (ed) *Education for Equality: Some Guidelines for Good Practice*. London: Routledge.

Hall, S., Cricher, C., Jefferson, T., Clarke, J. and Roberts, B. (1978) *Policing the Crisis: Mugging the State and Law and Order*. London: Macmillan.

Home Office (1999) *The Stephen Lawrence Inquiry: Report of an Inquiry by Sir William Macpherson of Cluny*. London: The Stationery Office.

Lane, J. (1989) 'The playgroup/nursery.' In M. Cole (ed) *Education for Equality: Some Guidelines for Good Practice*. London: Routledge.

Mac an Ghaill, M. (1988) *Young, Gifted and Black: Student–Teacher Relations in the Schooling of Black Youths*. Milton Keynes: Open University Press.

Mac an Ghaill, M. (1992) 'Coming of age in 1980s England: reconceptualising Black Students' schooling experience.' In D. Gill, B. Major and M. Blair (eds) *Racism and Education Structures and Strategies*. London: Sage.

Milner, D. (1983) *Children and Race, Ten Years On*. London: Ward Lock.

Richardson, R. (1990) *Daring to be a Teacher: Essay, Stories and Memoranda*. Stoke-on-Trent: Trentham.

Working Group Against Racism in Children's Resources (WGARCR) (1990) *Guidelines for the Evaluation and Selection of Toys and other Resources for Children*. WGARCR, 460 Wandsworth Road, London, SE8 3KX.

Working Group Against Racism in Children's Resources (1994a) Exclusions File – London Boroughs. Confidential document.

Working Group Against Racism in Children's Resources (1994b) Racial Harassment File – Eastern region. Confidential document.

Working Group Against Racism in Children's Resources (1994c) Discrimination File – Infant/Primary Schools. Confidential document.

Wright, C. (1987) 'Black students – white teachers.' In B. Troyna (ed) *Racial Inequality in Education*. London: Tavistock.

Wright, C. (1992) *Race Relations in the Primary School*. London: David Fulton.

Chapter 10

Mixed-race Children and Families

Nick Banks

Introduction

There is a growth in the number of mixed-race relationships. The Fourth National Survey of Ethnic Minorities (Policy Studies Institute (PSI) 1997) found that 20 per cent of married and cohabiting African Caribbean adults, 17 per cent of Chinese and 4 per cent of Indians and African Asians had white partners. The ensuing 'dual culture socialization' process makes mixed parentage children and families unique in the way this group influences notions of cultural homogeneity and notions of British 'racial purity'. Furthermore, the issue of being of mixed 'race' has become increasingly important due to the over-representation of these children in British social services care statistics (Barn, Sinclair and Ferdinand 1997).

This chapter will look at the historical factors surrounding mixed-race children and families and how these combine with the contemporary social context to affect the psychological dynamics and social pressures within such families. The chapter will also consider, through case study material, mixed-race children who find themselves separated from a parent and the dynamics that can exist within such acrimonious relationships. The chapter focuses on the psychological dynamics of parents and the social experiences of families as this is the context in which children live and are socialized. Discussion of strategies for direct work with children to promote a positive identity are considered in Chapter 7 of this book. The specific term mixed 'race' is preferred to other terms currently in use such as mixed 'parentage' as the latter term can be socially ambiguous and, as such, is not seen by me as a preferred term to describe a group which has yet to define its own identity.

Racialized Social Pressures and Personal Dynamics

Some researchers have argued that no distinction should be made be-tween children with one white and one black parent and those with two black parents since 'in this society any child who has the slightest taint of black is seen by the white majority as black' (Small 1986, p.92). Denial of a child's ethnic roots by white parents was said to give the child 'a white mask', and prevent 'exposure to his or her own self' (Small 1986, p.92). A similar view of the needs of people of mixed 'race' was advanced in the mid-1930s by Stonequist (1937). Stonequist saw people of mixed 'race' as being caught between opposing cultures, feeling they did not belong to either and yet wanting to belong to both. He believed that mixed-race people suffered pain and confusion from these experienced conflicts. It was Stonequist's view that resolving the conflict involved as-similating (making psychological connections) with the black group of origin. Park (1937), in opposition to Stonequist, stressed that there was a positive aspect to being of mixed 'race' in that it provided insight into two communities. However, the negative view of the identity develop-ment of mixed-race people has tended to predominate.

The social perception of children of mixed-race origin and their, most often white, mothers in Britain has historically been negative. Such children were typically seen as representing a threat to the social ('racial') purity of white British society. Early surveys indicated (Banks 1992) considerable hostility to the idea of white women in relationships with both African Caribbean and South Asian men. Interestingly, the earliest surveys were conducted exclusively with white people, presumably due to an erroneous belief that black people had a consensus of opinion be-lieving mixed-race unions to be desirable and positive. More recent sur-veys (PSI 1997) with both black and white ethnic groups have suggested that the level of blatant hostility may have subsided to a considerable de-gree. However, one must be cautious in accepting this more recent re-search as a positive indicator of change and acceptance of children and unions in (white) British society as the research measures opinions or at-titudes. The psychological research on attitudes indicates (Oskamp 1997) that an individual's claimed belief does not always correlate with his or her observed behaviour. It may be that people wish to appear 'po-litically correct' but when this projected facade is actually tested, say by a close relative such as a daughter or son intending to marry a person of a black ethnic minority group, the facade is dropped with previously hid-den or denied emotions coming too readily to the surface exposing the more accurate set of racialized beliefs that an individual holds about the subject. Certainly, when the opinions of white mothers in mixed-race relationships are sought (Banks 1996), it seems that they experience racism, often for the first time, from their family members and from wider society. In this particular publication, I sought the views of 16 white mothers between the ages of 17 and 23. With this small sample it was discovered that many experienced direct racism at the point that children arrived. It seems that the emotional connection with a black male became sexualized in wider society's view and they responded with verbal and sometimes physical aggression. The women in these relationships became sensitized to this and became wary of their presentation in public. The women with available and supportive partners developed better coping mechanisms than those with absent and/or non-supportive partners. Direct difficulties with the relationships with children arose where the partner was absent and the mother had wished for a continuing relationship or where the relationship was only short term and the mother was unwilling to consider contact with the father. The mothers with absent partners appeared psychologically 'trapped' with feelings of being unable to enter into a relationship with a white man due to having a black child and self-perceptions of being socially/personally unacceptable due to the overt sexualization stigma of their past being identified through having a mixed-race child. This social stigma made it particularly difficult for the women to 'reintegrate' into white society. Often the women did not feel able to form a further relationship with a black man due to associated negative experiences. Social and psychological isolation resulted in continuing and further difficulties in their relationship with their child. The sample in this study were women in a self-referring counselling relationship. Therefore, this negative experience will not be found by all those in mixed relationships and it is worth professionals and those contemplating such a relationship remembering that it is often those relationships with existing personal pathology and those formed with immature and unrealistic expectations or lack of social support that may fail due to social pressures. This is true of many relationships, mixed or not. However, there are additional social pressures, due to society's hostility and, in some cases, due to the 'racialized' pathology that enters into the relationship 'attraction' that can bring additional pressures to bear.

A lack of preparation for the direct experience of racism acts a destructive stressor in mixed-race relationships where there has been no prior discussion or experience. For example, encountering a racist slur while on public transport can be devastating, especially if one has previously taken a colour-blind notion that 'colour doesn't matter'. A parent without coping strategies or a parent that internalizes his or her anger is likely to discover that this impacts directly on their relationship with both children and partner. Such external pressure has the result, as is intended by the individual(s) who lands the insult, of potentially destabilizing a relationship. This is particularly so with a relationship that does not easily discuss the notion of 'difference'. A minimization or denial of difference has the effect of further undermining what may be an already weak relationship foundation. A lack of discussion, as well as not preparing the adults, does not allow for the preparation of children. For example, mixed-race children are likely to experience other children who enquire directly about their 'racial' difference, typically encountered in the nursery when asked by a white child 'Why have you got a white mummy?' This can be confusing or upsetting to a child who has not had the benefit of prior discussion and preparation. Mixed-race children who ask for clarification from parents who are themselves unclear and uncertain as to how to discuss issues of 'difference' will not be helped to come to terms with their difference in a way that will allow them to develop a positive personal or social identity. Without a positive frame of reference to understand their difference from others, they will be likely, much as their parents, to see 'difference' as negative and consideration/discussion to be avoided. Thus, 'difference' will be self-perceived as making them 'inferior' rather than objectively 'distinct' from children who are not mixed 'race'. Another result of lack of acknowledgement of 'difference' from the non-mixed-race family and child is that relational links with other mixed-race families and children are less likely to be established. Similarities will not be seen and the parents will continue on their colour-blind trail developing 'colour fear/avoidance' features when the topic is raised by others.

Personal dynamics and family dysfunction

It is useful to consider a case study showing specific conflict that may occur in a mixed-race family setting as a means to consider functional and dysfunctional ways of responding to conflict. This case study is not presented as having a 'typical' or commonly occurring family difficulty, but is provided to show the more dysfunctional dynamics for the purposes of learning case conceptualization skills.

Case study: Anita and Ahmed

The family make-up is of a 26-year-old Pakistani man, Ahmed, and a 23-year-old white English woman, Anita. They have a son originally named Asif with his mother later changing his name to Aaron. Ahmed was in a four-year relationship with Anita before having a son by her. Ahmed went to India two years into the relationship to enter into an arranged marriage with a Pakistani woman. On his return six months later, he continued his relationship with Anita. This was a major event in the relationship between Anita and Ahmed. It appears quite likely that Anita was not seen as a significant person by the extended family as her relationship with Ahmed appears to have been dismissed by the extended family requiring an arranged marriage. This must have been particularly painful for Anita, having the effect of undermining her confidence and self-esteem, living with and having a child by a man who had become married during their relationship and living within an extended family environment which had facilitated this arranged marriage. Anita became unhappy living with Ahmed's family and moved to find her own accommodation four months after the birth of Asif. Anita then attempted to live her own life but found that Ahmed would not allow this. She experienced Ahmed regularly stalking her. Ahmed admitted that he loved Anita and wanted to resume the relationship. Anita refused Ahmed contact with Asif due to his stalking behaviour and Anita's belief that a primary reason for Ahmed's wish for contact was to pursue attempts at maintaining a relationship with her. Ahmed went to court to fight for contact.

Cultural connections

Ahmed's criticism of Asif's mother was that Anita did not acknowledge Asif's Asian background and would not call him by his Asian name, preferring to call him 'Aaron'. In such cases there are often contradictions in attitude and behaviour. Some parents will attempt to adopt a colour-blind approach whereas other aspects of their behaviour highlight their colour-sensitive beliefs. Anita recognized that Asif would have difficulties related to his mixed-race appearance as she took the view that he would have fewer problems as he grew older if he used the name Aaron. In considering the likelihood of 'confusion' it may be more confusing for Asif to be known as 'Aaron' as, simply put, this name will 'not fit his face'. A European name is unlikely to cloak Asif in ethnic ambiguity. It will be his appearance that people will respond to as much as his name. Indeed, people, both adults and children, would most likely query the name and why this did not obviously fit his 'racially' perceived physical appearance.

Ahmed wished Asif to be brought up in the Muslim religion and become familiar with his culture by contact with him and his family. Anita wanted Aaron to be brought up in a western tradition and believed that learning an Asian language would be confusing and unnecessary for him. There is no evidence that bilingualism produces confusion in children; indeed there is much evidence to show that this is a very enriching experience, and that the sooner that children begin to learn a second language, the easier it is for them to comprehend its subtle and rich cultural meanings. As to whether it would be necessary is a separate issue. One would need to ask in considering this, what the disadvantages would be to Asif/Aaron if he were to learn an Asian language. There are unlikely to be any disadvantages, but many advantages. For example, learning an Asian language would allow Asif direct entry into aspects of Asian Muslim culture that would be hidden from him should he not learn his father's language. To give an example, there are culturally embedded meanings that exist that do not directly translate into English. The direct meaning of these aspects of culture would be lost to someone who did not have the specific language. Although the cultural/linguistic terms would not exist in English, the concepts may, but the cultural significance and meaning would be lost in attempting to convey the meaning in any language other than the mother tongue. Also, the speaking of an Asian language would allow Asif a greater cultural connection with individuals within the culture and the cultural group as a whole. Simply put, speaking an Asian language would give him a direct social connection and a sense of belonging, whereas not speaking the language would isolate him from the group and lessen his sense of belonging. This particular issue was one that Anita appeared to recognize hence her view that she wanted Asif to be seen as the son of his mother, not his Asian father. Clearly Asif would be the son of his mother but, regardless of Anita's viewpoint, is also the son of his Asian father. Anita appears to take a psychological stance of denial together with an attempt at 'exorcism' of Asif's Asian connections which she finds unacceptable due to her experiences with his father.

The literature (Banks 1996) suggests that aspects of pathology in the mother–son relationship may develop due to a spillover from pathological aspects in the parental relationship. My hypothesis was that the Asian presentation of Asif caused Anita personal difficulty due to him looking like his father and it was this aspect of Asif which Anita yearned (impossibly) to do away with. It may be that Anita's attempt to psychologically exorcise Ahmed from their son was related to some women's experience of having a child of mixed 'race' limiting their attractiveness to white men. Due to living in a racist society where mixed-race relationships are devalued, having a child of mixed 'race' allows individuals to make sexualized assumptions about a woman's (lack of) morals (Banks 1995, 1996). Thus, Anita may be limited in her future selection of a partner. There may be suspicion about any partner's motives or intentions towards her and also about a future partner's acceptance or treatment of Asif. This may be an unacknowledged source of anger in a mother which requires specialized support from a counsellor knowledgeable of social pressures in mixed-race unions.

Colour significance

It is very likely that Asif will cue into his mother's difficulties about his 'racial' difference from her and learn that these differences are a taboo topic that cannot be openly discussed. This will create difficulties for the child and for the mother–child relationship. When Asif wishes to discuss aspects of difference from mother perhaps with a trigger of children making comments and asking questions such as 'why are you a different colour from your mother?', Asif/Aaron will become hypersensitized to his obvious physical difference. It is often said that children do not notice colour. There is little evidence to support this belief. The evidence which has been in existence from as early as 1936 (Horowitz 1936) indicates that children do very much perceive differences in colour and can, towards the age of 7, locate these differences in an accurate social hierarchy (Clark and Clark 1939; Milner 1983). The available evidence suggests that children of mixed white/Asian background are lower down the perceived social hierarchy than children of white/African Caribbean background (Banks 1997; Gill and Jackson 1983; Milner 1983). This is to say that such children tend to be less accepted by Asian (and white) society. This appears to be related to the cultural and religious distance that these children are said to have from their perceived culture of origin. This may be related to the lack of mother-tongue language acquisition. The transmission of culture tends to be through the mother as the main agent of socialization and the proportion of mixed-race children (Asian/white) tends to be mainly with Asian fathers and white mothers (PSI 1997), therefore reducing the chances of the transmission of Asian culture. This raises the issue of even if Anita should agree that Asif should be raised in the Muslim faith how this would happen. Even with her agreement, from a practical point of view, unless Asif was living within Ahmed's family, it is an ideal that would never be achieved unless Anita was to convert to Islam. Simply put, there are many dietary requirements, religious expectations and 'cultural ways of being' that cannot be inculcated into a child's view of the world from a distant, unlived, day-to-day non-experience. Islam has to be practised and experienced within a cultural context to be understood and to be seen as relevant and important to a young child. Living outside a cultural/religious context, the positive significance of an Islamic perspective would not be received by Asif.

Anita took the view that if Aaron wanted to embrace his Asian roots when he was older and could decide for himself she would understand, but at age 4 she would not encourage it. Unfortunately, it is likely that Asif will have internalized many of the negative racist perceptions of Asian/Muslim culture and there will be little in his experience which will allow him to counter this to make unbiased decisions at a later point in his life. It is possible that due to negative social perceptions of Islam and 'Asianness' Asif would, without proactive positive support, develop a negative and internalized racist perspective of himself.

Theoretical Issues in Identity Development

Erikson (1959) stressed the importance of the congruence of personal or individual identity and group or communal identities if one was to form a mature, stable and healthy personality. For Erikson an optimal sense of identity was experienced as a sense of psychosocial well-being, 'a feeling of being at home in one's body, a sense of knowing where one is going, and an inner assuredness of anticipated recognition from those who count' (Erikson 1959, p.165). This latter aspect attributes a sense of psychosocial mutuality to identity, implying a reciprocal or mutual relationship with one's immediate community or peer group. A further development of the concept of identity was that of 'social identity' in the

1970s (Tajfel 1978) to explain in-group and out-group relations and social processes. Social identity has been defined by Tajfel (1978) as the individual's knowledge that he or she belongs to certain social groups together with some emotional and value significance to him or her of the group membership. Individuals become psychologically connected to their group through their self-definitions as members of the group. For a child of mixed 'race', this will be particularly important to feel part of both communities which is most likely to come initially through positive connections with both paternal and maternal families.

Gibbs and Moskowitz-Sweet (1991) suggested that mixed-race adolescents will tend to experience conflicts around five major psychosocial developmental tasks:

- the formation of a dual racial/ethnic identity
- conflicts with social marginality
- conflicts about sexuality and choice of sexual partner
- conflicts about separation from their parents
- conflicts about their educational or career aspirations.

Gibbs and Moskowitz-Sweet (1991) suggest that these conflicts may be shown in symptoms of anxiety, depression, academic under-achievement, substance abuse, and possibly even suicidal behaviour (Gibbs 1990). The research of Gill and Jackson (1983) in Britain does not lend support to these notions. Perhaps what is needed for the mixed-race child is that which is also needed for any black child (who is not directly mixed) to be able to navigate their way in white society. This ability could be termed 'bicultural competence' or even 'multicultural competence' which could be seen as the ability to understand and negotiate one's way in cultural environments requiring different ways of being whereby one adjusts one's behaviour to the norms of each culture in order to meet one's goals (de Anda 1984). However, it is uncertain whether this duality is psychologically viable.

There are relatively few studies of the identity development of mixed-race children. Wilson (1987), in Britain, published a study of 51 6–9-year-old British mixed-race children, with one white and one African or African Caribbean parent living with their birth mothers. Half the mothers were single, and most, but not all, were white. It is not clear how far the findings are generalizable to mixed-race families as a whole as the families were members of 'Harmony', a specific social support organization for mixed-race families and thus very much exposed to and knowledgeable about issues regarding 'race' and the well-being of their mixed-race children. Wilson (1987) found that the children tended not to see themselves as black or white but as 'half-caste or brown'. However, 70 per cent of the children gave some indication of a preference for being white or, in a few cases, black. A positive mixed-race identity seemed to be associated with living in a multicultural area. Wilson suggested that this was because there may be sufficient numbers of mixed-race people to make 'mixed race' a viable racial identity.

With any intending mixed relationship both parents will need to address a number of issues about their view of their children and how they will be responded to by the white parent. In order to prepare the mixed-race child to have a positive view of their black mixed-race self the following criteria should be carefully considered:

1. Will the parents have adequate skills, knowledge and understanding of issues of difference in the sense of acknowledging cultural, historical and physical distinctiveness in an open and positive way?

2. Will the white parent have the necessary (non-racist) attitude/mind-set? Racist or ethnocentric attitudes in a parent will harm the child's emotional and cognitive development. In suggesting that a parent may have racist attitudes, I am suggesting that the more subtle, difficult to identify racist attitude (such as not wanting to acknowledge a child's ethnic/colour difference and the significance of this to a child's development as in the case of Anita) may exist. Cultural arrogance or missionary rescue type beliefs may also reflect a covert racist value base.

3. Will both parents be able to consider the value of living in an environment which does not translate the child's 'ethnically unique' characteristics i.e. 'difference' into 'odd' or 'unusual'? The area of residence may be an important aspect of support for the child's social, psychological and physical 'connectedness' with black communities.

4. Will the parents have frequent informal and natural social connections with black individuals and communities?

5. Will the parents be able to proactively and defensively prepare the child for racist social reality?

In specifically considering a white parent's ability to engage successfully with the psychological development of their black mixed-race child one needs a suitable theoretical framework. An empirically based theoretical model for the assessment of white racial identity development has been proposed by Helms (1990) in the USA with a sample of over 500 participants. I have discussed this framework in more detail in a previous article (Banks 1999). In this chapter I wish to consider another framework for considering both the black and white parents' development of the ability to engage with 'racial' difference.

Mixed-race relationship development model

It is useful to consider how the parent may enter into a relationship and the process whereby that relationship may change over time. A stage model is proposed. This model is yet to be empirically supported and is devised from clinically based observations. Thus, this model is tentative and is offered as a means to conceptualize the route individuals may take and the different outcomes that result.

Stage 1: Oblivious to Social Meaning

This is not necessarily a lack of awareness of the existence of racial boundaries, as this is one of the explicit foundations of social division, but a lack of awareness of the meaning and depth of racial boundaries and the relationship implications. This separation in meaning allows the individual to consider the possibility of a mixed relationship without threat to self or, depending on the circumstances, fear of social reaction.

Stage 2: Curiosity

Curiosity may stem from an attraction to the individual for his or her personal qualities or be the result of attraction to forbidden fruit with either unconscious or acknowledged sexual undertones. Attraction to aspects of the culturally exotic may also be involved. Here, there is an awareness of racialized social boundaries. The individual believes the boundaries do not apply to them or can be successfully managed by situational or short-term engagement. Pregnancy at this stage is likely to have serious negative consequences for the child due to a lack of commitment between the parents and the implications for the white mother having a black child being unconsidered.

Stage 3: Engagement

This involvement may be at a surface level of physical fascination or sensation-seeking with limited/short-term infatuation. Engagement may develop into a genuine emotional connection and commitment but there may continue to be a lack of acknowledgement and consequent discussion about the social implications of the relationship and the implications for the socialization of the children.

Stage 4: Realization

This stage and the next stage of 'withdrawal' in the relationship development are those which markedly differentiate the relationship of the mixed-race couple from one with no racialized difference. Here, the individuals encounter a threat or challenge to their relationship. The threat may be the experience of the first racial slur. The challenge may be what is intended to be a constructive questioning regarding their intention of long-term commitment. Several reactions may follow: there may be a reaction that begins to undermine the security of the relationship by sowing the seeds of doubt about its social viability; there may be a reaction which causes the couple to question/debate the implications for themselves and any children in a racially hostile community context. Discussion of this is likely to strengthen the relationship if the individuals have the knowledge/understanding of the likely implications. Without this knowledge the discussion will only serve to support the foundations of denial further. Having parents who enter the stage of 're-alization' without informed awareness may have drastic implication for the socialization and acceptance of mixed-race children as with the case study involving Ahmed and Anita. The individuals may proceed to Stage 5 ('withdrawal') or bypass this to move to Stage 6 ('commitment'). Movement to Stage 5 or Stage 6 is dependent on the degree of personal 'turbulence' caused by social threat and the couple's ability to manage this by open discussion of the feelings and fears this arouses in both.

Stage 5: Withdrawal

A developing awareness of the implications of social hostility and rejection may cause the relationship to break down. Without the presence of children the consequences are no greater than with any relationship lacking commitment that breaks down with a realization of lack of compatibility or personal disinterest. However, the breakdown in a relationship that is not related to personal circumstances/choice and is the result of racist social pressure has implications for the development of a racially tolerant society.

Stage 6: Commitment

This stage can be reached only when the couple have moved beyond a cognitive understanding (as achieved in Stage 4 ('realization') of their mixed-race relationship social status and have discussed the implications for the 'management' of this at crisis points e.g. when encountering social hostility. As well as a cognitive appreciation, a developing emotional linkage that transcends both exotic curiosity and social division is required before commitment is consolidated.

Conclusion

The progress the parents make in developing strategies to cope with social hostility and those strategies which they use to discuss difference with their child will help build the child's sense of uniqueness and confidence. This will be necessary for individual psychological security and family relationship development. A family with children of mixed parentage has additional tasks to accomplish to ensure positive psychological development for their children. This task is one that needs open, at-ease discussion for children not to feel ill at ease. The parents of mixed-race children will need to consider their own barriers, if any, to this discussion and move through a process to help them gain additional confidence in achieving the necessary tasks.

References

Banks, N. (1992a) 'Techniques for direct identity work with black children.' *Adoption and Fostering 16*, 3, 19–25.

Banks, N. (1992b) 'Some consideration of racial identification and self esteem when working with mixed ethnicity children and their mothers as social services clients.' *Social Services Research 3*, 32–41.

Banks, N. (1995) 'Children of black mixed parentage and their placement needs.' *Adoption and Fostering 19*, 2, 19–24.

Banks, N. (1996) 'Young single white mothers with black children in therapy.' *Clinical Child Psychology and Psychiatry 1*, 1.

Banks, N. (1997) 'Social workers' perceptions of racial difference.' *Social Services Research 1*, 26–32.

Banks, N. (1999) 'Transracial placements and the assessment of white carers.' *Educational and Child Psychology 16*, 3, 55–67.

Clark, K.B. and Clark, M.K. (1939) 'The development of consciousness and self and the emergence of racial identification in negro preschool children.' *Journal of Social Psychology, S.P.S.S.I Bulletin 10*, 591–599.

de Anda, D. (1984) 'Bi-cultural socialisation: factors affecting the minority experience.' *Social Work 99*, 101–107.

Erikson, E.H. (1959) *Identity and the Life Cycle: Selected Papers by Erik Erikson, Volume 1 Psychological Issues.* New York: International Universities Press.

Gibbs, J.T. (1990) 'Bi-racial adolescents.' In J.T. Biggs and L.N. Huang (eds) *Children of Colour: Psychological Interventions with Minority Youth.* San Francisco, CA: Jossey-Bass.

Gibbs, J.T. and Moskowitz-Sweet, G. (1991) 'Clinical and cultural issues in the treatment of bi-racial and bi-cultural adolescents.' *Families in Society: The Journal of Contemporary Human Services 72*, 10, 579–592.

Gill, O. and Jackson, B. (1983) *Adoption and Race: Black, Asian and Mixed Race Children in White Families.* London: Batsford/BAAF.

Helms, J. (1990) *Black and White Racial Identity.* Westport, CT: Greenwood.

Oskamp, S. (1977) *Attitudes and Opinions.* Englewood Cliffs, NJ: Prentice Hall.

Park, R. (1937) 'Introduction.' In E. Stonequist, *The Marginal Man.* New York: Scribners.

Policy Studies Institute (PSI) (1997) *Ethnic Minorities in Britain: Fourth National Survey.* London: PSI.

Small, J. (1986) 'Transracial placements: conflicts and contradictions.' In S. Ahmed, J. Cheetham and J. Small (eds) *Social Work with Black Children and their Families.* London: Batsford.

Stonequist, E. (1937) *The Marginal Man.* New York: Scribners.

Tajfel, H. (1978) 'Social categorisation, social identity and social comparison.' In H. Tajfel, *Differentiation between Social Groups: Studies in the Social Psychology of Intergroup Relations.* London: Academic Press.

Wilson, A. (1987) *Mixed Race Children: A Study of Identity.* London: Allen and Unwin.

Chapter 11

Adoption of Children from Minority Groups

Harry Zeitlin

Case study: Meera

Meera was born in southern India and is very dark skinned. She was adopted by an affluent white Anglo-Saxon Church of England family at 6 weeks. The mother had other natural children and though the girl bonded with the mother, the mother did not bond with her. They never discussed with Meera her origins, culture or heritage, religion or difference in appearance from the rest of the family. The rejection progressively affected her behaviour giving reason to place her further and further from the heart of the family unit. At 12 she came into the care of the local authority. She was placed with a woman of African Caribbean origin, who was a Jehovah's Witness, of low income and a single mother. She was kind and caring but frequently took supportive comment as a criticism of her based on prejudice against black people. After a suicidal attempt by Meera, a proposal was made to place her with a recently immigrated Indian Muslim family.

Introduction

This case history raises nearly all of the issues relevant to adoption and fostering of children from minority groups, but it is almost impossible to examine them without immediately entering into controversy. The whole subject has become one of emotional debate, partly because of the media sensation-seeking and partly because of understandable feelings of resentment against prejudice and 'racism'.

Same-race placement has been put forward as the determining principle in adoption. Thoburn (1988) stated that

> Although babies should be placed as early as possible, there is reason to be hopeful that they will settle in with a new family when a suitable family is found, if care is taken over the introductory period…it is preferable, even for babies, for a same race placement to be made after some delay, than to make a transracial placement. (Thoburn 1988, p.78)

No evidence is offered either to support the bad outcome for transracial adoption or the lack of effect of delay in placement and ignores current research on attachment. There is also a tendency to a simple polarized argument for and against placement of black children with white families. This policy is often taken further so that any 'black' child must be placed in a 'black' family, if unable to live with the birth parents. Children of 'mixed' parentage are usually considered as black for the purpose of placement decisions.

One of the greatest problems is confusion over terminology. Such fostering and adoption have variously been referred to as transracial, transcultural and mixed ethnic. Unfortunately there is a lack of consistency in the use of the terms race, ethnicity and culture, each being used with variable meaning but also interchangeably. Though for some the problems seem quite clear with regard to themselves, for example about being black in a majority white community, or about specific religious persecution, the same problems arise with regard to a wide variety of other people of different national origins and cultures. Those would include, among many others, Turks, Chinese, American Indians and, depending on the majority community, nearly every religion.

These issues matter greatly when considering placement for a child. The phrase 'same-race placement' is easy to say but exactly what is meant is obscure and it is a term born more in response to social prejudice than anything else. In view of the confusion it is valuable to review briefly the meaning of the terms and then to consider the impact of the relevant factors on placement.

Race and Racial

The word 'race' is freely used and often without regard to meaning. Dictionary definitions give various meanings from 'a group of persons, animals or plants connected by common descent or origin' to 'a genus, species'. Much of the present social usage derives from nineteenth-century ethnologists and Pritchard in 1845 wrote:

> The principal object of the following work [*The Natural History of Man*] may then be described as an attempt to point out the most important diversities by which mankind, or the genus of man, is distinguished and separated into different races, and to determine whether these races constitute separate species or are merely varieties of one species. (Pritchard 1845, p.10)

Strictly speaking, as noted by Darwin (1871, p.241), racial difference really implies genetic incompatibility, a different species. As there are no two human groups where cross-mating produces diminished fertility in this sense there is only one human race.

Tizard and Phoenix (1989) comment that the term 'race' is 'socially constructed and contentious', but found 'no alternative for its use in a society where it has deep political and psychological meaning'. For the most part it seems that the term is used to imply people with a common national heritage and who share certain physical characteristics, but with very uncertain implication as to associated cultures. As far as possible here reference instead will be made to physical characteristics, culture, country of heritage, culture of heritage and where possible the use of the terms race and ethnic will be interpreted in these terms.

Ethnicity

Dictionary definitions give 'Ethnic: pertaining to nations, gentile, heathen' and 'Ethnology: science of human races, their relations and characteristics'. Not a great deal of help except perhaps in the reference to nations. Unfortunately when applied to the British nation we immediately run into a total lack of consistency with physical characteristics. British origins were Nordic, Saxon, Roman etc. with a range of appearance from flaxen haired to swarthy Mediterranean. Today a significant proportion of the British population take their origins in Africa or Asia and much of the open debate centres on being black or white. However there is no agreed definition of what being black constitutes except as non-white. What is more important is that such categorization is based on xenophobic hostility, is neither logical nor exact, and is not a helpful basis on which to examine the best interests of children unable to stay with their natural parents. Certainly many people see themselves as being black and would be so described by others. However, many others in British society would neither be able to decide whether they are black or white nor wish so to categorize themselves. There is no evidence to support the idea that there is a 'black race' compared with white other than politically, and in discussing placement of a child, if the importance of being black in British society is because it identifies a section of society for hostility and prejudice, then the real issue is to help children cope with prejudice.

Apart from skin colour there is a wide variety of genetically determined physical characteristics which are related to 'ethnic' or 'racial' groups, including aspects of stature and physiognomy and to which social stereotypes are applied. Stereotyping of this nature is made by well-meaning professionals as well as more hostile members of society, with assumptions about cultural practice and experience. It would be incorrect to assume that all Semites are of the same religion or that black Asians share a common culture with black African Caribbeans. In any case as soon as a family migrates to a different majority culture the children will have a different experience to that of their parents even if they adhere strictly to their culture of heritage.

Culture

Both Pritchard (1845) and Darwin (1871) mixed issues of physical status with those of culture. Culture can be seen as referring to improvement through education or training. It usually applies to patterns of behaviour that are linked to national and religious customs. The cultural experience of children should be distinguished from the cultural associations linked to 'national' characteristics or heritage as these have different implications for the children. The former, being part of a child's personal experience, is more relevant to learned coping styles and the latter to a sense of historical identity. In the case study quoted, Meera's heritage was of Indian culture, though across India that differs greatly. Her religion of heritage might have been Muslim or Christian but statistically more probably Hindu. In reality no one knew and false assumptions were made. Her experience was of Christian culture, but that was Church of England and very different from Jehovah's Witness. However, talking to Meera it was apparent that there were many other areas of culture that were important to her, not the least being that she had become poor and missed celebrating Christmas.

The policy of black with black assumes not only a black race but also a single black culture, another stereotype as there is no unifying 'black culture' but a wide and rich range of very different cultures. An appreciation of the particular child's experience becomes more relevant than a blanket policy. It is also hazardous to generalize about the ways that children react to differences between their culture of origin and majority culture as for example Weinreich (1983) found that there were differences not only between Asian and West Indian groups but also between male and female within those groups.

Confusion of issues

Closer examination of the use of these terms indicates that there is considerable confusion of the issues relating to placement of a child. Each of the items needs to be considered separately to avoid transferring that confusion to the child (Alstein *et al.* 1994). Alstein and colleagues noted that there were dangers of making assumptions that became self-fulfilling and stressed the need for self-awareness among social workers involved in adoption placement.

It even remains difficult to find a terminology to deal with the problems. Transracial/ethnic/cultural adoption is somewhat cumbersome and perhaps the terms euharmonic and euharmony for those matching in every respect is preferable, otherwise specifying the mismatch condition relevant.

As food for thought you might at this point consider the following question. If the choice is between a black Christian family or a white Muslim family with which would you place a black Muslim child?

This chapter will address the problem from a general point of view, though with particular focus on 'black' children. With regard to adoption and fostering the issues that are entangled can be summarized by the list in Table 11.1 and we can proceed to examine what evidence there is to prioritize each in importance when planning placement.

Table 11.1 Confusion of issues

Race	Unhelpful ambiguous term now linked with prejudice
Ethnic	Too varied in usage
Physical appearance	Does not indicate important areas of culture
Culture	Culture of heritage may differ from that experienced
Identity	Normally based on various factors, not usually just appearance; differences between personal and assigned
Reasons for adoption	Relate to special needs of the child
Attachment/ stability/consistency	Where in prioritization of matching?

Fostering and Adoption

It is essential to stress that the most important approach to fostering and adoption is to address the root causes that result in parents being unable to care for their children. However, children do and will continue to need alternative care and three factors make it necessary to address the problems of 'mixed race adoption'. First, there is a shortage of suitable minority group families compared with the numbers of children needing alternative care. Second, at present there is greater risk for some minority group children to need alternative care compared with the rest of the community (Jenkins and Diamond 1985). That means that the biggest pool of families is majority group whereas a relatively greater proportion of minority group children need alternative families. Third, the increasing variations of heritage and culture from mixed parentage make placement into dissimilar families difficult to avoid.

If children do have to be in alternative care, there are aspects of placement that need to be considered before looking at the question of match. Though it would not be appropriate here to review all issues relevant to adoptions, there are some generally accepted principles. The younger the child, the lower the rate of placement breakdown. The more problems within the natural home that the child has been subject to, the more the impact of separation and uncertainty. Children who have spent some time in institutional care are more likely to be over-affectionate but also later have difficulty in forming close relationships. From personal clinical experience children who either spend prolonged periods in temporary care or move through a series of short-term carers become increasingly rigid, untrusting and emotionally distant. Some of the aspects of adoption common to all placements are listed in Table 11.2.

Table 11.2 Aspects of adoption common to all placements

Reason for placement	Need to be taken into account
Bereavement Parental illness/incapacity Abuse/neglect Beyond parental control Special needs	
Age of child	Adoption outcome better when placement before age 3; after age 5 not likely to make too much difference between fostering or adoption
Number of previous placements	More placements, less trust
Period of time in temporary care	Longer time gives more relationship problems
Emotional or behavioural disorder	Special demands on alternative parents

What might go wrong for minority group children

Tizard and Phoenix (1989) considered the anxieties relating to black children in white families:

1. Black children living in white families fail to develop a positive black identity. Instead they suffer from identity confusion and develop a negative self-concept, believing or wishing they were white.

2.   Unless they are carefully trained, white families cannot provide black children with survival skills that they need for coping with racial prejudice in society.

3.   The children will grow up unable to relate to black people and at the same time will experience rejection by white society.

Identity

Issues of identity and its development are of great importance in any adoption but how central is racial or ethnic identity and should it be the main means of personal identification? In the 1950s, Erikson (1968) laid the foundation for conceptualization and research on identity formation. He saw identity formation as part of the developmental process by which choices could be made by the individual:

> The young person in order to experience wholeness must feel a progressive continuity between that which he has come to be during the long years of childhood and that which he promises to become in the anticipated future; between that which he conceives himself to be and that which he perceives others to see in him and to expect of him. (Erikson 1968, p.)

Marcia (1980) further developed Erikson's ideas and construed identity as

> an internal, self constructed organization of drives, abilities, beliefs, and individual history. The better developed this structure is, the more aware the individual appears to be of their own uniqueness…the less developed this structure is, the more confused individuals seem to be about their own distinctiveness from others and the more they have to rely on external sources to evaluate themselves. (Marcia 1980, pp.159–187)

Ideas have progressed in some aspects pushed by the issues concerning 'ethnic identity'. The idea of a single composite identity is replaced by one with several components or domains. If we look at the available means by which children, as individuals, gain their identity, these would include gender role, family values, social grouping, occupation, religion, political ideology, relationships and personal values. The various components of identity are not developed or fixed at the same time. Gender identity, for example is set very early in life, whereas career-based idenity evolves much later, at least for most. Fairly fundamental to identity formation are rather diffuse feelings of being valuable, and of having desirable personal characteristics. Most children in western society are not primarily identified by their appearance but by being good at reading, skilled at football or kind and loving, while some of course are identified by being aggressive or violent. Early reinforcement of those same types of quality enables children to evaluate more constructively characteristics that might be seen as negative by others (Jacobs 1978).

Tizard and Phoenix (1989) challenged the value of the concept of 'positive black identity' as being too simplistic with regard to the way in which children identify themselves. Early research based on forced choice between seeing self as black or white led to some incorrect conclusions. When children were given a range of appearances to match themselves with, they had from an early age quite accurate independent awareness of their skin colour that was more precise and different from a black–white categorization (Jacobs 1978). In a study of 130 black pre-school children Spencer (1984) found that the children were able to conceptualize and compartmentalize a view of self that is independent of attitudes surrounding the evaluation of their racial group. Scott (1986) found that strong personal identity rather than group identity is associated with good outcome in terms of low rates of disturbance.

Children of mixed marriages, 'black' and 'white', are of special concern. Currently there is a pressure that they should be classified as black and that they should see themselves as so. The argument is that society sees them as black and they will be better off if that is their self-perceived identity. Arnold (1984) found that 11 out of 28 interracial children rated themselves as black, but 12 saw themselves as interracial and 5 as white. As a whole the children expressed an uncertainty about their racial identification but those who saw themselves as interracial showed greater emotional and psychiatric stability. They also scored higher on self concept.

Identity and self-esteem

Self-esteem is related to identity in a very uncertain manner. A simple model is that strong positive identity leads to high self-esteem but it does not always seem to work like that. Though black children are not of particularly low self-esteem (Gill and Jackson 1983), and Rasheed (1981) found little correlation between ethnic identity and self-esteem, Casey (1986) established that strong identification with a minority group has an adverse effect. This is not confined to groups identified by skin colour and Casey's (1986) data, for example, refers to Italian and Polish second and third generation immigrants in America. Stein (1984) compared 91 adoptees at age 15–18 with matched non-adopted children using self-rating scales for identity and self-image. It was the quality of family relationships in both groups that was predictive of positive identity outcome rather than the adoptive status.

The political writers correctly noted that people with black skin will be classified according to that skin colour by at least a proportion of society. They argue that a black identity should be encouraged as the primary means of identification. However such identity is an assigned one and difficult to separate from stereotypes and prejudices. The danger is that central identification in that manner results in the individual being controlled by the assigned identity rather than owning and being proud of the attributes that had been used to classify them.

Negative identity

Erikson (1968, p.174) wrote also about choice of a negative identity: 'They choose instead a negative identity i.e. based perversely on all those identifications and roles which, at critical stages of development, had been presented to them as most undesirable or dangerous and yet also as most real'. However, that is based largely on the supposition that identity formation is based on a series of choices. In this case it is not so much a negative identity as a negative connotation of the identity assigned. How then can children achieve a positive identification with those characteristics used as a source of prejudice? How can strong ethnic/cultural identity be developed as an asset rather than something that isolates the individual from other parts of society and restricts individual exploration and growth?

First, the child should be secure within a safe environment. It is for secure individuals with clearly identified assets in a safe environment, that ongoing exploration of identity is safe and effective. Those individuals can cope with the uncertainty involved. Second, for many, early positive identity formation is protective particularly from adverse assigned identity. That identification should be with a range of individual positive characteristics as well as with the culture of heritage (rather than race or those physical characteristics that have been used for prejudice). Third, failure to form elements of personal identity based on positive attributes, early in the process of independence, leaves children vulnerable to a range of emotional and behavioural disturbances including aggressive behaviour, drug abuse and depression. Fourth, ethnic and cultural domains of identity become important valuable personal assets against this background. Finally, if care professionals assign identity because society uses that identification for prejudice, children receive a very mixed message about the value of that aspect of personal identity.

The issue of identity can become circular. Identifying because of assigned identity based on prejudice will lead to angry defensiveness which in turn leads to segregation and then back to seeking to impose a segregated identity. In this way a group of angry people unable to deal with prejudice or participate in a dialogue is developed.

Outcome studies for fostering and adoption

There are relatively few good systematic data on long-term outcome for 'crossed adoption': most still confuse culture, heritage, appearance etc. What data there are, however, have a remarkable consistency, showing no major differences in outcome for matched and non-matched 'race' adoptions on a variety of measures (Moore 1986; Womak and Fulton 1981; Wrobel 1990). Overall it appears that some 80 per cent of such adoptions are satisfactory in terms of adult adjustment, though obviously what is meant by that is open to debate. Womak and Fulton (1981) studied 28 transracially adopted (TRA) black children comparing them with 13 non-adopted black children. They found no significant differences on measures of development or of racial attitude. Wrobel (1990) reported that all 78 transracially adopted adolescents in his study rated themselves positively, males more strongly so than females, and good communication with the mother was central to positive self-esteem. Berridge and Cleaver (1987) from a study of foster home breakdown concluded that ethnicity (referring to black or 'mixed race') was not strongly related to outcome though there was a small excess of foster breakdown for transracial placement. They noted that the rates of disturbance in adopted children were actually quite low and that the majority did well. This seems to be a common factor in what studies have been reported, even those that anticipate later problems (see Table 11.3).

In adoption some children become 'searchers' for their family and culture of origin but these tend to be those who have experience of instability and difficulty in developing individual identity (Stein 1984). The associated psychological disturbance is best dealt with by minimizing periods of uncertainty and instability and promoting identification with the family of adoption. Kim (1980), reporting on problems with three Korean children adopted by white North American families, noted that the children had experienced major cultural change which, though usually ignored, could well explain the children's disturbance. Given the wide range of cultural, ethnic and social factors associated with people of any one skin colour or national origin, the stereotyped associations that ignore the real experience of the child are hazardous. However, more research is needed on the effects of 'cultural dissonance' as well as physical dissimilarity.

Table 11.3 Summary of outcome studies

Womak and Fulton 1981	Comparison of TRA and non-adopted black children: no significant difference in development of racial attitudes; early placement and open social attitudes relate to good outcome.
Berridge and Cleaver 1987	Ethnicity not strongly related to foster breakdown; rates of disturbance low; most (80%+) do well.
Wrobel 1990	TRA black children rated themselves positively; communication with mother important.
Stein 1984	Search behaviour greater with physical mismatch but mainly linked to family relationship difficulty; less with early placement, stability and open social attitudes.

Good Adjustment in Transracial Adoption

Womak and Fulton (1981) proposed that the good outcome in their study was largely due to the stability given to the adopted children by early placement. They noted that the adopters that they studied were of higher than average socio-economic status and thought that they also showed relatively more open social attitudes.

Physical match does have relevance. Stein (1984) compared 91 adoptees at age 15–18 with matched non-adopted children using self-rating scales for identity and self-image. It was the quality of family relationships in both groups that was predictive of positive identity outcome rather than the adoptive status. Stein (1984) did find that search behaviour (looking for the family of origin) among adoptees was more likely where there was a heightened sense of physical dissimilarity from the family. That occurred however when there were also unsatisfactory family relationships and tended to be those who had experience of instability and difficulty in developing individual identity. The associated psychological disturbance is best dealt with by minimizing periods of uncertainty and instability and promoting identification with the family of adoption. Early placement, stability and open social attitudes were also important factors for good adjustment.

Jacobs (1978) studied interracial black–white adoptions and found that there were a number of factors that were supportive of positive interracial self-concept formation. These had three main elements: a good relationship with the adoptive mother, early strong reinforcement of the child's skills and character and a policy of open discussion of the child's origins and of ethnic and racial issues (see Table 11.4).

Table 11.4 Summary of factors linked to good adjustment

Good communication with mother

Early ego-enhancing treatment

Assistance in verbalizing racial material

Supportive interest in expression of racial ambivalence

Multiracial associations

Interracial label for the child

Early age of adoption

Coping with Racism

It is assumed that it is best to place a child who may experience prejudice with a family who have been subjected to prejudice. While racism is common and highly distressing to those subjected to it, there has been little systematic study of the effects of racism on children or on the best means of psychological defence. A number of studies have concerned ethnic identity and its effect on racial attitudes (Branch 1982; Heavan 1978; Jahoda and Harrison 1975), but not on the well-being of the child. Some effects have been noted within the educational system with impairment of teacher's relationship, peer group environment and educational achievement (Comer 1989; Stephen and Rosenfeld 1978). Racism has also been linked to antisocial behaviour with the suggestion that unfairness of opportunity resulted in 'displacement' behaviour directed against social rules (Simons and Gray 1989). Children subjected to intense racial animosity in concentration camps during the Second World War also showed marked behavioural effects (Kestenberg and Breener 1986; Roseman 1984). For both of these it is difficult to separate the components of social deprivation, separation and loss though these themselves are indirect effects of racism.

What indications there are suggest not surprisingly that the same factors that are linked to successful adoption placement are also related to dealing with racism. It is important for children to feel valued in their own right and not primarily because they are part of a minority group. The children should know that they are adopted from an early age and should be taught to be proud of their appearance, culture and heritage. There should be open discussion that racism occurs in society but also help to distinguish adversity that is not due to racism or prejudice – a task easier said than done. Membership of mixed social groups based on interests other than ethnicity can help. This form of approach has been criticized as bringing children up to be 'human beings' and denying that they are black. It must be quite clear that that is unequivocally not what is proposed – rather that 'the parents convey to their child that they, themselves, do not judge and relate to people on the basis of their skin colour, but they should tell the child that many people in the society do' (Jones and Else 1979).

Placements that do break down

While the rate of breakdown is not significantly greater than for 'euharmonious' adoption, there are some possible markers for special reasons. In two transracial adoptions that broke down a principal factor was the reason for adoption being an altruistic wish to do good (Cassel and Zeitlin 1995). Choulot and Brodier (1993) report four cases of failed adoption of foreign children; they found that older age adopting parents and lack of counselling were related factors.

Apart from breakdown of placement, some children become

> searchers for their biological parents. Search behaviour is slightly more common where there is a physical dissimilarity between adopters and adoptee. However it seems that the search

behaviour within this group was more linked to poor relationship with the adoptive mother. (Stein 1984, p.2908)

Education for practice in a Multiethnic Society

One approach to practice is to employ professionals who are representative of minority sections of the population served. To some extent that can be helpful where there is a large and relatively uniform recent immigrant population. Special knowledge of the language and culture can aid communication and understanding. It may also help in recruiting substitute families from minority groups. There are, though, hazards in such an approach. It assumes a relevance of the professionals' own cultural experience though there may be major differences between the culture of a successful professional social worker and an immigrant family of similar heritage. There are also many communities with immigrants from several source countries. Most importantly, professionals should be selected for their professionals skills first and additional linguistic and special cultural knowledge second.

It is more appropriate that training should include an approach to evaluating and understanding the special needs of children from 'ethnic groups'. That would include an analysis of the issues, access to relevant literature, skills to listen to the child, awareness of personal feelings about the situation and a preparedness to enlist the help of those who do have special knowledge. The aim should be as much to prepare practitioners raised in minority groups to work with 'the majority' as the reverse.

Recommendations for practice

- Training should be available for professionals relevant to the special problems of minority groups.
- Training should include the means of helping people deal with prejudice.
- Professional advice should be based on research and empirical evidence and not on political attitude.
- Assessments for fostering or adoption should consider separately the relevance of physical match (including skin colour), 'racial' identification, culture of origin and the social and cultural experience of the child.

- The closer the match between the child and alternative family the better.

- Placement with a caring stable family is of prime importance.

- Wherever possible a match with the child's experienced culture should be made.

- If possible without undue delay in placement, a physical match with the adoptive family is helpful.

- Significant delay in placement while seeking a same-race family is not justified.

- Fostered and adopted children should be encouraged and helped to take pride in their national and cultural origins.

- Adoptive and foster parents should be counselled to help children develop a positive identity based on personal skills and attributes rather than one that is based solely on appearance or identification with a minority group. Children should be helped to be proud of personal characteristics including skin colour.

- Parents of children from minority groups should be counselled to help their children be aware of social prejudice. (Adapted from Zeitlin *et al.* 1991)

Conclusion

If a child can be matched on physique and culture with a family who are stable, loving and consistent and who will accept guidance on helping the child deal with being adopted and with prejudice that they might experience, then that is best of all. The closer the match, the more 'euharmonic', the easier the task for the child and parents.

The pessimism over placement of children with physically dissimilar families – 'transracial' adoption – is unjustified and the majority do well. There is a shortage of families of Asian or African origin ('black families') and certainly every effort should be made to recruit more families from 'minorities'. However, until there is a sufficient pool of minority group families able to foster or adopt, it is better to make the best match for culture and to avoid undue delay trying to match race.

Once a child has been placed with a family, the task commences of helping that child cope with being adopted (or fostered), with the differences between his or her self and the adoptive family, and with such issues as prejudice in society. That applies no matter how close the match between the child and family; it cannot be assumed that experiencing prejudice trains a person to cope with that prejudice. There are guidelines that can help and professional support should be available to all families.

Children in minority groups should first be helped to identify themselves by the same types of criteria as all other children and then to use their heritage and 'racial' characteristics as part of their developing and maturing identity. They will then be more able to own and be proud of those characteristics that are used by others as a source of prejudice. While we are far from it at present, we should not lose sight of the goal of all members of society being proud of their individual heritage but not separated from others by it.

References

Alstein, H., Coster, M., First Hartling, L., Ford, C., Glascoe, B., Hariston, S., Kasoff, J. and Grier, A.W. (1994) 'Clinical observations of adult intercountry adoptees and their adoptive parents.' *Child Welfare 73*, 3, 261–269.

Arnold, M.C. (1984) 'The effects of racial identity on self concept in interracial children.' *Dissertation-Abstracts-International 45*, 9A, 3000.

Berridge, D. and Cleaver, H. (1987) *Foster Home Breakdown.* Oxford: Blackwell.

Branch, C.W. (1982) 'A cross-sectional longitudinal study of the development of racial attitudes among black children as a function of parental attitudes.' *Dissertation-Abstracts-International 43*, 3B, 846.

Casey, C. (1986) 'Ethnic identity and self esteem in second and third generation Polish and Italian sixth grade children.' *Dissertation-Abstracts-International 46*, 11A, 3273.

Cassel, D. and Zeitlin, H. (1995) 'Two cases of placement breakdown in transcultural adoption.' Unpublished report.

Choulot, J.J. and Brodier, J.M. (1993) 'Risk of failure in uncontrolled adoption of foreign children.' *Ann. Paediatr 40*, 10, 635–638.

Comer, J.P. (1989) 'Racism and the education of young children.' *Teachers College Record 90*, 3.

Darwin, C. (1871) *The Descent of Man.* London: John Murray.

Erikson, E.H. (1968) *Identity, Youth and Crisis.* New York: Norton.

Gill, O. and Jackson, B. (1983) *Adoption and Race: Black, Asian and Mixed Race Children in White Families.* London: Batsford.

Heavan, P.C. (1978) 'The social attitudes of a group of South African children.' *South African Journal of Psychology 8*, 30–34.

Jacobs, J.H. (1978) 'Black/white interracial families: marital process and identity development in young children.' *Dissertation-Abstracts-International* *38*, 10B, 5023.

Jahoda, D. and Harrison, S. (1975) 'Belfast children: some effects of a conflict environment.' *Irish Journal of Psychology 3*, 1, 1–19.

Jenkins, S. and Diamond B. (1985) 'Ethnicity and foster care: census data as predictors of placement variables.' *American Journal of Orthopsychiatry 55*, 2, 267–276.

Jones, C.E. and Else, J.F. (1979) 'Racial and cultural issues in adoption.' *Child Welfare 58*, 6, 373–382.

Kestenberg, J.S. and Breener, I. (1986) 'Children who survived the Holocaust.' *International Journal of Psychoanalysis 67*, 3, 309–316.

Kim, S.P. (1980) 'Behaviour symptoms in three transracially adopted Asian children: diagnosis dilemma.' *Child Welfare 59*, 4, 213–224.

Marcia, J.E. (1980) 'Identity in adolescents.' In J. Adelson (ed) *Handbook of Adolescent Psychology*. New York: John Wiley.

Moore, E.G.J. (1986) 'Family socialisation and the IQ test performance of traditionally and transracially adopted black children.' *Developmental Psychology 22*, 317–326.

Pritchard. J.C. (1845) *The Natural History of Man*. 2nd edn. London: Hippolyte Ballière.

Rasheed, S.Y. (1981) 'Self esteem and ethnicity in African American third grade children.' *Dissertation-Abstracts-International 42*, 6B, 2604.

Roseman, S. (1984) 'Out of the Holocaust.' *Journal of Psychohistory 2*, 4, 555–567.

Scott, S.L. (1986) 'Personality correlates of personal identity in black children.' *Dissertation-Abstracts-International 46*, 8B, 2823–2824.

Simons, R.L. and Gray, P.A. (1989) 'Perceived blocked opportunity as an explanation of delinquency among lower-class black males: a research note.' *Journal of Research in Crime and Delinquency 26*, 1, 90–101.

Spencer, M.B. (1984) 'Black children's race awareness, racial attitudes and self-concept: a re-interpretation.' *Journal of Child Psychology and Psychiatry 25*, 433–441.

Stein, L.M. (1984) 'A study of identity formation in the adopted.' *Dissertation-Abstracts-International 44*, 9B, 2908.

Stephen, W.G. and Rosenfeld, D. (1978) 'Effects of desegregation on race relations and self esteem.' *Journal of Educational Psychology 70*, 5, 670–679.

Thoburn, J. (1988) *Child Placement: Principles and Practice. Community Care Practice Handbooks*. Aldershot: Wildwood House.

Tizard, B. and Phoenix, A. (1989) 'Black identity and transracial adoption.' *New Community 15*, 3, 427–437.

Weinreich, P. (1983) 'Emerging from threatened identities: ethnicity and gender in redefinitions of ethnic identity.' In G.M. Breakwell (ed) *Threatened Identities.* Chichester: John Wiley.

Womak, W.M. and Fulton, W. (1981) 'Transracial adoption and the black preschool child.' *Journal of the American Academy of Child Psychiatry 20*, 4, 712–724.

Wrobel, G.E.M. (1990) 'The self-esteem of transracially adopted adolescents.' *Dissertation-Abstract-International 51*, 8B, 4093.

Zeitlin, H., Harris-Hendricks, J., Sein, E. and Garralda, E. (1991) 'Child psychiatry in a multi-ethnic society: principles of good practice in fostering and adoption.' From the *Report of the Working Party of the Child and Adolescent Section of the Royal College of Psychiatrists.* London: Royal College of Psychiatrists.

CHAPTER 12

Residential Care for Ethnic Minority Children

Harish Mehra

Introduction

In this chapter, the term 'black' is used to describe people who share similar experiences of belonging to ethnic minority groups in the UK and being easily recognizable as such. Therefore in this sense black is used as a political term. Similarly the term 'mixed parentage' is preferred to the more often used term 'mixed race'.

Race Relations Act 1976

In the Race Relations Act 1976 (Section 71) there is a duty placed on local authorities

> To make appropriate arrangements with a view to securing that various functions are carried out with due regard to the need to eliminate unlawful discrimination and to promote equality of opportunity and good relations between persons of different racial groups. (Home Office 1976, p.28)

Since the Race Relations Act 1976, the quality of service delivery to black clients has not dramatically changed; rather the national picture is, as Roys (1988, p.224) highlights, 'one of piecemeal activity or no serious activity at all'. Antiracism is essential for all children's sake.

> An anti-racism strategy is an ongoing process. It needs constantly to be reviewed and challenged by all who profess to care about the well-being of children and their families. Such a strategy needs to be integrated into all aspects of provision, play, staffing,

admissions, discipline, and assessment. If we fail to do so, we fail all of children and continue to contribute to the pain that racism causes. (Durrant 1986, p.135)

Social Services Inspectorate

Furthermore, Social Services Inspectorate (1980) issued a letter to all the directorates of social services stating:

> Social Services must address and seek to meet the needs of children and families from all groups in the community. Society is made up of people of many different ethnic and racial origins and of different religious affiliations. The provision of services which will reach all members of the community calls for the development within Social Services Departments of awareness, sensitivity and understanding of the different cultures of groups in the local community, and an understanding of the effects of racial discrimination on these groups. These principles apply to services to help children to remain within their own families as well as to services for children in care and their families, so that children are not admitted to care through lack of appropriate and effective Social Work support for the family. This is especially important in the light of indicators that children from certain minority ethnic groups are over-represented among children in care. (Social Services Inspectorate 1980, pp.1–2)

Children Act 1989

With the Children Act 1989 (Department of Health 1989) agencies are required, in all decisions in respect of a child they are looking after, to have regard to the child's religious persuasion, cultural and linguistic background and racial origin, and to the wishes and feeling of parents and other adults who have played a significant part in the child's life, as well as to the wishes and feelings of the child (Section 22/5/c). A number of changes are also bound to happen with the introduction of the following:

- Best Value, Quality Protects, Performance Assessment Framework
- Care Standards Act 2000 (Department of Health 2000)
- Local Government Act 1999 (Home Office 1999)

- Crime and Disorder Act 1998 (Home Office 1998)
- Disability and Discrimination Act 1995 (Department of Health 1995)
- New Assessment Framework – Children Act 1989 (Section 47 – Cause for Concern and Section 17 – Child in Need) (Department of Health 1989).

In addition, the government has asked Social Services, National Health Service, Education Department, Housing Department, police and primary care groups to work jointly. The local authorities are required to implement all these changes and the issue of equality is not ignored in adopting these new requirements.

For the ethnic minority child, the care which is provided needs to recognize the different cultural content of both physical and social needs of food, hair and skin care, clothing, religion, education and history. Overall the child's emotional, psychological, religious, physical and social needs require to be met in a way which enables the child

- to develop a positive identity for him/herself as an ethnic minority child
- to develop the necessary linguistic, cultural, religious and social skills to function effectively as an adult in a multiracial, multicultural society
- to acquire skills to cope as both child and adult in a society in which the child is likely to encounter racism, prejudice and disadvantage
- to enable the child to come to terms with living apart from the birth family.

Any child in care has a particular need to build and sustain a positive self-identity, and if children are placed in an environment where people of their kind are held in low esteem or rarely encountered at all, the outcome will be a marginalized identity. Rejection by many white peers, so frequently encountered at the stage of adolescence or young adulthood, is most likely to lead to an identity confusion. Also, children may try to resist the negative projections of the ethnic majority both in relation to their colour and as regards their being in care, by determinedly defiant behaviours that put them at risk of serious sanctions and/or of exploitation by others.

> A central issue facing most black families (regardless of class and health) is how to prepare their children to deal with their devalued racial status in a way which will be most beneficial to their overall emotional and social growth and development. Socialisation of children is now doubly challenging for the black family for now it must teach its young members not only to be human and not dislike white people (the dominant group) but also how to be black with pride. (Ahmed 1985, p.17)

In order to meet the needs of and help the development of any child, black or white, it is essential that the service operates with adequate knowledge, understanding, sensitivity, intelligence and, most importantly, the ability to empathize.

> It is doubtful that the majority of well intentioned white care-takers, be they residential staff, foster or adoptive parents, can understand the pain of apparently small hurts that come through racially prejudiced behaviour towards the child of others, and offer comfort, 'the ultimate survival tool', rather than tension or rage. Not having internalised these survival mechanisms, the child grows up without needed defences or learned coping behaviours. (Small 1984, p.171)

Inequalities

Inequalities of provision at the institutional level and inequalities of treatment in the world outside the residential care combine to give black children their perception of themselves which itself becomes a hindrance in the way of racial equality. Very few of them have been able to grasp that their positions are socially constructed and do not just happen. Not only is there a need for appreciating the fact that the ethnic minority consumers in such institutions often become objects of racism but also it is necessary to recognize that the racism in the wider society is reflected in and reinforced by racism in social services institutions.

It is important to emphasize the need for proportionate matching of staff to children, otherwise it would disproportionately disadvantage black children in care who would lose the capacity to identify, feel with and communicate readily with members of their community of origin. This would also reduce the strangeness felt on first arrival in care. Furthermore, there is a need for specific training in the care of ethnic minority children to ensure competence at the basic level of physical care.

Otherwise the staff may not be aware even of the matters of day-to-day importance such as the need to avoid dry skin by the use of moisture creams or oils. They may not be able to carry out specialized hair care for younger children or to produce enjoyable food. It may also be more difficult for them to act as role models for the children. Similarly young people who are of mixed parentage cannot push aside the white side of them but knowing they are black can be positive. To stop this identity problem, the teaching and learning have to come from the social workers whether they are black or white, as well as themselves. There is already a vast body of knowledge regarding the issues surrounding mixed parentage and its difficulties which need to be assimilated by the worker in order to meet the needs appropriately (see also Banhatti and Bhate, Chapter 3 in this volume).

Ethnic minority children in care may be disproportionately disadvantaged by the location of residential provision, which is often outside areas of black settlement in the suburbs or in rural areas. This is relevant to 'matching' difficulties but may also geographically distance the children from other black people. It is important for children's feelings of well-being as well as for their behaviour that they are afforded relief from the pressure of pervasive whiteness.

The following case study, which is not atypical of an Asian family on social workers' caseloads, highlights the issues discussed above.

Case study: Gurvinder

When Gurvinder's case was allocated to me, he had already been in local authority care for the previous four years. Now he was 13 years old. He was not living with foster parents but had been placed in a local authority residential home. He liked to call himself Gary and strongly objected to his original name Gurvinder. He hardly had any contact with his father, stepmother or his siblings. His father, younger brother and sister had all been feeling desperate to meet him regularly. In fact, the family really wanted him to return home and live with them.

It was revealed that Gurvinder was taken into care when his father was divorced and Gurvinder started displaying disruptive behaviour in the school. Gurvinder's mother did not contest the custody. She refused to have anything to do with him or have access to him. Following this decision, she tried to avoid the label of being a divorcee, which made her path easier for remarriage in her cultural context. When Gurvinder had started exhibiting some behavioural difficulties, there were no extended family members from his father's side residing in Britain. If there were, they would have supported and helped in looking after Gurvinder. After the divorce, his father remarried but Gurvinder and his stepmother did not develop a good relationship.

When this case was referred to the social services department, a social worker of white ethnic background, who had very little knowledge of racial and cultural issues, was allocated to deal with it. Instead of exploring the possibility of any in-depth work in terms of building up relationships, even with the help of an Asian social worker or a consultant on race and cultural issues, Gurvinder was taken into local authority care. Again no real efforts were made to find an Asian foster family for him. This must have been an easy and convenient solution for the social worker but, for Gurvinder, this was the beginning of his alienation and loss of his family, language, religion, food, culture and ethnic identity.

During the last four years of being in care, he did not have any input of Asian culture and there were no provisions or opportunities in the residential home or the programmes organized for him, to expose him to Sikh religion, Asian food or to maintain any contact with the Asian community or his own family. All the children in the residential home were white and Gurvinder was living an excluded life. To be accepted by his co-residents and social workers, he was doing his utmost to become a white child. He started to develop friendships with white children and their parents, who sometimes used to visit them. Eventually, he was successful in strengthening his relationship with one white parent whose child was also residing with Gurvinder in the local authority residential home, which was located in an all-white community. Gurvinder was now allowed to visit this white family and spend weekends with them. Gurvinder started to call these white parents mummy and daddy. He refused to meet his father, who tried several times to contact him on the telephone and in person. Social workers (both residential and from the area office) did not feel the need to alter this development.

On my first visit to Gurvinder, he refused to see me. He informed his residential social worker and the manager of the residential home that he would like to have a white social worker. I did not insist at this point but informed the residential social worker and Gurvinder that I would discuss this issue with my line manager. My line manager and I agreed that I should continue to work with Gurvinder but with acute sensitivity and care. This decision was communicated to the residential home manager, residential social worker and Gurvinder.

On my second visit I had a general discussion with Gurvinder and also made a strong recommendation to the manager of the home to arrange for an Asian residential social worker to work with me jointly. I then had several meetings with this new residential Asian social worker and developed a number of strategies.

During my subsequent visits, I started to explore Gurvinder's feelings about his identity. He was stating outright: *'I am British. My name is Gary. I don't like Pakis. All Asians are Pakis.'* I remained calm and asked Gurvinder that if all Asians are Pakis, then what about his father? Is he a Paki too? He could not answer me. I did not force him to reply. The other question I posed to him: *'Gurvinder, I accept you were born in Britain and you have a British passport and you call yourself British. Suppose you are walking alone down the road and confront a gang of National Front youths. How would you convince them that you are British and not Asian? In addition how would you hide your skin colour and your features?'* Once again he did not answer. At this stage I left him and made an appointment to see him in the next couple of weeks. During this period, the residential social worker was kept informed of all the developments and was advised to assist and counsel Gurvinder so he could also understand and remain in touch with some of these important issues being discussed.

While this was proceeding Gurvinder's new-found white parents telephoned me several times to say that Gurvinder was upset since I had been allocated to his case and threatened to make an official complaint against me. In discussion with my line manager we felt it was essential to pursue our plan despite this resistance and obstruction. Our extensive efforts and negotiations between different parties were successful in holding a meeting between

Gurvinder and his father. Gurvinder's father, younger brother and sister were overjoyed to see him. Gurvinder's father was anxious to have Gurvinder back home immediately but we insisted that any reintegration of Gurvinder with his family had to be a slow and well-worked-out process for it to be successful. The frequency of meetings between Gurvinder and his family were therefore gradually increased; first it was at three-weekly intervals, then at two-weekly and eventually at weekly intervals before he started spending weekends with his family.

His father disclosed to Gurvinder that since he was the eldest son in the family, the father had already bought a house for Gurvinder as a wedding gift. The father also shared how he had felt lost without Gurvinder and that if Gurvinder wished to start a business, his father would be delighted to help him financially to set up a business, or if Gurvinder wished to continue his studies, his father would be equally delighted to finance this. For us it took a year before Gurvinder was successfully rehabilitated with his family. He and his family at the final reunion were extremely delighted and we were happy to close our files.

Nearly six months later I met Gurvinder and his father while shopping. Father emphasized that they had no problems whatsoever now; Gurvinder was planning to pursue his further studies. He spoke Punjabi at home, enjoyed eating Asian food and attended the Sikh temple every Sunday without fail. Gurvinder's father pressed my hand and said, *'I am indebted to you, you brought my son back to me. I can never forget this in my life.'*

Matters of Policy

Childcare social workers and their managers can break the process of racism only by acknowledging that it exists, deciding that it is wrong and making a commitment to change. To refuse to do so negates ethnic minority children and contradicts the caring role which the work demands. Most local authorities in Britain have an equal opportunity policy which is applicable to all the departments including social services. The Commission for Racial Equality (1978) suggested that an equal opportunity policy is aimed at developing positive measures to eliminate overt discrimination, as well as conditions, requirements or practices which are discriminatory in operation. It has the legislative support of the Race Relations Act 1976 (Section 71) which makes racial discrimination unlawful and establishes the basis on which equal opportunities may be pursued.

Unless there is a common core of values which underpin social work practice informed by equal opportunity, social workers, I think, are likely to operate in idiosyncratic ways. It is essential that such values become central to social work practice and not 'added on' or marginalized. It is also important to be clear about what is meant by equal opportunity. Jewson and Mason (1987) make the distinction between liberal and radical conceptions of equal opportunity. The latter focuses on equality of outcome and understands fairness to exist when numbers of different groups are distributed in proportion to their presence in the wider population.

There is a need to focus on what the equal opportunity outcomes are of working with ethnic minority children in residential care. Jenkins (1989) points out that the pursuit of equal opportunity as a formal statement has only symbolic value creating an image of success. It is important that the policy statement is combined with strategies of implementation. He emphasizes that although a voluntarist approach (i.e. organizations and agencies etc. taking steps themselves to adopt equal opportunity policy) is vital, it has severe limitations. He argues that equal opportunities can be solved only by recognizing that it is a political problem. For example, we need to look outside the boundaries of individual organizations since individuals within organizations are influenced by popular racism and the way equal opportunity and antiracism are portrayed as something that will disadvantage whites.

Social workers and their managers may have internalized negative perceptions about antiracism. The media portrayal of antiracism as being associated with the so-called Labour 'loony left' and attempts by right-wing intellectuals to discredit it by referring to antiracism as indoctrination have become part of 'common sense' (Flew 1984; Honeyford 1982; Lewis 1988).

Many social services departments may even have antiracist policies. The question is whether these departments actually draw on antiracism concepts, implement them and closely monitor them. Also, who does the monitoring? Do the people who monitor it have adequate knowledge and understanding of racism? Brandt (1986) has explored how these concepts are concerned with power, justice, gender, equal human rights, oppression, structural inequalities, racist ideologies, institutionalized racism, equality, liberation and emancipation. Many black people and practitioners believe as Dominelli (1988) argues that white social workers should not work with black or ethnic minority families until they have demonstrated their ability to practise antiracist social work. The implementation of policies and Acts becomes more important as the racist ideologies may be in operation which may have led to ethnic minority children in residential care feeling powerless and experiencing a deep sense of injustice.

Lane (1990) emphasizes:

> Issues of child care/education are high on the national agenda. There are many national and local organizations in the field that are in the process of adopting or having adopted equality of opportunity policies. Local authorities are in likely positions to monitor what is happening in their own areas, to make information widely available and to ensure that, together with other organizations which are committed to racial equality, both the latter and the spirit of both pieces of legislation are enacted... Despite the lack of resources the extra requirements put on staff as a result of legislation, authorities can make the task easier at the outset, defining the task to be done within the framework of the law. Such definitions, rather than ad hoc responses, will make it possible both to see what needs to be done and to take appropriate measures and permanent steps to eliminate discrimination and provide a service based on principles of equality. (Lane 1990, p.49)

Conclusion: Some Guidelines

If social care practice is to meet the needs of a multiracial society, the development of an antiracist practice is essential. Here are some of the dimensions of crucial importance in developing such practices:

1. Implementing and monitoring antiracist policies and Acts along with antiracist training for all the members of the department, including senior managers, with the emphasis on the credibility of minority ethnic community's norms and lifestyles.

2. Talking through emotional and cultural issues, valuing and acknowledging cultural identities, heritage and histories of ethnic minority people.

3. Meeting the cultural, religious, linguistic, skin care, hair care and dietary needs of the ethnic minority children in care.

4.   Enabling ethnic minority children in care to take pride in their race, skin colour, physical features, religious, linguistic and cultural identity.

5.   Acknowledging and understanding the implications of discrimination and racism upon ethnic minority children in residential care, for example lack of personal growth, dignity, worth and power.

6.   Examining the use of language, personal norms and values, which may be degrading and stereotyping to ethnic minority children and people. Promoting positive images of ethnic minority people and supporting those who take a stand against any kind of discrimination and racism.

7.   Declaring antiracist policies to the liaising statutory and voluntary agencies, ensuring that the child's environment is in line with the departmental policy. It needs to be acknowledged that one central fact is that the accumulative and persistent effects of racial prejudice in society is the psychic assault on ethnic minority people. These attacks take many forms, e.g. name calling, spitting, beating, shouting and can sometimes include torturing, maiming and killing.

8.   Ensuring that committed social workers and their managers, whether from the ethnic majority or the ethnic minority, have a network of support within the department, in other local authorities and from people and organizations in society.

References

Ahmed, S. (1985) 'Black children in day nursery: some issues of practice.' *Focus* *33*, 17–20.

Brandt, G. (1986) *The Realisation of Anti-Racist Teaching*. London: Falmer.

Commission for Racial Equality (CRE) (1978) *'A Home from Home': Some Policy Considerations on Black Children in Residential Care*. London: CRE.

Department of Health (1989) *The Children Act*. London: HMSO.

Department of Health (1995) *Disability and Discrimination Act 1995*. London: HMSO.

Department of Health (2000) *The Care Standards Act 2000*. London: The Stationery Office.

Dominelli, L. (1988) *Anti-Racist Social Work.* London: Macmillan Education.

Durrant, J. (1986) 'Racism and the under fives.' In V. Coombe and A. Little (eds) *Race and Social Work.* London: Tavistock.

Flew, A. (1984) *Education, Race and Revolution.* London: Centre for Policy Studies.

Home Office (1976) *Race Relations Act.* London: HMSO.

Home Office (1998) *Crime and Disorder Act 1998.* London: The Stationery Office.

Home Office (1999) *Local Government Act 1999.* London: The Stationery Office.

Honeyford, R. (1982) 'The end of anti-racism.' *Salisbury Review 1.*

Jenkins, R. (1989) 'Equal opportunity in the private sector: the limits of voluntarism.' In R. Jenkins and J. Solomos (eds) *Racism and Equal Opportunity Policies in 1980s.* Cambridge: Cambridge University Press.

Jewson, N. and Mason, D. (1987) 'Monitoring equal opportunities policies, principles and practice.' In R. Jenkins and J. Solomos (eds) *Racism and Equal Opportunity Policies in 1980s.* Cambridge: Cambridge University Press.

Lane, J. (1990) 'Sticks and carrots.' *Local Government Policy Making 17,* 3, 40–49.

Lewis, R. (1988) *Anti-Racism: A Mania Exposed.* London: Quartet.

Roys, P. (1988) 'Social services.' In A. Bhat, R. Carr-Hill and S. Ohri (eds) *Britain's Black Population.* Aldershot: Gower.

Small, J. (1984) 'The crisis in adoption.' *International Journal of Social Psychiatry 30,* 1–2, 171.

Social Services Inspectorate (1980) *Letter Issued to Directors of Social Services* [c.1(90)2]. London: Department of Health.

Chapter 13

Practical Approaches to Work with Refugee Children

Jeremy Woodcock

Introduction

Since the ending of primary immigration, one of the few ways in which people from developing countries can secure residence in the west is to enter as an asylum seeker. As a result policy and practice toward asylum seekers and refugees have become a hot political issue. Governments routinely enact legislation to deter asylum seekers, which conflicts with their legal obligations to uphold human rights. Consequently, the political climate toward asylum seekers and refugees in host countries is often hostile and xenophobic and a lack of hospitality permeates every layer of welfare provision, from social security and health to schooling. Practitioners working with refugees and asylum seekers find themselves caught in a conflict in which good practice is made difficult because of the scarcity of resources caused by government policy. Consequently, the only way of really providing a meaningful service is to take a human rights perspective that offers a source of practical well-being to refugee children and families and at the same time advocates for their rights. This chapter will demonstrate some ways of providing such a practical approach alongside a human rights perspective.

The Vulnerability of Refugee Children

By virtue of their lack of status, refugee children are extremely vulnerable. Their vulnerability has legal, emotional and practical aspects, which tend to amplify one another. Legally, children who are asylum seekers have far fewer rights than indigenous children. Furthermore, it is almost certain that they will have been exposed to a range of emotional events, which may include massive loss, disruption, fear and huge, unexpected changes. At the same time they will face practical difficulties as basic as entitlement to housing and welfare rights, difficulties with schooling and problems with health-care provision.

Triple Jeopardy

Each of the different aspects of vulnerability described above – legal, emotional and practical – are amplified by triple jeopardy. An understanding of triple jeopardy can help practitioners conceptualize some of the underlying reasons that make refugee children more vulnerable. As the concept implies, triple jeopardy has three aspects:

1. Refugee children will have been through terrifying experiences, which because of their disturbing nature will be difficult for them to hold in mind or put into words.

2. Their parents or carers find it just as difficult to hold those experiences in mind. In addition refugee adults very often do not know their way around the 'system' and how to find help.

3. Child mental health services find it very hard to hold the terrifying, overwhelming and atavistic nature of refugee experiences in mind. Furthermore, their services are usually not set up to deal with the overwhelming quality of refugee children's vulnerabilities and the multitude of loss, deprivation and horror plus all the practical dilemmas that refugee children and families bring.

When these three factors of jeopardy found in children, their parents or carers and children's services coincide, they add up to a situation in which refugee children's needs are overlooked, pushed out of mind or not engaged with because they are too difficult.

Triple jeopardy can take a number of different forms. Very often it takes the form of 'gaze aversion' which results in a service or individual practitioner failing to engage with the reality of a child's experience and their needs. For instance, a 12-year-old unaccompanied refugee child was referred to a community paediatrician by a social services department because they were worried about the impact of his terrible experiences upon him, including the violent death of his mother and siblings.

The paediatrician, however, did not consider the young person's experiences or wonder about his emotional vulnerability but merely checked to see if he was carrying any infectious diseases that could be transmitted to the indigenous population. A similar example is of a refugee child with enuresis who was referred to a child health clinic but the wider picture of terror and warfare in which her symptoms could be understood was not taken into account.

Another example of triple jeopardy is of a 6-year-old refugee child in school who was acting aggressively and drawing pictures of warfare his teacher found so disturbing that initially she really wanted to ignore his communications and blamed the child for being difficult. Nevertheless, when she understood the circumstances that generated the boy's behaviour, she enriched her approach to him in a way that was more inclusive of his experience, took on board the real experience in his drawings and acknowledged what his aggressive play meant – hiding from soldiers and bombs. As a result the boy's behaviour gradually normalized as he integrated his extraordinary experiences with the help of his teacher's understanding.

In another example, a family with multiple physical and psychological needs living in temporary accommodation in a particular area for over 18 months was never offered a service by the local health or social services department, because they were deemed as temporary residents and about to move. In a similar example three children from a family seeking asylum were refused places in local schools because they were deemed to be in temporary accommodation. In both these examples, what was most pernicious was not the temporary residence but that education, health and social services had a mind-set that deemed the temporary nature of refugee residence as so transitory and legally ambiguous that they thought they were right to deny them legitimate rights to services. In fact, no matter how temporary their stay, asylum-seeking and refugee children and families *are* absolutely entitled to education and health services and to social services when there is a statutorily defined need – in practice this qualifies them to the same rights as the indigenous population.

A Human Rights Perspective

In order to provide effective welfare for refugee children practitioners should carefully consider how their service might be contributing to triple jeopardy and what interventions are necessary to prevent it. One of the first and most effective preventive steps that can be taken is to formulate practice within a *human rights* perspective. This promotes the idea that we are all entitled to a health service that guarantees a basic standard of well-being and dignity of life, irrespective of culture, background or immigration status. It can be difficult to maintain such a perspective, however, because much government rhetoric positively discriminates against refugees. This has created a climate in which it is only too easy for practitioners to think of refugee children and families as unwanted, temporary and marginal with dubious entitlement to services. Furthermore, government legislation has actually discriminated against refugee children. For instance, when Britain ratified the United Nations Convention on the Rights of the Child the government added an exclusion, which states that the rights enshrined in the convention do not apply to children who have temporary immigration status. Thankfully, in practice, most local authorities have read the children's legislation as having a priority over the government's exclusion. As a result in most circumstances refugee children are provided with services they require when they are brought to the attention of health and social services. Nevertheless, there is compelling evidence that refugee children are also routinely overlooked and pressure is required to persuade health providers and local authority services to engage actively (Woodhead 2000).

Reviewing Services

Many practitioners probably need to review what prevents children and families living in their catchment area from making use of the full range of interventions that their services have to offer. This can lead to practical steps to make services more accessible to refugee children. The information-gathering aspect of a review can also provide valuable information for practitioners as well as raising their consciousness about salient issues in the lives of refugee children and their families.

The review should seek the views of refugee children and families as well as potential referrers, local schools, refugee community organizations and non-governmental organizations (NGOs) such as the Refugee Council. It might also include making working relationships with human rights lawyers, who are very often on the frontline in encounters with vulnerable refugee children. This in turn can contribute to a raised awareness about human rights and immigration law and how these are likely to interact with mental health issues.

Another step that can be taken to make services more accessible is to ensure that notices explaining services are provided in languages spoken by refugees. Yet another step can be the collection of knowledge about refugee experiences, specific to the groups settled in the area. This might include an understanding of typical life stories, cultural, religious and political histories, parents' and carers' attitudes to children's health and developmental issues and their hopes and anxieties about life in exile with their children. This work will have to hold in mind an understanding that refugees will have frequently had to contend with repressive authority in their homeland and immigration control in this country that is suspicious of their motives for seeking asylum. These can contribute to them being wary of representatives of state authority, however benign.

Supporting Practitioners

Consultation and supervision are very important ingredients in work with refugee children and families. Their importance must not be underestimated. One-off consultation can help with familiarization and orientation to the new aspects of the work but regular ongoing supervision is very important, particularly for staff who work with children and families who are survivors of torture and organized violence. Such work is really difficult to bear without good regular supervision which appreciates how to respond to the way the work can get under the skin of the practitioner. Furthermore, managers should not underestimate the extent to which work with refugee children and families challenges very experienced staff, who often feel quite deskilled by the huge scale of emotional and practical difficulties that face refugee children and their parents. Encouraging multidisciplinary assessment and joint working arrangements are also good ways of supporting staff, as are providing a space for regular peer consultation for the work as it develops and access to helpful resources, some of which are discussed below.

Providing interpreters

A most important realization is that most work with newly arrived refugee children and families will require work with interpreters. This is often very off-putting for practitioners who are not used to working alongside interpreters and having to rely for communication on colleagues who probably do not have mental health training. But because interpreters are crucial to clinical work, it is important that practitioners develop the means actually to enjoy their work with them. It does not really help to think of interpreters merely as the conduit for a conversation between oneself and the family. Rather, it helps to think of them as an ally, co-worker and consultant on the richness of the intercultural communication that will develop as the work progresses. A good piece of advice is to use the same considerations when choosing an interpreter as one would when choosing a co-worker. But while regarding interpreters as full colleagues, it is also important to recognize that they are unlikely to have had a deep training in mental health work. Consequently their capacity to reflect and conjecture about very emotionally demanding material and their own emotional responses to the work are likely to be less robust than those of trained colleagues (Dearnley 2000). Because of this, it is important that the practitioner provides space with the interpreter for preparation and reflection before and after each session. One should also be prepared to make concessions to less skilful responses to the work, in rather the same way as one would with a new, perhaps recently trained, colleague. Finally, in order to facilitate them being fully involved in the work as co-workers one should involve them in all consultations connected to the family, including joint supervision whenever possible.

Holistic Practice

It is enormously helpful to one's professional insight and one's ability to engage in fruitful work just to realize how fragmenting refugee children's experiences will often have been. For instance, a 9-year-old refugee child had to be abandoned by her fleeing parents at the border of their country because there was not room in the vehicle for the onward journey nor enough money to bribe border guards. She was put into the hands of a priest, who managed to get her to her paternal grandfather. When the war in their country died down, the priest was able to get the child to a maternal aunt who lived in the capital. Meanwhile her parents were devastated because she was completely out of touch. War completely disrupted communications within the country for over a year. Furthermore, when they did re-establish contact it took another year for them to be reunited. She flew to another European country at the invitation of a paternal uncle and then was able to cross the channel to her parents. When she arrived in Britain the parents were forced to be rehoused by the local authority because they were then deemed to be a 'family' rather than a 'couple'. Consequently they were uprooted from the neighbourhood with which they had become familiar. They also had to change their GP and the hospital that had been treating the mother for the consequences of persecution. The family then underwent another two moves before becoming finally settled.

That sort of fragmentation of life experience is not at all unusual for refugee children and families. Consequently, it is helpful to think holistically and to use the sort of systemic thinking familiar to family therapists as a framework to hold the different contexts of refugee children's lives in some sort of perspective. It is also wise not to prioritize any particular domain but rather to map out their interrelatedness. For instance, practitioners will not be able to engage in all the practicalities of refugees' difficult and fragmented life experiences, but at least they can show that they can hold them in mind. For instance in the example above initially we were very active in finding medical help for the family and acting as advocates with the social services and housing departments. We saw that work as an essential adjunct to the psychotherapeutic work we were doing. As the family became more emotionally secure and adapted we provided advice on how to get services, but left them to advocate on their own behalf. All the time, however, we saw their ability to master practical needs as a backdrop that made sense of their psychotherapeutic progress. As such, psychological adaptation and integration were mirrored by practical adaptation and integration.

Offering a secure base

The notion of the secure base emerged from the work of Bowlby (1988) on the quality of the emotional attachment between mother and child. Ongoing research has established that the key factors in the provision of the secure base are the parents' capacity to provide physical and emotional care, their ability to provide continuity and consistency and their emotional investment in the child's life (Cassidy and Shaver 2000). For refugee children these are very likely to be disrupted by the practical circumstances caused by massive loss and change. At the same time, refugee parents can be so distracted by what they have been through and the challenges ahead that they may be too upset and emotionally preoccupied to provide the quality of attachment that they once enjoyed with their children.

In response to this one of the most effective interventions is for the practitioner to act as a 'secure base', becoming like a 'grandparent' to the child and family system. Furthermore, because of the practitioner's status as a professional person he or she can be a powerful ally and a gateway to the solution of many practical dilemmas. This may involve helping the family to solve practical problems that prevent them from enjoying good health, adequate housing or income.

Crucially, the provision of a secure base may also involve ensuring that refugee children and families are represented by competent asylum lawyers. This may seem a rather odd involvement for a child health specialist. The highest context in all refugee work however is the overarching need for safety. Unfortunately, there are just too many unscrupulous or incompetent lawyers and immigration advisers involved in asylum work. Consequently, because the asylum legislation is very harsh and since the most basic cornerstone of a child's security is freedom from the fear of refoulement it arguably becomes a duty of care to make sure that a child and family are properly represented. (Refoulement is the technical legal term for returning a refugee to the country in which they faced persecution.) Furthermore, asylum lawyers often find it helpful to have a medical or psychological report on a child or family, which can add to the evidence of the persecution that they have endured. Inevitably providing such a report will shape the therapeutic relationship and it is usually best to integrate the work involved into the therapeutic work as a process of dialogue, conscientization and witnessing (Agger 1992).

The art of listening to refugee children

Enabling the emotional security for a refugee child and family involves basic child mental health skills:

- listening, with an ear attuned to both the inner world and the outer world, which will demand rigour and subtlety as one unravels their connectedness

- exploring in a non-judgemental way the things that constrain the parents in providing good emotional care for their children

- problem-solving those constraints through advice, suggestion, reassurance and interpretation, which indicates that the practitioner understands and can stand alongside them in their emotional difficulties

- attending to the child's experience and helping to provide an explanatory narrative that makes sense of a world that has become senseless because of persecution and loss.

Often, listening can seem very demanding. It can be because the horrible content of their experiences naturally makes us not want to listen. It may be because stories of loss and change put us in touch with personal or family scripts that are sensitive or taboo. Sometimes politics puts us off, for instance, uncomfortable reminders that western intervention (or non-intervention) has contributed to regional instability that has led to war. Or perhaps we may feel discomfort about the constraints on the service we have to offer because of government legislation or agency policies. Another area is the sheer complexity of refugee children's experience and the very valid question, 'Where to begin?'

Because listening is such a critical skill that can enable children to validate and integrate their experience it will pay to spend some time in reflection with colleagues, in supervision or in consultation, to work through some of the constraints. For instance in one consultation to an organization that had just begun work with refugee children, workers felt very deskilled. Ongoing supervision with a few cases over a number of months that contributed to their knowledge base, affirmed their existing child mental health skills and gently teased out some of the personal sensitivities to the work enabled them to establish a very effective service.

Loss and change

Enabling a child and family to mourn is an important skill to develop. Initially it may involve thinking about what prevents mourning. For instance, it is very difficult to mourn loved ones who died in violent or shameful circumstances. Work might therefore need to be done to process traumatic material before the mourning process can be properly entered into. Equally it is difficult to mourn when the child or parent has not been able to see or bury the dead, as very often happens when refugee families have loved ones who are 'disappeared' or executed in prison. In those circumstances work can be done to adapt and create mourning rituals that fit the circumstances and this can help the grieving process (Woodcock 1995). Equally, simply giving 'permission' to children and adults to talk about the dead can be enormously facilitative because often, particularly with violent deaths, there is a belief that grief can be a damaging thing, rather than a natural, although inevitably painful, process of letting go.

It is very likely that family members will have differing loyalties to homeland and exile, which can generate huge tensions, especially in

families with adolescent children. If this is so it can be helpful to enable
the children and family to unpack the dilemmas of having to live between two cultures. One cannot be prescriptive but by enabling issues to
be put into words, progress can be made in sorting out some of the mud-
dles and tensions. This can be particularly challenging because there are
no prescribed ways of moving from one culture to another (Eastmond
1993). Often people cling to ways of life that are not adaptive or helpful.
Families will need time to mourn changes and the rhythm of mourning
may vary between family members, with one holding onto the instrumental, practical, future aspects, while another clings to the past (Sluzki
1979). It also helps to provide a space in which multiple positions can
flourish (Papadopoulos and Hildebrand 1997) and a secure base, which
allows for play and experimentation in the knowledge that whatever
conflicts emerge can be expressed in the safe certainty that care and
emotional security will remain ensured by the family as a whole
(Byng-Hall 1999).

Idioms of Suffering

Refugee people from other cultures often have different idioms in which
they signal and respond to distress. It is tempting to translate these into
western psychological concepts, but it is important to respect different
idioms as having their own unique meaning, which may not be reduced
into a western psychological language (Bracken 1998). The practitioner
should think about western psychological thinking not only as a set of
truths but equally as an idiomatic way of expressing experience. Differing idioms are rich in metaphors that may connect or run parallel to
one another and allow for meaning to be negotiated and co-constructed.
None offers a superior vision, just different ways of understanding
things. For instance, refugees are often religiously observant and derive
comfort and meaning from their beliefs: learning how to understand
them can give the practitioner an insight into unique ways of facing adversity rather than being prescriptive about western ideas about psychological health and resilience. In fact, most often, being open and
transparent about one's own assumptions models a way of communicating openly and collaboratively that can mutually inform the therapeutic
process. This happened in a case where a family understood misfortune
in terms of sorcery and I understood their adversity in terms of loss of attachment. Ultimately, our understandings flowed together as they
learned what I meant by the effects of the severing of emotional connec-

tions and I understood how they used sorcery to conceptualize, communicate about and regulate hidden conflict.

Trauma as a Social Construction

The persecution and massive loss that refugee children and families experience will predispose them to suffering a traumatic response to those events, which it is tempting to evaluate solely within the criteria of post-traumatic stress disorder (PTSD). The broad criteria of PTSD, intrusiveness, avoidance and arousal, offer a very helpful guide, but they need to be used tentatively and critically as a useful part of the practitioner's wider repertoire. People will experience extreme events in a range of idiomatic and socially constructed ways. At the heart of trauma, in so far as it emerges as a psychological entity, is the disruption of the attachment nexus, that bit of us that can be described as 'basic trust' or the 'inner parent', which mediates the inner and outer world (De Zulueta 1993). The practitioner may find it helpful to use cognitive, medical, psychoanalytic or systemic ways of thinking about trauma. It also helps enormously to place any such professional thinking in the context of a 'socially constructed' narrative, in other words a story with many layers and 'chapters' that make sense of unusual and fragmentary experience. This is because extreme events in people's lives often make most sense when they can be brought forth as a story and woven into the texture of their ongoing life (Woodcock 2000). But practitioners should not necessarily pursue the child or family's story as a text that *must* be brought forth and *must* make sense as a factual narrative. One should allow it to come forth by working in the here and now of their relationships with each other, with their histories, their futures and their relationships with oneself. Practitioners can weave themselves in and out of the 'meta', or bird's-eye-view, position – relating, observing, intuiting, making hunches, seeking connections not only in what one thinks and says but also in how one acts and relates to the child and family.

Adversity and Resilience

In getting to the UK refugee children and families will have made use of remarkable survival skills. They will have been resourceful, courageous, cautious and perhaps devious. Simultaneously they may have been frightened, powerless, overwhelmed, abandoned and grief-stricken. They will have lived on the edge between utter deprivation and survival.

Escape and flight will have made use of very active survival skills. Exile can be a much more passive experience:

- waiting in anxiety to be granted asylum

- waiting to be reunited with parents, children or other family members

- being dependent on local authority or central government services for help with housing and living expenses

- having few, if any, choices over major decisions such as where to live, which school or college the children attend or which GP one gets

- being fairly powerless communicating with people because of lack of competence in English

- therefore being reliant on interpreters to give one a voice and act as advocates.

Experience suggests, unless they are completely psychologically over-whelmed, that both children and adults are far more resilient when they adopt an active style of coping (M. Rutter 1985). Even passive waiting can be done actively because what often counts is the inner disposition. Thus active coping will include experiencing some degree of choice over major decisions; being able to problem-solve actively in collaboration with others; being connected into networks which offer some degree of social and cultural familiarity. It will also involve being able to talk about ongoing problems – being able to talk and reflect on past experiences both good and bad and being able to grieve actively. It will also involve being able to make discernible progress and to plan and have some sense of control over the future. It is probably very important with parents who are not coping because they have been overwhelmed by grief, anxiety or trauma to link strategies for psychological health with active coping strategies in practical domains, for instance, helping parents make good choices about local schools, enabling them to understand education practices here and how to communicate with teachers about their children's needs or how to access health care on behalf of themselves and the family. Such emotional and practical support with parenting can facilitate a sense of achievement and well-being for parents who are bewildered by the new situation of exile.

Coming to terms with adversity may mean that children and parents have to face very painful feelings. Practitioners may find they enter a labyrinth of their experiences alongside them (Woodcock 2001). As they do it is important to take time to map out and connect to their past and present strengths, however depleted. These will be useful resources to be in touch with on behalf of child and family when the work gets tough. In this respect it is also vital to draw out their beliefs, values and basic worldview, which are important resources for survival. Equally, practitioners must attend to their political, religious and spiritual values. The unique aspects of a child and family's genogram (family tree) will provide information about their resources. Furthermore, genogram-making should be tried collaboratively as life-story work completed by the child and family in a way that maps out relationships and their meaning and qualities over time. For young children, drawings are a marvellously helpful form of self-expression. They can be free drawings that enable children to express their preoccupations and help toward making sense. Otherwise they can be theme centred, tackling themes such as 'My family back home', 'My family in exile', 'My journey to London' and so forth. Play therapy approaches to theme-centred work with children will be very fruitful (Cattanach 1994).

Adolescents

Refugee adolescents often face the dilemma of living in two cultures. One is the culture of homeland, sometimes preserved rather rigidly in the home, and the other is the culture of exile. Most adolescents are adept at making the transitions. Some may suffer, however, because they experience their parents as being overly rigid or because schools and colleges do too little to understand or support their cultural heritage.

All families have to negotiate change because no culture stands still. But in exile many rules about meeting partners, mixing with the opposite sex, or degrees of interdependence are all likely to be challenging and different. Furthermore, the way that parents and adolescents make rules about how to change the rules may no longer work very well. In one family the unspoken rule about change was that extended family gatherings would set the tone of any change. Group disapproval would indicate if a change were too great. In exile the extended family was not available to provide such opportunities for subtle and gradual change, which led to a build-up of tension. The parents feared they were going to 'lose' the next generation to the culture of exile, when their hope was that the children would carry their culture forward in a way in which they could take collective pride. Family therapy helped the fears of the parents and the frustrations of the children to emerge in a safe therapeutic environment. Gradually, over time, the family sessions acted as a sort of substitute for the lost traditional family gatherings. The two therapists became a bit like a surrogate aunt and uncle, helping with the process of change – through discussion, emotional support and showing an understanding of both the parents and their adolescent children and by providing checks and balances to the direction and pace of change.

Unaccompanied Refugee Children

Many children arrive in exile either completely alone or accompanied by siblings, often sent by parents who are afraid that their children will be engulfed by war in their home country. Older children may have knowledge and insight into the common-sense reasons for sending them abroad. Younger children may be quite confused. Either way, the emotional separation from families and networks is most acute among these children. Unfortunately they are often failed by social services departments (SSDs) which treat them as falling into the grey area of child welfare policy caused by the British government's reservation on the International Rights of the Child. Consequently children are treated as if they do not satisfy the 'habitual residence test' and therefore departments will not take full responsibility for their well-being. Often SSDs are suspicious about their motives for exile, or they do not believe that older children are minors and seek 'expert' medical advice about their age before being willing to help. This is done despite the fact that physicians are extremely cautious about medically assessing the age of children, especially older adolescents, because the physical signs of age cannot be clearly defined. Often, even very obviously young children are accommodated by SSDs in bed and breakfast accommodation with no care plan, no links with the refugee community and no adult responsible for their daily needs.

There is however some good practice in this area with social work teams devoted to the welfare of unaccompanied children. The British Agencies for Adoption and Fostering (BAAF) has a specialist worker whose task is to develop good practice and recruit carers from refugee communities. The Child and Adolescent Team at the Medical Foundation for Care of Victims of Torture has also contributed enormously to the development of good practice and has a befriending project for unaccompanied refugee children that seeks to recruit carers from refugee communities. Finally, the Refugee Council has a panel of befrienders who act as advocates on behalf of unaccompanied refugee children, making sure they have adequate legal representation, linking them in with refugee communities, pressing SSDs to take up their cases and networking with voluntary organizations, schools and colleges in order to get the best care for these children.

Refugee Children in Schools

The refugee child's need for normalization can perhaps most easily be met in school, especially in those that have well-thought-out arrangements for pastoral care and policies for integrating refugee children. However, if schools have little experience, refugee children can find themselves suffering from alienation and marginalization. In addition, the effects of political persecution may cause some children to be withdrawn in behaviour or prone to fits of anger, or they may appear to act oddly, as described in the example given above in the section on triple jeopardy. Apparently unusual behaviour may increase their visibility as victims and expose them to racism and bullying. This in turn can contribute to low self-esteem and a continuation of the dynamics of persecution. Sometimes a child's experience may emerge in play, in story writing and through drawings with an immediacy of expression that may shock the class teacher and other children. When such material can be acknowledged, safely contained and worked through the curriculum and in extra pastoral support, there can be a good outcome. For instance, with the help of his class teacher a Kurdish boy produced a booklet entitled 'I am from Kurdistan' which included the story of his family and people and his journey through persecution into exile. It became a curriculum resource for the class and helped the boy to establish himself in the school in an affirmative way. Schools can also make themselves more welcoming to refugee pupils by providing adequate English as a second language (ESL) teaching. Another strategy is for schools to provide good cultural materials and information as part of the general curriculum. These are readily available from sources such as the Refugee Council (J. Rutter 1991a, b), the Minority Rights Group (Warner 1991, 1995) and from UNICEF and Save the Children. Another strategy is to make parents and refugee community leaders welcome in the school, so that refugee people have a visible presence. Further suggestions on work with refugee children in schools can be found in J. Rutter (1994) and Melzak and Blackwell (2000).

Another way forward is the excellent work that has been provided by child mental health practitioners working alongside teachers and with children in schools (Howard and Hodes 2000). This work provides a backup to the school's pastoral services by offering consultation and classroom interventions on children who worry teachers and direct intervention with children and their parents in the school setting when that is *really* necessary. Because of triple jeopardy, routine school health surveillance is important because it can also pick up refugee children who may have health problems but have missed out on what is available through their GP or community health services.

Conclusion

The number of refugee children arriving in the UK is rising annually and there is evidence that good practice is being developed in this undoubtedly complex work but this has significant resource implications (O'Shea *et al.* 2000). The theme of this chapter has been about the multidimensional nature of work with refugee children and how to work as a practitioner from a human rights perspective. This will go some way towards addressing their needs. The underlying message however must be that refugee children will never get a good enough service until they are regarded first and foremost as children, rather than as aliens and strangers. To do that means that child health services need to reach out. We may eventually thank refugee children for teaching us all to relearn that most fundamental and human skill.

Resources for Refugee Children and Families

Several of the books referred to in this chapter are good resources for refugee children and families. For children in school Jill Rutter's work is indispensable. Rachel Warner's series written for the Minority Rights Group is excellent for informing children and teachers about lives of refugee children from various countries. For troubled children, Sheila Melzak and Richard Blackwell's book published by the Child Psychotherapy Trust is both a knowledgeable and accessible guide. Naomi Richman's (1988) book is also an indispensable guide. For refugee children and families who are affected by trauma Woodcock (2000) provides a helpful 'expert' view. Other general resources for refugee children can be obtained from the Refugee Council, Save the Children Fund and UNICEF. Specialist help and advice on refugee children's health can be had from the Child and Adolescent and Family Teams at the Medical Foundation for the Care of Victims of Torture. London is increasingly well resourced for help with refugee children. There are many refugee community groups and health projects in both main-stream and voluntary sectors that offer services to refugee children. The Refugee Council in London will have an up-to-date list of these agencies as well as agencies around the UK. For unaccompanied refugee children the befriending projects at the Refugee Council and at the Medical Foundation may be able to help as well as the specialist project for unaccompanied refugee children within the BAAF. Even though the manual written by Sarah Uppard and Celia Petty (1998) applies mainly to unaccompanied refugee children in countries of first asylum, and therefore mostly children in refugee camps in developing countries, they provide sound advice that is equally applicable in western countries. Finally, the tracing service of the Red Cross provides a vital service in reuniting seperated refugee families.

Most of the above agencies have information services that can be contacted by telephone (details are readily available via directory enquires) and many now provide information on dedicated websites.

Jeremy Woodcock

Medical Foundation for the care of Victims of Torture,
Star House,
104–108 Grafton Road,
London NW5 4BD

and

School for Policy Studies,
University of Bristol,
8 Priory Road,
Bristol BS8 1TZ
Jeremy.Woodcock@bristol.ac.uk

References

Agger, I. (1992) *The Blue Room: Trauma and Testimony among Refugee Women: A Psycho-Social Exploration.* London: Zed Press.

Bowlby, J. (1998) *A Secure Base: Clinical Applications of Attachment Theory.* London: Routledge.

Bracken, P. (1998) 'Hidden agendas: deconstructing post traumatic stress disorder.' In P. Bracken and C. Petty (eds) *Rethinking the Trauma of War.* London: Free Association.

Byng-Hall, J. (1995) 'Creating a secure family base: some implications of attachment theory for family therapy.' *Family Process 34,* 45–56.

Byng-Hall, J. (1999) 'Family and couple therapy: Toward greater security.' In J. Cassidy and P. Shaver (eds) *Handbook of Attachment: Theory, Research and Clinical Applications.* London: Guilford.

Cassidy, J. and Shaver, P. (eds) (2000) *Handbook of Attachment: Theory, Research and Clinical Applications.* London: Guilford.

Cattanach, A. (1994) *Play Therapy.* London: Jessica Kingsley.

Dearnley, B. (2000) 'Psychotherapy in translation: one clinician's experience of working with interpreters.' *Bulletin of the Society of Psychoanalytical Marital Psychotherapists 7,* 19–22.

De Zulueta, F. (1993) *From Pain to Violence: The Traumatic Roots of Destructiveness.* London: Whurr.

Eastmond, M. (1993) 'National conflict and refugees: re-creating Chilean identity in exile.' In H. Lindholm (ed) *Ethnicity and Nationalism: Formation of Identity and Dynamics of Conflict in the 1990s.* Göteborg: Nordnes.

Howard, M. and Hodes, M. (2000) 'Psychopathology, adversity and service utiliization of young refugees.' *Journal of the American Academy of Child and Adolescent Psychiatry 33,* 368–377.

Melzak, S. and Blackwell, R. (2000) *Far from the Battle But Still at War: Troubled Refugee Children in School.* London: Child Psychotherapy Trust.

O'Shea, B., Hodes, M., Down, G. and Bramley, J. (2000) 'A school-based mental health service for refugee children.' *Clinical Child Psychology and Psychiatry 5,* 2, 189–201.

Papadopoulos, R. and Hildebrand, J. (1997) 'Is home where the heart is? Narratives of oppositional discourse in refugee families.' In R. Papadopoulos and J. Byng-Hall (eds) *Multiple Voice: Narrative in Systemic Family Psychotherapy.* London: Duckworth.

Richman, N. (1998) *In the Midst of the Whirlwind: A Manual for Helping Refugee Children.* Stoke-on-Trent: Trentham.

Rutter, J. (1991a) *Refugees: We Left Because We Had to: An Education Book for 14–18 Year Olds.* London: Refugee Council.

Rutter, J. (1991b) *Refugees: A Resource Book for 8–13 Year Olds.* London: Refugee Council.

Rutter, J. (1994) *Refugee Children in the Classroom.* Stoke-on-Trent: Trentham.

Rutter, M. (1985) Resilience in the face of adversity: protective factors and resistance to psychiatric disorder. *British Journal of Psychiatry 147,* 598–611.

Sluzki, C. (1979) 'Migration and family conflict.' *Family Process 18*, 379–390.

Uppard, S. and Petty, C. (1998) *Working with Separated Children: A Field Guide.* London: Save the Children.

Warner, R. (ed) (1991) *Voices from Kurdistan/Eritrea/Somalia.* London: Minority Rights Group.

Warner, R. (ed) (1995) *Voices from Angola/Sudan/Uganda/Zaire.* London: Minority Rights Group.

Woodcock, J. (1995) 'Healing rituals with families in exile'. *Journal of Family Therapy 17*, 397–410.

Woodcock, J. (2000) 'Refugee children and families: theoretical and clinical approaches.' In K. Dwivedi (ed) *Post Traumatic Stress Disorder in Children and Adolescents.* London: Whurr.

Woodcock, J. (2001) 'Threads from the labyrinth: therapy with survivors of war and political oppression.' *Journal of Family Therapy 23*, 2.

Woodhead, D. (2000) *The Health and Well-Being of Asylum Seekers and Refugees.* London: King's Fund.

CHAPTER 14

Community and Youth Work with Asian Women and Girls

Radha Dwivedi

Introduction

Most of the women who migrated from the Indian subcontinent (India, Bangladesh and Pakistan) usually had to suffer lengthy separations before they could join their husbands. They had to travel long distances to the British high commissions and then undergo rigorous and intensive interviews, much of which they felt were totally irrelevant and impertinent. On arrival in the UK their experiences of further interrogation by the immigration officials, humiliating medical examinations and sometimes even detentions and fear of deportation added to their distress.

Adjusting to the new environment is not very easy. Not only is the weather astonishingly different, but so too are the dress code, social and welfare structure, health service provisions, cultural values and so on. These and many other issues can easily become stressful. Many were shocked by some of the things they saw in the UK.

Language barrier

For many women the language barrier can be a formidable obstacle. Some may be able to read or write English but not able to speak it fluently. Even those who have a good grasp of English may find local accents difficult; this is compounded by the difficulty in understanding the accents of Asians and Africans from other areas. The wide variety of dialects and languages spoken in India makes communication in their native languages equally difficult.

283

With the breakup of their close-knit communities of origin, Asian women find it hard to deal with the changed structure of society, especially the way it affects language. They may not be able to approach or find any one with whom they could share or express their feelings and difficulties. There are therefore immense problems in dealing with official bodies such as the social security, social services, police, school and so on. They may not even be aware of such agencies or the advice bureaux that could offer them support. Becoming aware of opportunities for training or jobs and applying for such things are therefore very difficult tasks.

Day-to-day life

Public transport, road crossings and traffic, buying clothes, food or even ordering milk can be very different and unfamiliar. Shopping can be equally difficult in the beginning, as one may not know where to go to buy the desired items. One may not think of a post office in a grocery store. Many cannot read the names of items or ask for them in English. The appearance of things may confuse them. For example shoes for men and for women may sometimes seem very similar and they may purchase the wrong type through being too shy to ask. Most shops look alike and finding what they are looking for may be a daunting process. Returning goods is even harder as this involves some understanding of the system and rituals involved in such transactions.

Even little things like what saris to wear for different occasions can become problematic. In their previous environments these decisions were straightforward, but those social cues are no longer available or applicable in the UK. The result is that some can be overdressed for the occasion, such as visiting their doctor wearing an expensive silk sari along with all the jewellery. The disorientation they feel from not knowing what is and what is not acceptable or the 'done thing' can be very unsettling. This can also lead to being ridiculed by others. Even places where the community is predominantly Asian, varying degrees of westernization and having different regional backgrounds from Asia lead to feelings of isolation.

Thus, the day-to-day activities, which were in fact the high point of the day in their previous societies, now become difficult and burdensome in the UK. The shopping trip was a great social occasion, getting on a rickshaw and visiting the hustle and bustle of the market. The shopkeepers were well known to them and they often went in groups and chatted. Such activities provided a relaxing change and a light relief from other tasks. Here, the life and excitement in such an outing are usually missing and it becomes just another fearful and burdensome task. They are no longer able to have long chats with the milkmen, argue with the laundry ladies, or haggle with the vegetable sellers. Such social interaction played a highly supportive role in women's emotional stability; its loss is a major contributory factor to their loneliness and isolation.

Work

Another factor causing isolation in the UK is their work environment. Unemployment is high among Asian communities, especially among women. University degrees from the Indian subcontinent are usually not recognized so women are employed far below their potential and end up doing menial jobs from lack of encouragement. They often find only unskilled, repetitive types of jobs with poor working conditions, pay or opportunities for further training. Employers or managers invariably put extra pressure on them demanding completion of even more in the same time allowed. These women do not feel confident in standing up for their rights. They have little or no idea of their own rights and feel helpless and trapped. Sometimes these women work from home and this leads to further isolation and vulnerability.

In the Indian subcontinent where they lived before, the roles and responsibilities of men and women were very clearly differentiated. The housework was usually shared by all the women. They also knew what other work was or was not appropriate for them to undertake. For example, some women could fetch water from the well, feed and milk their goats, buffaloes or cows, sow seeds and so on. Some activities, for example, driving heavy vehicles and digging or ploughing were, however, seen as inappropriate, heavy and burdensome and were not undertaken by women.

There was usually a good understanding between employer and employee to accommodate the cultural needs that may arise in special circumstances. Various relatives also played their important social role in such situations, e.g. pregnancy, illness, death of a relative and other life events. There was a great deal of team approach to work. Women from the same household or neighbourhood in a village could approach a potential employer together for work such as planting rice in a group. Thus knowing each other so well gave them support and strength and this approach was further enthused by group singing. If disagreements arose,

the quarrels were rarely suppressed, in fact, these were expressed immediately so that a resolution of any conflict could take place more openly
and spontaneously.

In Britain, their isolation is further exacerbated by their husbands
working unsociable shifts and overtime to maintain a living wage. Much
of the housework and chores are then left for the wives, the burden being substantial if they take on some employment themselves. These are
usually low-paid jobs as already described. The pressures are even worse
if they are looking after aged parents in extended family situations.

Housing

Of immediate significance to their welfare is housing. If they are lucky
enough to have a house of their own then more often than not it will be
cold with faulty heating, draughty, in a poor state of repair and unkempt.
Often families have to make do with rented accommodation with just
one room. Here they cook, work, live and sleep in crowded conditions.
They also have to answer to the landlord who may make excessive demands and take advantage of such helpless immigrants. Moving in with
relatives or friends is usually impractical as they are often themselves trying to cope with already crowded conditions. The waiting lists for council houses are long and availability is very low. Sometimes they are forced
to stay in makeshift accommodation including bed and breakfast or
cheap hotels. This is obviously stressful and has serious implications for
their health and interpersonal relationships within the family. It also has
serious effects on the quality of the children's education. Schooling may
become haphazard and children find it difficult to do their homework in
such conditions.

It is true that not all Asians emigrating to the UK undergo such hard-
ships, but a significant proportion do. It seems that the immigrants from
Bangladesh arriving in the UK have experienced the maximum difficulties. They also have the greatest level of unemployment.

Racism and isolation

Another serious problem is the experience of racial harassment and
abuse, which leads to suffering, isolation, hatred and discomfort felt by
these families. They develop fear and anxiety through having to live in
the environment that such attacks create. The families most affected include those just settled and widowed or single women. They live in con-

stant fear of verbal and physical abuse and are afraid to let their children go out. There are numerous examples of such incidents including sealing doors from the outside and smashing windows with stones at night. Racist elements may try to beat up Asian children on the way home from school. In the area I work I have come across many examples of harassment. For example one incident involved the house of a Bengali family, which was completely sealed with tape, and all their rubbish scattered in the back garden. Another Punjabi family suffered for some time with stones being thrown through their windows by a 9-year-old boy. They therefore find it very difficult to become part of their new environment; they feel threatened and extremely isolated.

The dramatic difference in almost every aspect of their lives in comparison with what they were used to before and the loss of the supportive social network means that they find very little to hold on to and there is an intense feeling of insecurity. This is compounded by the lack of communication due to a poor grasp of English and other Asian languages. Before, in their societies of origin, they took part in a variety of rituals, customs, traditions and celebrations, which were helpful in dealing with their feelings and stress. For example crying together was the most natural way between close friends and relatives to express sympathy or share each other's feelings. Usually a large number of people participated in celebrations of childbirth, weddings, funerals and so on and shared various responsibilities for organizing these activities. Such things are no longer possible in Britain because of the loss of the close links between the neighbours that existed in their societies of origin. In the UK it would appear very awkward and out of place if dozens of women got together and started to cry with someone recently bereaved.

When they lived in the Indian subcontinent the family included the whole of the extended family – uncles, aunts, parents, children and grandparents often living together in large and complex households. The women felt secure and well supported and knew who to turn to if they had any problems. Before marriage the girls felt well protected. They received proper guidance as regards education, morality and behaviour appropriate for girls, expectations of roles and responsibilities in marriage, various domestic skills and so on. Old people were seen as experienced, wise, important and highly respected. They usually lived with their children and grandchildren in an atmosphere of care, warmth and affection for each other and of striving for harmony. The theme of familiarity extended to the village life as well because people living in a village knew each other well. The relationships were close, almost like an extended family. People learnt about the way various relationships should be formed, for example the relationships between parents and their children, mother-in-law and daughter-in-law, younger ones and older ones, students and teachers, and between the neighbours and village kinsfolk and so on. These relationships were governed by well-known rules which were learnt through observing others, and through parental guidance. Thus these codes of conduct became instinctive with a natural sense of what is right and what is wrong in a particular situation.

Asian parents worry that their children may reject their family values regarding education, marriage, interpersonal relationships, self-development and so on. As they themselves had a rather different upbringing, which instilled rigorous moral standards, they begin to feel apprehensive about the possibility of their children not persevering with these traditional moral values. When the children's presentation, manners, attitudes, thoughts and ideas diverge markedly from traditional patterns and from what the parents perceive as culturally appropriate and correct, they may fear the loss of their close links with their children.

The children may feel that other children have more freedom such as about staying out late and may think that their parents are being unfair or unkind. On the other hand, the parents may not have had any experience of childhood in the UK and may not know what is safe and could be permissible. Their fears may also be fuelled by media stories of violence, kidnapping or road accidents. In their countries of origin they would have felt comfortable to allow children to go out to the market, see friends or attend festivals because of the security of a close-knit community and of knowing what they were likely to encounter. In the UK they are now very unsure.

Sometimes in desperation, some parents put pressure on their children to comply but this may only make matters worse and the children may become more distant due to the lack of a close social network that could help them appreciate each other's points of view and feelings, as might have happened in their previous societies. The so-called helping professionals further strain the relationships in the name of teaching children independence or of 'rescuing' them. Family arguments can deteriorate the home environment and this can become so stressful that the youngster may run away from home.

Community and Youth Work Principles

Social and community work within such a community requires the right attitude, if it is to be successful. A community or youth worker needs to develop enough understanding, respect and commitment to the community. A thorough understanding of both the complex problems and their cultural strength has to be the basis of the whole approach. Only through knowing how they feel and the traumas that they are going through and have suffered already, can the worker make a resolute effort to help. If a worker is simply going through the motions of running a community project, without a sincere commitment to the community and real people involved, the project is likely to fail, no matter how hard it is 'sold' or how many leaflets and other publicity materials are distributed. I have personally seen numerous examples of failed attempts at such community work. Although the workers may blame the community for their lack of cooperation, I feel that this is more likely to be due to the lack of sincerity and unskilful and uninformed approach of the worker involved.

Establishing credentials

In the beginning one has to get to know some individuals from the community who are in need of support and help them as far as possible. This would help to establish the sincerity and the credentials of the worker. In community work actions speak louder than words. Because of auto-extension and the sense of curiosity in the community, the news of the worker's sincerity begins to spread around. Thus by interacting on a personal basis with individuals, the workers have to expose themselves, their values and commitment to the community in order to build up a good working relationship with members of the community on a larger scale. Even in organizing group programmes it is essential to make personal contact with people, making them feel respected and valued for what they are. On the contrary I have known workers who have been arrogant in their approach. They have felt uncomfortable visiting people's homes or mixing with the community. There is the need for not only a constantly supportive attitude but also great sensitivity to people's feelings and above all immense humility. If enough preparation and work with individuals in the community have not been accomplished, the planned group programmes will be difficult to start or such groups are likely to break down.

In organizing group activities or programmes the worker initially needs to be personally available to see through all aspects of the group's activities, such as collecting members from their homes to take to the meeting point, personal contact out of hours and being present at every activity, function or outing. This is more difficult to keep up than it sounds as people can create many obstacles even in the face of the worker's very good intentions. In fact, these are testing times. One can fail by losing temper or patience under such pressures. Any inappropriate or non-cooperative behaviour, instead of being reacted to with sanctions or telling off, has to be taken up in group discussions to explore various perceptions, points of view, underlying feelings and so on. This then becomes a social learning opportunity for individuals and worker alike.

Sensitivity

When the members begin to develop trust in the worker they start to disclose their underlying feelings (such as of frustration, anger, hate and jealousy) as and when they arise in the group settings. Eventually their chronic and complex difficulties and also the reasons for their certain behaviours are shared in this supportive atmosphere. By being aware of the mood of the group in the context of their culture and language, the worker can begin to avoid potentially difficult situations by intervening at the right time in a skilful way. If excessive or uncontrolled quarrelling or disputes break out without resolution, the members will see the worker as weak and incompetent. Loss of trust in the worker can easily lead to the collapse of the group.

As more and more problems, simple or complex, come to be shared, the strategies for solving these are evolved. Some would need active help from the worker, others the mobilization of group resources. This can easily test the limits of the worker's capabilities and may include work outside the worker's understanding or competence. It is especially important to ensure that these particular problems are solved even if they require extra time and effort and gathering of external resources. This will further help the strengthening of trust. Some, however, may not express their desires or wishes but may still expect the worker to fulfil the same regardless.

Professionalism

It is also essential to arrange opportunities for learning certain skills, and for outings, recreational events, festival celebrations, use of local leisure facilities and staging of group events. The idea may be to get them into activities such as swimming or learning sewing, which they would enjoy but had been hesitant to get involved in before. In organizing such activities or lessons it is essential to make sure that the instructors or teachers are skilled, competent and sensitive to the particular needs of the group. It is therefore crucial that these events are professionally led. This means, for example, a professional sewing teacher is employed and the proper equipment is used or that talks are given by experts who specialize in their fields.

Initially there may be a great deal of resistance but it is the enthusiasm of the worker that helps them to attend at least the first few sessions. Once they manage to get a taste of these few sessions and start to enjoy the activities and the opportunities gained by coming out of the house, they quickly become self-motivated. After the first few sessions they become confident in the worker as they see the deeper benefits of the activities. This confidence helps the worker in establishing further trust. They also begin to see that it may be possible to start to break the cycle of depression and isolation. As they begin to appreciate the benefits of such activities for social interaction they themselves start to put in their own efforts to make sure that they attend, such as by making their own transport arrangements.

Group work

The effect of such activities, along with group work with its emphasis on interpersonal social education and counselling, can be extremely profound on the entire community. The benefits of careful preparations for establishing the group, solving of individual problems with due care and other such interventions begin to spread throughout the community outside the group. The positive changes in individuals' behaviours also have an impact on the relationships in the community and become examples for them. This leads to the recruitment of new members and the spread of self-help activities. These developments can be enhanced by working outside the group environment in liaison with key community members to smooth the progress of change.

Groups for children

Groups for children follow similar principles. They are best started after the adult groups are established to allow the parents to gain confidence and trust in the worker. When the adults have begun to trust the worker and feel safe with the worker's values and attitudes, they would then feel comfortable in allowing their children to join the groups organized by the worker. The content of the psychoeducational activities of such groups should again depend on the group's perceived needs. If such activities are not made interesting or adequately researched they will not be supported by the youngsters and will fail to continue. The worker should be careful to respect the parents' wishes and the cultural needs of the children and use the opportunities to explain the parents' traditional values, norms and parental behaviours. Similarly it is essential to explore, understand and empathize with the youngsters' feelings, points of view, hurts, dilemmas and so on.

Sometimes it is not obvious to the children that their parents, to whom the wisdom of their traditions has been passed on for many generations, are trying to do the same for the children's benefit. The children, because of the outside influences of the school, media and so on, may not fully appreciate this, leading to conflicts between the children and their parents. Similarly when a child does not adopt the traditional dress, food or hairstyle the parents may fear that their child has become alienated. Thus both children and their parents need help in understanding each other better and appreciating each other's difficulties. Parents need assistance in transmitting their culture to their children in a new environment like this, in a way that will be acceptable and understandable to the children.

The worker should also remember that the children do not have enough opportunities for going out and it is because of the fact that the parents have developed enough trust in the worker that the children are attending these group activities, with their recreational or educational opportunities. As it is a precious time, every effort should be made to use the time as constructively and enjoyably as possible.

Case study: Community and Youth Work

In the past, I did voluntary work to teach English as a second language to Asians in a small English town. At the end of these sessions the women gradually began to approach me with some of their practical problems. For example, someone's child was being racially abused at school or someone had received a letter from the school regarding a child's irregular attendance, poor homework or school dress. They wanted me to accompany them to the school, which I did. Someone had difficulty with getting permission for their close relative (such as a son's wife) to come to the UK and I helped them contact the appropriate helping agency. Seema, a Punjabi woman, was extremely worried about her 11-year-old daughter Reeta. Reeta, who was a very withdrawn and quiet child, did not mix with other children. Reeta's older brother had already been taken into care and Seema was very angry with and suspicious of the so-called helping agencies. I gave her a listening ear.

Similarly women needed my help in dealing with their bank, social security office, arranging appointments with their GPs, approaching the racial equality officer, clarifying problems with their gas, electricity and so on. Many had sleepless nights; others suffered from various aches and pains. Someone did not get enough housekeeping money from her husband, someone's husband was very violent, someone's child was being refused school dinner and so on. Most of these were single women, but married women too had a number of difficulties. Their minds were too preoccupied to be able to concentrate on English lessons. I myself had plenty of time, so I began to spend a couple of hours listening to the problems, giving whatever advice I could offer and afterwards took them to the relevant agencies and helped them in their dealings with these agencies.

I then decided to organize a social group for these women and approached the social services for help. The local social services department, too, were aware of the problem and had already made several unsuccessful attempts to organize such a group. Their previous attempts had failed because they concentrated more on gathering the women together to form a big crowd rather than genuinely helping them with their difficulties. The educational activities that they had organized were rather insensitive to the women's actual needs and abilities. For example a sewing teacher used profuse handouts that the women could not read. Having personally known many of these women and their difficulties, I was more in touch with their needs, their strengths, their abilities and their suffering.

With the help of the local social services department, I managed to organize a group for the women. These included Hindus and Muslims, young and old, women who had originated from Bangladesh, Punjab, Pakistan, Gujarat or East Africa. The group activities began to take place in the local social services accommodation, so that the women would come in contact with the social workers to provide opportunities for mutual familiarity and learning from each other. I made sure that there was enough space and comfortable sitting arrangements, facilities for refreshments and transport provided by the department. I looked after them with a lot of affection, humour, regard and respect.

At first I picked them up from their homes but they were seldom ready when I arrived. In fact, they would wait for me to come to their house before they would start to get ready. Later I learnt that they did not actually believe that I would really turn up. They had had so many disappointments in their lives that they had become ultrasensitive. During the group discussions I began to discuss these issues. Then we talked about the time that could be saved if people were ready. To my delight, it really began to happen. Then they began to wait in small groups and even to telephone our receptionist to apologize if they could not attend, so that we didn't make any wasted journeys. Similarly they began not to mind being collected by someone else and at times made their own way.

The same pattern of response was reflected in a number of other areas while working with this group. Initially I made tea and snacks which I offered to each one of them, treating each person as the most respected guest. Gradually we turned this into a learning and teaching exercise about different regional dishes. Someone would teach others how to cook a certain dish. They all began to be involved with great curiosity and enjoyment and most of the tasks related to shopping, cooking, serving, washing up, and so on began to be shared. Similarly people began to try out different regional songs and even dance, humour and jokes. Although they had different mother tongues such as Gujarati, Bengali, Punjabi, Hindi and Urdu, we began to manage somehow through Hindi/Urdu as a link language. This became the high time of their week providing the enjoyment they had been missing from their lives so sadly before.

In the beginning, whenever I organized any skill-based educational activities (for example sewing, swimming and so on) I met with a great deal of resistance. But I made sure that the teacher was professionally skilled and qualified and that I fully prepared and supported the teacher. Soon the women began to enjoy learning, also because the social atmosphere that had already been created was maintained in the new environment as well.

I organized day trips to places, lectures by visiting speakers on relevant topics such as health issues, benefits, police and so on. We began to visit some of these agencies together and we even enjoyed a week's holiday together. They began to help each other more, for example, looking after someone's child, pushing a disabled person's wheelchair, taking care of an elderly person and so on. A number of small subgroups were formed across age, language or religion. They began to pick up a bit of English, a lot of confidence in approaching agencies and a great deal of understanding about so many other things. They learnt not to ask the minibus driver to turn or to stop immediately without due notice on these trips. Little achievements, like managing to make or cancel an appointment with their GP or police officer entirely by themselves with the use of broken English, were fully acknowledged.

Most importantly they began to tolerate each other's idiosyncrasies, moods, manners, customs and so on. They began to notice and support each other, share one another's pain and comfort each other. Either individually or in the group setting, they began to discuss a number of their deep-rooted difficulties.

Case study: Uma

Uma, a 28-year-old single depressed mother with a young child, had been attending this group. I knew her from my English as a second language classes. She had had a violent husband with a drinking problem who deserted her when she became pregnant. She had grown up in India and had no other support here. She went to the women's refuge and finally found a council house to live in but felt extremely hurt, bitter, isolated and depressed. She had frequently visited the surgery with various aches, pains and fears of all sorts of infections. She was frequently suicidal. However, through attending the sewing classes that I organized for the group, she turned out to be very skilled in sewing. She had never touched a sewing machine before but she put a great deal of effort into learning it. She began to make dresses for her child and for herself, very professionally. Before she would have been seen as rather unkempt and neglected and was unnoticed by other community members; now however, people began to take a great deal of notice of her and of her tailoring talent. The sewing teacher was also very pleased with her. Her hairstyle changed and she began to look really smart. Similarly when I organized swimming classes, she became equally interested.

Uma began to share with the group her intimate feelings, about her relationship with her child, her confidence or lack of it before, her anger and her life, her new-found pride in her sewing skills and so on. Her relationship with and her handling of her child was now unbelievably better. She at times would still get bouts of depression but now she realized that she could recognize these earlier and do something to manage her feelings better. She was now interested in studying for her GCSEs and in training to become an instructor.

Case study: Seema and Reeta

One could see a gradual and similar transformation in almost all the women. As mentioned earlier, Seema had been extremely angry and hateful of the social work agencies. She was a single mother with three children. Her son had a medical condition for which he received treatment but then began to exhibit behaviour problems, which gradually escalated and led to the involvement of a social worker. Seema felt that her son became delinquent because of the fact that the social worker arranged for him to go on a holiday with other extremely delinquent boys. He was now in care with negligible contact with the family and she felt that she had lost him. Her daughter Reeta was often withdrawn, quiet and shy and Seema felt that she might lose her too. Through attending the groups Seema developed a great deal of confidence and a tremendous improvement in her self-esteem. Her relationship with Reeta began to improve as she began to enjoy the group and then enjoy the company of her daughter too.

Seema became very keen for her daughter to experience similar groups as well. Other women felt the same for their children, especially their girls. I therefore started a weekly girls' group after school for young people of 12 years and above. The girls appeared really motivated to attend and very keen in various

educational, recreational, social and other activities that we
arranged. They valued the opportunity to discuss their feelings
and understand their parents' points of view, working out ways
of clarifying, sharing, exploring and negotiating with their
family members and others. There were nearly 20 girls attending
and more wanted to come but we could not find a bigger place. I
then started another girls' group through the Youth Service.
Many had had enormous difficulties, some had recently arrived
from Bangladesh, some missed their fathers, some felt extremely
restricted, some were scapegoated in their community and some
were still feeling hurt by the family violence that they had
witnessed a long time ago.

Reeta remembered the physical abuse she and her mother
experienced at the hands of her drunken father. Although it
happened several years ago and her parents were no longer living
together, the memory of these traumatic experiences was still
very distressing for her. As she began to share these feelings
either in the group or outside with me she began to take interest
in her day-to-day activities as well. She talked about her worries
for her mother and how her mother felt lonely. She felt angry
about the freedom her brother had. She was annoyed by the
visitors in the house and how this interfered with her homework.
As I began to take interest in her educational progress, she started
to use these opportunities with more and more delight. She
shared her fantasies and fears. She had recently attended some
weddings where some relatives had enquired about her wishes.
She became very anxious thinking that her mother was going to
arrange and force her to marry soon. The intensity of her feelings
tended to stop her from discussing a lot of these things with her
mother. She would wonder 'Does my mother not like me?' 'Does
she want to get rid of me?' and so on. I tried to explain that most
Asian parents tend to feel responsible for their children's
marriage out of their true love for their children. They have their
children's welfare at heart and would hate to force anything like
this.

My suggestion was 'Try to explain your feelings, your likes and
dislikes to your mother, I am sure she would not like to do
anything against your wishes.' Gradually she began to try. Reeta's
experience of her father was so negative that she worried that her
own husband could turn out to be like him. Through the

discussions in the group and her relationships outside she gradually began to learn that all men may not be like her father. She began to enjoy other things in her day-to-day life as well and to realize that there was more to life than constantly worrying about one's future marriage or husband. In the women's group I encouraged Seema to listen and to explain her feelings to Reeta. In the girls' group I encouraged Reeta to do the same with her mother, with occasional comments on how they appreciated their heart-to-heart talks. I still treasure the happiness that it brought into every aspect of their lives.

Conclusion

I thoroughly enjoyed being part of both the groups and continued to run them until I took up my current post. Now they have a life and independence of their own. Many new members have joined the groups. Others have emotionally matured and left. These groups do a great deal for the community as a whole, as the members also begin to take interest in the welfare of the wider community.

Chapter 15

A Conceptual Framework of Identity Formation in a Society of Multiple Cultures

Applying Theory to Practice

James Rodriguez, Ana Mari Cauce and Linda Wilson[1]

Introduction

In the United States increased immigration from Asia and Latin America and higher birth rates among ethnic groups than whites suggest a demographic shift where people of colour will represent 47 per cent and whites 53 per cent of the US population by the year 2050 (Martin and Midgley 1999). Ethnic minorities already make up the majority in many major cities, and in some urban centres one in six newborns are multiracial (US Bureau of the Census 1992, cited in Root 1996). These trends have prompted interest and empirical research on ethnic identity development, which has not ever dealt with the issue of young people in foster care where challenges to ethnic identity development are prevalent. In the field of foster care, the over-representation of young people of colour, the high number of biracial youth and the prevalence of cross-cultural placements compel practitioners and caretakers to attend to ethnic identity formation in young people to support exploration of a significant aspect of them. What is ethnic identity development? How does it develop in children and young people? How is ethnic identity a healthy and important aspect of development? What does it mean for children and young people in foster care? What can practitioners and caretakers do to foster it?

This chapter addresses these questions in two sections. The first section outlines a conceptual model of identity formation in a society of multiple cultures that synthesizes theory and research in ethnic identity development and ethnic socialization. The paradoxical process of developing an individual sense of self that is based on group membership and shaped by external forces is detailed. In the second section we explore the implications and challenges of ethnic identity for young people in foster care. This section is based on interviews with young people in foster care, alumni, caretakers and practitioners. Since most of the available research on ethnic or racial identity for young people in foster care focuses on the issue of transracial adoptions, the interviews represent a fresh contribution to the field.

Conceptual Overview

A trend in research and theory on the psychosocial development of ethnic minority children and young people is to view development as a complex product of individual and contextual influences. Spencer's (1999) identity centred ecological (ICE) perspective is exemplary of this trend. Likewise, our model is based on ecological systems theory (Bronfenbrenner 1977), which views development as embedded within various systems of influence. Figure 15.1 represents three layers of context. The central circle illustrates the dynamic, almost paradoxical, struggle at the self-system level to develop a sense of individual identity based on the knowledge of and the significance attached to group membership (Tajfel 1981). This process at the self-system level is influenced by the process of ethnic socialization, which occurs at the microsystemic level as the individual interacts with significant others in the environment. In this respect, the self is viewed as extended and interactional, and not narrowly individualistic (Stevenson *et al.* 1997). The outermost circle, the macrosystem, reflects how government policies, media stereotypes, prevalent societal values and beliefs, and popular culture interact with the micro- and self-systems to affect the processes at other levels. In this chapter we focus on the processes associated within and between the microsystem representing ethnic socialization and the self-system representing ethnic identity development.

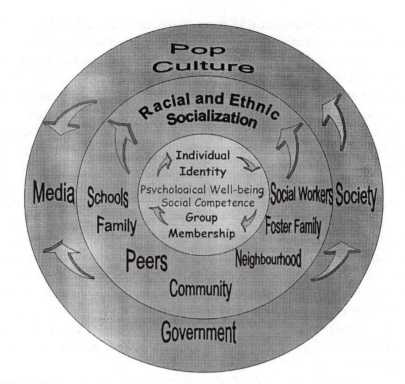

Figure 15.1

Ethnic Socialization

Ethnic socialization includes the messages that children and young people receive from significant others that influence the way they behave, think and feel about their group membership. The process of ethnic socialization can be direct and indirect, tacit and explicit, and ultimately, these proximal socializing influences affect social identities and self-concept and influence the way that young people interact with others in society (Knight *et al.* 1993b, c). Work with African American young people by Stevenson and his colleagues (Stevenson 1997, 1998; Stevenson *et al.* 1997) suggests that messages may be proactive and protective. Proactive messages highlight cultural history and individual talents, and encourage children and young people to succeed as a function of their individual abilities drawing from traditional cultural strengths. Protective messages prepare youth for life as minorities in a racially conscious and hostile society. In combination, proactive and protective messages lead to adaptive socialization, which promotes healthier psychological outcomes by ensuring that cultural values, norms and traditions are passed on from one generation to the next, and builds a realistic awareness of injustice without thwarting hope for the future.

Proactive and protective messages refer to the content of messages; however, messages also differ in context and form. The context refers to whether messages are planned in advance or reactive. Planned messages are purposeful, generally proactive, and are necessary because negative ethnic and racial stereotypes prevail in the media, and although ethnic-specific books are more common in our time, positive ethnic images are generally represented less. Reactive messages are typically delivered in response to circumstances or to capitalize on a particular 'teachable moment', as when children come home from school distraught over being made fun of because of their race. The form of messages can be explicit or subtle. This distinction is important because adults, in general, will be less aware of the subtle messages that they pass on to children and youth (Ellen E. Pinderhughes, personal communication, 24 June 2000). By avoiding any conversations about race or ethnicity or ignoring situations that arise, adults may unintentionally send a subtle message that race or ethnicity is unimportant or not to be discussed openly. Figure 15.2 provides some examples of messages by type, context and form.

The three primary goals of ethnic and racial socialization are to promote cultural traditions, to prepare children and young people to deal with racism and discrimination, and to prepare them to get along in the mainstream (Bowman and Howard 1985; Boykin and Toms 1985; Spencer 1983; Stevenson, Reed and Bodison 1996; Thornton *et al.* 1990). Boykin and Toms (1985) refer to these goals as the triple quandary that black parents must face in raising their children, but these goals have implications for the socialization process for many racial and ethnic groups in US society.

Research in ethnic and racial socialization suggests that parents who strongly identify with and value their ethnicity desire the same for their children. Such parents strive to raise children who value their ethnic heritage (Bowman and Howard 1985; Dennedy-Frank 1982; Knight *et al.* 1993a; Stevenson *et al.* 1996). Moreover, children and adolescents who are socialized about race and ethnicity are further along in identity development than children who are not (Knight *et al.* 1993a; Marshall 1995; Spencer 1983) and they demonstrate more positive mental health outcomes and competencies (Parham and Helms 1985a, b; Phinney and Chavira 1995; Pyant and Yanico 1991; Taub and McEwen 1992).

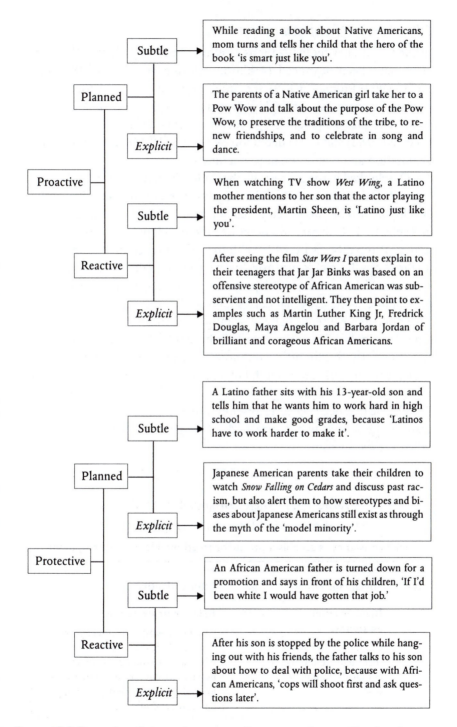

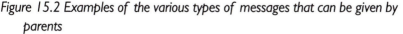

Figure 15.2 Examples of the various types of messages that can be given by parents

Ethnic Identity Development

While various conceptualizations of ethnic and racial identity development have been advanced (Atkinson, Morten and Sue 1998; Cross 1971, 1991; Phinney 1989), the process typically involves four stages: relative unawareness, emerging awareness, exploration and commitment. The process parallels ego identity formation described by Erik Erikson (1968) and expanded upon by Marcia (1980) in that it involves exploration and commitment to a defined identity.

Overlooked in the process of ethnic identity development is the process of social constancy, which is a necessary precursor to ethnic identity development. The two developmental processes are shown side-by-side in Table 15.1. Column one describes the development of social constancy, or the process by which children of colour come to understand that race or ethnicity is intrinsically fixed and immutable. The development of social constancy overlaps with the early stages of ethnic identity development. The ages that correspond to the stages of ethnic identity development are intentionally wide ranging to illustrate that the process typically can, but does not necessarily have to, follow a sequential process from early childhood to adulthood. The process may begin in later adolescence or early adulthood, but adults can revisit stages (except for relative unawareness) throughout the course of their adult lives (Parham 1989). The first two stages, relative unawareness and emerging unawareness, can be seen as two interrelated sub-stages of a more general stage called pre-exploration.

Table 15.1: Stages of social constancy and ethnic identity development

Social constancy is seen as a precursor to ethnic identity development.

Age[a]	Social constancy[b]	Age[a]	Ethnic identity[c]
2–5	**Race or ethnic awareness** Child becomes aware that there are different races or ethnicities[d]	2–16	**Relative unawareness** Child or young person recognizes race or ethnic differences, knows what race or ethnicity he or she belongs to, but race or ethnicity has low salience and is not yet an important aspect of life

3–6	Race or ethnic self-identity Child identifies as a member of a specific race or ethnicity	5–21	Emerging awareness Child or young person comes to understand the *social* significance of race or ethnicity (e.g. that race or ethnicity is an important facet of the social order)
3–9	Race or ethnic constancy Child realizes race or ethnicity are immutable and will not change with time	9–25	Exploration/identification Child or young person begins to develop an understanding and appreciation of the *personal* significance of race or ethnicity in his or her life
		14–25	Commitment Young person develops a positive commitment to membership in ethnic or racial groups and accepts the positive and negative aspects of both his or her own group and that of others

Notes:

a Approximate

b These stages are based on the work of numerous researchers and theorists (Garcia and Hurtado 1995; Knight et al. 1993b, c; McAdoo 1985, 2000)

c These stages represent an amalgamation of the work of numerous researchers and theorists (Atkinson et al. 1997; Cross 1971, 1991; Phinney 1990)

d Children typically are aware that there are different races before they recognize different ethnicities. Likewise, we believe it is likely that children of colour in less stigmatized ethnic groups or those with more white-like appearances may progress through the early stages at a slower pace.

Relative Unawareness

Research indicates that by the age of 5 children become aware of aspects of their social identity like gender, race and ethnicity, and by the age of 6 they can self-identify by these categories (Ocampo, Bernal and Knight 1993). However, children of this age are typically unable to understand the personal meaning and implications of race or ethnicity within the larger society, although they can behave in ways that indicate some understanding of racial and ethnic hierarchies (Garcia-Coll and Garcia 1995; Pinderhughes, personal communication, 24 June 2000). Though relative unawareness is likely parallel to the development of social constancy, it does not strictly apply to young children. There are a number of ways that relative unawareness can surface even into adulthood (Cross 1991). Assigning low salience to race and ethnicity, viewing one's ethnic group membership as a social stigma, having a negative reference group orientation, and defining oneself purely from a Eurocentric cultural perspective are ways that people of colour can display attitudes associated with this stage.

Emerging Awareness

Emerging awareness occurs after an experience or accumulation of experiences that lead to an abandonment of attitudes associated with relative unawareness (Cross 1991; Helms 1990). There is a sober realization that in society people of colour are treated differently because of their racial or ethnic background. The existence of this stage is contested in the literature, but taken together these first two stages represent pre-exploratory identity development.

Research suggests that relative unawareness and emerging awareness are prevalent and are evident into late adolescence. In a sample of high school students in California, more than half expressed attitudes consistent with relative unawareness (Phinney and Chavira 1995). Another study found that emerging awareness is a common stage among college students (Kohatsu 1993), which supports the importance of context in understanding ethnic identity development. People of colour find themselves exposed to predominantly white or mixed settings for the first time during college. The shifting ethnic composition from one context to another can significantly influence ethnic identity development generally and this stage in particular.

Exploration

Ethnic minority adolescents at this level of development embark on a deep exploration of their cultural heritage. They search for information about traditions and practices, desire intimacy with others of the same race or ethnic group, and search for a positive sense of identity (Phinney, Cantu and Kurtz 1997). Ethnic identity may be a source of self-esteem for young people (Phinney *et al.* 1997), and they may feel euphoric and proud as they explore positive aspects of their racial and ethnic group membership. However, this stage can be associated with negative views of the mainstream in general (Phinney and Devich-Navarro 1997) and whites specifically (Cross 1991; Helms 1990). Such feelings may stem from historical knowledge and personal experiences of racism and discrimination.

The major struggle for youth at this stage of development is balancing deep exploration with ways of functioning in the mainstream where ethnocentrism, a feature of this stage of development, is frowned upon. Studies with Latino and Asian Americans indicate that the conflicting demands of two cultures may lead to psychological distress (Ramirez 1984; Sung 1985). In black college students, this period of intense identification can result in low self-regard, low self-actualizing tendencies, high anxiety and hostility (Parham and Helms 1985a, b). Such stress may result from coping strategies that are inadequate for functioning in the mainstream or dealing with perceived and real racism and discrimination.

Commitment

At this stage the individual is mostly secure in his or her ethnic identity. Reinforcement and gratification stemming from group membership increasingly emanate from within (Helms 1990). Young people with a secure racial or ethnic identity exhibit higher levels of self-esteem (Phinney and Chavira 1992) and multicultural competence (Berry and Kim 1988; LaFromboise, Coleman and Gerton 1993; Oetting and Beauvais 1991; Phinney and Devich-Navarro 1997; Ramirez 1984) and are better able to deal with racism and discrimination (Phinney and Chavira 1995; Stevenson 1997; Ward 1990).

Commitment is not necessarily the conclusion of development. In a society of multiple cultures, where race and ethnicity are so salient, there is a high likelihood that a person of colour may revisit prior stages of development, except relative unawareness. For this reason, it may be imprudent to discuss ethnic identity in terms of stages; it may be more appropriate to think of ethnic identity as states that change from one context to another. The reference to stages here has been to offer an ideal type model, but how does the context of ethnic identity development mediate this processes described?

Ethnic Identity for Children and Young People in Foster Care

Progress toward the development of a coherent identity in general, and ethnic identity in particular, for children and young people in foster care, is challenging due to the stress and impermanence that results from being separated from one's birth family (SalahuDin and Bollman 1994). A youth who has experienced multiple placements is exposed to multiple separations and parental figures. With each separation, security and stability is diminished, and the youth must cope with the sense of failure and rage associated with loss (Steinhauer 1991), which increases the likelihood that subsequent foster placements will disrupt and identity development will be hindered. However, a stable positive relationship with foster parents can help the youth internalize new images of himself based on how he believes he is seen by them (Steinhauer 1991), which can positively influence identity formation and promote healthy ethnic identity.

What is a Healthy Sense of Ethnic Identity?

In a society of multiple cultures, young people often think about their racial or ethnic group membership through 'racialized discourses' (Phoenix 1997), and some unhealthy attitudes and behaviours may develop. Young people may deny being a member of their racial or ethnic group, claim membership of a group other than their own, view group membership as a social stigma, and even promote negative stereotypes of their group. While some young persons refuse to affiliate with members of their own ethnic group, others affiliate exclusively with members of their own group. Lastly, many young people of colour struggle to cope with racism or discrimination. They may internalize it or be unable to distinguish between racist and non-racist events. In the face of the complexities associated with ethnicity and race, and the challenges that children and young people in out-of-home care face, how does ethnic identity form among young people in foster care?

To answer this question we interviewed staff, foster parents and young people from Casey Family Programs which provides long-term foster care services. These interviews occurred in staff meetings, focus groups and individual interviews. Though not part of a formal course of research, these interviews provided some insights into the issue of ethnic identity development for young people in foster care.

The focus of our inquiry was on the individual interviews of social work practitioners who, because of their long-standing relationships with youth, often have a keen understanding of their psychosocial development. We asked practitioners to identify young persons from their caseloads who met four criteria for a healthy ethnic identity. A young person with a healthy ethnic identity was defined as one who

- identifies as a member of a particular ethnic group or groups
- has a generally positive attitude about being a member of the group or groups
- affiliates with members of his or her group but can interact with members of other groups
- is able to cope with racism and discrimination.

The following are themes that emerged from our interviews, with additional vignettes and comments gathered from focus group interviews with caregivers and young persons.

The Importance of Birth Family Work to a Healthy Ethnic Identity

Case study: John

John, a 17-year-old Mexican American youth, has been in foster care since he was 4 years old. Following a school suspension for pushing a teacher, John told his social worker that Mexicans 'don't wimp out of situations; [violence] is our way of doing things.' He tells his social worker that his father was that way, even though he has had little contact with his biological father since he left his family of origin. John's description of his father was reliable; he was violent and promoted violence as a way to solve problems. (practitioner interview 1999)

Nearly all practitioners indicated the importance of birth family work in helping children and young people develop a healthy ethnic identity. Research suggests that a high level of contact and identification with birth parents is associated with higher self-esteem among adolescents in foster care (SalahuDin and Bollman 1994), but research has never explored the relationship between ethnic identity and birth family contacts. The birth family can mediate the process of ethnic identity development in a number of ways.

Biological family turmoil, especially when experienced early in life, can adversely affect the cycle of attachment–identification–identity formation. The process of identity formation is based on this cycle, which starts with the ability to attach to others: primary caretakers at first but other adults and peers later on. After attachment there is a period of identification where the individual begins to think and act like the primary caretaker. Ultimately, identity is the result of a secure sense of self based on the attachments and identifications one makes with significant others throughout the life-span; it is particularly important from birth to age 6, but continues well beyond these years.

Without healthy secure attachments early in life, children can develop an inability to develop secure trusting relationships with others. For children in foster care family loss, chaos, conflict and inconsistency can result in a negative initial picture of the self (Steinhauer 1991) that can persist into later identity development phases. Young people like John can develop worldviews and constructions of their own cultural traits that are based on distorted and incomplete attachments. The result could be diminished social functioning and stigmatized ethnic identity. Children and young people in foster care are particularly susceptible since they will naturally have gaps in information.

One aspect of treatment for John should deal with the constructions of what it means to be Mexican based on patterns of identification with his father. In a family therapy session with his biological sisters, they shared that his father could be nurturing and reminded him of enjoyable times that John spent with his father during his early childhood years. This intervention allowed John to reconstruct his perception of what it means to be Mexican American. Birth family contacts and information provide a deeper, three-dimensional picture of the family of origin and especially of the birth parents.

Birth family work was also emphasized by social workers and foster parents who anticipated future conflict. They understood the inevitability that children in foster care will eventually wonder about or take a greater interest in their birth family history. Social workers facilitated birth family contacts or gave birth family information as much and as often as they could throughout a child's placement, out of concern that waiting could set the stage for giving too much difficult information all at once or to avoid resentment and conflict later in placement. One foster mother stated that if she waited for adolescence to do birth family work, her foster daughter would have cause to ask, 'Why didn't you give me this information when I was younger?' (staff meeting 1999).

Birth family contacts can facilitate ethnic identity in more subtle ways as well. One social worker told the story of a white foster mother who was driving along with her 10-year-old Native American foster child, following a visit to his birth mother. 'You really like my mom,' said the foster child, to which the foster mother responded 'Yes' (practitioner interview 1999). In this case, the message the foster mother gave the child through her interactions with the birth mother was proactive and subtle. The birth parent contact provided the foster parent with an opportunity to model care and acceptance of difference. The foster mother accepted and showed care for the birth mother, which gave the child approval to show acceptance and care as well. Because the foster mother was white and the birth mother Native American, there was also a subtle message supporting positive intergroup understanding. Had the foster mother been cold or disapproving of the birth mother, the subtle message sent to the child could have been that it is bad to be Native American.

Birth family contacts were also seen as the only way for children and young people to learn to value or have a connection to their culture of origin. One white foster mother stated that by maintaining contacts with the birth family, her Native American child participated in many of the cultural traditions of her tribe, including the naming ceremony (staff meeting 1999). Some social workers pointed out that socio-economic status, income, region of the country, ethnic make-up of the neighbourhood and type of community (rural, urban or suburban) all account for differences in culture within racial or ethnic groups. A social worker from the south of the USA noted that there are great cultural differences between black families in rural versus urban settings. In this respect, birth family contacts are as crucial in same-race placements as they are in cross-cultural placements. In the process of development, the average child identifies with his or her family and its attitudes, values and characteristics (Fenichel 1945). Birth family work can provide children and young people with some continuity by acting as a bridge between the culture of the family of origin where they first celebrate their ethnicity (McAdoo 1997) and the culture of the family or families to which they go.

Developmental Issues in the Formation of a Healthy Ethnic Identity

Case study: Nina

Nina, a 10-year-old Native American girl, is driving in the car with her foster mother and states 'I don't want to be Native American any more.' (practitioner interview 1999)

Social workers repeatedly discussed the issue of timing in relation to understanding the processes of ethnic identity development. Nina's social worker noted that her statement was common for children of colour at her age. Such comments can be explained in terms of social constancy, wherein children at about the age of 9 or 10 can fully understand that their ethnicity is something that will not change. If a child in foster care has been teased or ridiculed for the colour of her skin, she may begin to deny or avoid thinking about being a member of that ethnic group. Denial or avoidance can curtail discussion and/or exploration of one's ethnic identity. Though Nina's social worker did not mention social constancy theory, she recognized the dynamic interaction of age and development and suggested that intervention should be redirected at exposing Nina to images of Native Americans that are positive and affirming.

Timing was also considered important in talking to young people about race and ethnicity. One social worker described the experience of Charles, a 16-year-old biracial (African American/white) youth who avoided discussions about race (practitioner interview 1999). He expressed to his social worker some hesitance to accept that he was half white. He had lived with his white biological mother until he was 4, then went to a number of different foster homes. He spent the majority of his life in a biracial foster home that disrupted when that couple separated. He identified himself as black but rarely wanted to talk about race beyond that. When there was a school dance, he was invited by an African American girl but he decided to go with a male friend instead. Though many factors could explain Charles's behaviour, the social worker recognized a connection between his hesitance to date the African American girl and his hesitance to deal with his racial identity. She decided not to force a conversation about the issue because she realized that Charles was socially immature, and expected that once he did decide to start dating the opportunity to have discussions related to ethnic identity would follow.

Most social workers recognized that it is often appropriate to respect a youth's lack of interest in talking about race, ethnicity or culture, but this should not be cause to avoid addressing the issues. Social workers found that persistence pays off. For example, one African American social worker reported that she likes to expose the African American youth on her caseload to different types of activities such as motivational speakers, conferences of black professionals or graduate students, art shows or performances. She observed that the young people are not always enthusiastic at first, but they will often remember such activities and bring them up for discussion later in the course of placement (practitioner interview 1999). A common observation of many social workers and foster parents was that they valued 'teachable moments' and either created them or used naturally occurring ones to discuss race, ethnicity and culture.

Personal Attributes Associated with a Healthy Ethnic Identity

Social workers often described youth who displayed a healthy sense of ethnic identity as possessing certain personal attributes, including confidence, friendliness and the ability to use others as resources. They noted that these characteristics were directly and indirectly related to the young person's ethnic identity. One social worker stated that she would add, as an additional criterion for a healthy ethnic identity, the ability and confidence to express the uniqueness of one's ethnic group membership to people outside the group.

A causal link between ethnic identity and confidence or self-esteem is not supported consistently by research (McAdoo 2000; Phinney 1991). However, among the social workers interviewed, the confluence of ethnic identity and attributes like confidence were seen as having some protective value for young people. Angie, a 17-year-old African American in kinship foster care, was being teased by her cousins about trying to 'act white' because of the way she dressed and because many of her friends at school were white (practitioner interview 1999). According to her social worker, Angie met all the criteria of a young woman with a healthy sense of identity: she attended an all-African American church, she participated in African American cultural events in the community. In time, she began to affiliate more with other African American students, but continued to hang out with her white friends as well. Throughout the period when she was being teased, she maintained a strong connection to her ethnic community and her sense of ethnic identity remained intact.

Characteristics of the Placement that Promote a Healthy Ethnic Identity

Whether a young person is placed with extended family members, in a same-race placement with unrelated caretakers, or in a transracial placement, ethnic identity can and does develop, although the type of placement does account for some qualitative differences. Certainly some types of placements can provide more opportunities to ensure critical features of ethnic identity development in the context of foster care. For example, kinship care can provide children and young people with direct birth parent contacts and accurate information about absent parents via stories or recollections. In addition, when parents are not available or there is little available information, kinship care providers can help children and young people process intense feelings and assuage rescue fantasies. Angel, a 12-year-old Mexican/Filipino adolescent in a kinship foster home, expressed his desire to save his mother from her drug addiction (practitioner interview 1999). The social worker reported that Angel's aunts told him that they too wanted to help his mother, but that she had to try to help herself first. The aunts' involvement provided Angel with the knowledge that close family share in his concern for his mother, and that she will have the safety net of the kinship system available, which lessens the burden on him to save her. The social worker pointed out that this situation continues to cause the child psychological distress, but it is lessened by the aunts' interventions.

Despite the putative utility of kinship foster care, it is not a panacea for all the challenges to ethnic identity development. Some children who were described as not having a healthy sense of ethnic identity were also in kinship care. A common characteristic of all homes of children with healthy ethnic identity could be divided into proactive and protective socialization practices. Proactive socialization in these homes consisted of exposure to culturally relevant events like museums, movies or books that portrayed members of the young person's race or group in meaningful and authentic ways. The homes also promoted the value of culture in general by exposing the children to cross-cultural events. They provided role models of people of the same ethnic group who themselves had a healthy sense of ethnic identity, and the adults had high expectations for success. Protective strategies included the ability and willingness to discuss race and at times to examine their own biases about other groups. Lastly, the caretakers were ready to listen when children and young people felt they were being discriminated against and investigated and acted on racism and discrimination when it occurred.

Some people we spoke to expressed doubts that children and young people in cross-cultural placements could develop a healthy sense of ethnic identity, particularly those where the foster or adoptive parents were white and the child or young person is of colour. Children and adolescents in foster care are often placed in situations that reduce the likelihood of developing a healthy ethnic identity. Folaron and Hess (1993) found that foster families of biracial children were generally unassessed regarding the racial composition of their neighbourhoods, school districts or religious organizations, their sensitivity to cultural issues, the extent of racism within the families, and the families' willingness and ability to become involved in multiracial and diverse cultural experiences.

There has been little research on the effects of foster care on ethnic identity for children of colour (McRoy 1993), but transracial adoption studies suggest that adopted children suffer no ill-effects of overall psychological well-being, but they tend to be more acculturated to white mainstream society and identify less with their racial or ethnic group. Our interviews suggest that transracial placement presents challenges to foster parents concerned about ethnic or racial identity for the children and young people they care for, but they can be overcome. One of the social workers we interviewed worked with a white long-term foster care mother who was raising a Native American girl. The following are some of the characteristics this foster mother displayed and some of the things she did that contributed to the girl's healthy identity. First, she was persistent and patient in birth family contacts, enduring some years of feeling alienated from them until she was finally accepted. In addition, she expressed a respect for Native American culture and traditions and was willing to learn more about them. The foster mother had clearly planned ahead regarding the child's ethnic identity development, anticipating that the girl would eventually want to learn about her culture at a deep level.

Conclusion

This chapter should be viewed as a starting point in understanding how ethnic identity development unfolds within the context of the foster care system. The issues raised should serve as cause for further enquiry for two reasons. First, ethnic and racial identity research has grown over the years – though it continues to struggle to gain legitimacy in the field of psychology – but there is surprisingly little research that looks at the vulnerable population of children and young people in foster care who are particularly susceptible to ethnic identity developmental challenges. Second, because they are susceptible to these challenges, young people in foster care can, by virtue of the very challenges that require attention, offer insights that can add to our understanding of the ways that ethnic identity development forms. For example, our interviews suggest that adolescents in foster care can develop a healthy sense of ethnic identity irrespective of placement. Further examination of the features of the young person, the placement and interventions by practitioners could help to provide some insights into the various developmental trajectories towards ethnic identity that youth may follow. This research should be longitudinal and include mixed methods approaches because of the difficulties that arise when attempts are made to measure ethnic identity or ethnic socialization (W.E. Cross, 24 January 2001, personal communication).

In addition to the research implications of the model, training and assessment criteria should be established to guide caseworkers and foster parents who work with and care for children and young people of colour. At the very least, this chapter should promote discussions about specific dilemmas regarding ethnic identity development among caseworkers and foster parents. One shortcoming of current forms of multicultural training within large organizations is to take a 'cookbook' approach to culture and train practitioners to work with children, young people or families from specific backgrounds. An identity-focused approach to training should be different. Rather than training practitioners to understand the child's or young person's culture to gain understanding about the client, a practitioner would have to explore how a child or young person views and constructs a personal identity in relation to his or her group membership.

References

Atkinson, D.R., Morten, G. and Sue, D.W. (eds) (1998) *Counseling American Minorities*, 5th edn. Dubuque, IA: McGraw-Hill.

Berry, J.W. and Kim, U. (1988) 'Acculturation and mental health.' In P.R. Dasen, J.W. Berry and N. Sartorius (eds) *Health and Cross-cultural Psychology: Toward Applications.* Newbury Park, CA: Sage.

Bowman, P.J. and Howard, C. (1985) 'Race-related socialization, motivation, and academic achievement: a study of Black youths in three-generation families.' *Journal of the American Academy of Child Psychiatry 24*, 2, 134–141.

Boykin, W.A. And Toms, F.D. (1985) 'Black child socialization: a conceptual framework.' In H.P. McAdoo and J.L. McAdoo (eds) *Black children: Social, educational, and parental environments.* Beverly Hills, CA: Sage.

Bronfenbrenner, U. (1977) 'Toward an experimental ecology of human development.' *American Psychologist 32*, 7, 513–531.

Cross, W.E. (1971) 'The Negro-to-Black conversion experience: toward a psychology of black liberation.' *Black World 20*, 9, 13–27.

Cross, W.E. (1991) *Shades of Black: Diversity in African-American Identity.* Philadelphia, PA: Temple University Press.

Dennedy-Frank, D.P. (1982) *Mexican-American Parents: Transmittors of Ethnic Identity.* Ann Arbor, MI: University of Michigan Press.

Erikson, E.H. (1968) *Identity: Youth and Crisis.* New York: W.W. Norton.

Fenichel, A. (1945) *The Psychoanalytic Theory of Neurosis.* New York: W.W. Norton.

Folaron, G. and Hess, P.M. (1993) 'Placement considerations for children of mixed African American and Caucasian parentage.' *Child Welfare 72,* 2, 113–125.

Garcia, E.E. and Hurtado, A. (1995) 'Becoming American: a review of current research on the development of racial and ethnic identity in children.' In A.W.J. Willis and D. Hawley (eds) *Toward a Common Destiny: Improving Race and Ethnic Relations in America.* San Francisco, CA: Jossey-Bass.

Garcia-Coll, C.T. and Garcia, H.A.V. (1995) 'Developmental processes and their influence on interethnic and interracial relations.' In W.D. Hawley and A.W. Jackson (eds) *Toward a Common Destiny: Improving Race and Ethnic Relations in America.* San Francisco, CA: Jossey-Bass.

Helms, J.E. (1990) *Black and White Racial Identity: Theory, Research, and Practice.* New York: Greenwood.

Knight, G.P., Bernal, M.E., Cota, M.K., Garza, C.A. and Ocampo, K.A. (1993a) 'Family socialization and Mexican American identity and behavior.' In G.P. Knight and M.E. Bernal (eds) *Ethnic Identity: Formation and Transmission among Hispanics and Other Minorities.* Albany, NY: State University of New York Press.

Knight, G.P., Bernal, M.E., Garza, C.A. and Cota, M.K. (1993b) 'A social cognitive model of the development of ethnic identity and ethnically based behaviors.' In G.P. Knight and M.E. Bernal (eds) *Ethnic Identity: Formation and Transmission among Hispanics and Other Minorities.* Albany, NY: State University of New York Press.

Knight, G.P., Bernal, M.E., Garza, C.A. and Cota, M.K. (1993c) 'Family socialization and the ethnic identity of Mexican-American children.' *Journal of Cross-Cultural Psychology 24,* 1, 99–114.

Kohatsu, E.L. (1993) *The Effects of Racial Identity and Acculturation on Anxiety, Assertiveness, and Ascribed Identity among Asian American College Students.* College Park, MD: University of Maryland.

LaFromboise, T., Coleman, H.L. and Gerton, J. (1993) 'Psychological impact of biculturalism: evidence and theory.' *Psychological Bulletin 114,* 3, 395–412.

McAdoo, H.P. (1985) 'Racial attitude and self-concept of young black children over time.' In H.P. McAdoo and J.L. McAdoo (eds) Black children: social, educational, and parental environments. Beverly Hills: Sage.

McAdoo, H.P. (1997) 'Racial attitude and self-concept of young black children over time.' In H.P. McAdoo and J.L. McAdoo (eds) *Black Children: Social, Educational ,and Parental Environments.* Thousand Oaks, CA: Sage.

McAdoo, H. (2000) *Conceptual Framework Roundtable: Casey Family Program.* Seattle, WA: Casey Family Program.

McRoy, R.G. (1993) 'Racial identity issues for Black children in foster care.' In S. Logan (ed) *The Black Family: Strengths, Self-help, and Positive Change.* Boulder, CO: Westview.

Marcia, J. (1980) 'Identity in Adolescence.' In J. Adelson (ed) *Handbook of Adolescent Psychology.* New York: Wiley.

Marshall, S. (1995) 'Ethnic socialization of African American children: implications for parenting, identity development, and academic achievement.' *Journal of Youth and Adolescence 24,* 4, 377–396.

Martin, P. And Midgley, E. (1999) 'Immigration to the United States, Population Bulletin 54, 2. Washington, DC: Population Reference Bureau.

Ocampo, K.A., Bernal, M.E. and Knight, G.P. (1993) 'Gender, race, and ethnicity: the sequencing of social constancies.' In G.P. Knight and M.E. Bernal (eds) *Ethnic Identity: Formation and Transmission among Hispanics and Other Minorities.* Albany, NY: State University of New York Press.

Oetting, E.R. and Beauvais, F. (1991) 'Orthogonal cultural identification theory: the cultural identification of minority adolescents.' *International Journal of the Addictions 25,* 655–685.

Parham, T.A. and Helms, J.E. (1985a) 'Relation of racial identity attitudes to self-actualization and affective states of Black students.' *Journal of Counseling Psychology 32,* 3, 431–440.

Parham, T.A. and Helms, J.E. (1985b) 'Attitudes of racial identity and self-esteem of Black students: an exploratory investigation.' *Journal of College Student Personnel 26,* 2, 143–147.

Phinney, J.S. (1989) 'Stages of ethnic identity development in minority group adolescents.' *Journal of Early Adolescence 9,* 1–2.

Phinney, J.S. (1990) 'Ethnic identity in adolescents and adults: review of research.' *Psychological Bulletin 108,* 3, 499–514.

Phinney, J.S. (1991) 'Ethnic identity and self-esteem: a review and integration.' Special issue: Ethnic identity and psychological adaptation. *Hispanic Journal of Behavioral Sciences 13,* 2, 193–208.

Phinney, J.S., Cantu, C.L. and Kurtz, D.A. (1997) 'Ethnic and American identity as predictors of self-esteem among African American, Latino, and White adolescents.' *Journal of Youth and Adolescence 26,* 2, 165–185.

Phinney, J.S. and Chavira, V. (1992) 'Ethnic identity and self-esteem: an exploratory longitudinal study.' *Journal of Adolescence 15,* 3, 271–281.

Phinney, J.S. and Chavira, V. (1995) 'Parental ethnic socialization and adolescent coping with problems related to ethnicity.' *Journal of Research on Adolescence 5*, 1, 31–53.

Phinney, J.S. and Devich-Navarro, M. (1997) 'Variations in bicultural identification among African American and Mexican American adolescents.' *Journal of Research on Adolescence 7*, 1, 3–32.

Phoenix, A. (1997) '"I'm White! So what?" The construction of Whiteness for young Londoners.' In M. Fine, L. Weis, L.C. Powell and L.M. Wong (eds) *Off White: Readings of Race, Power, and Society.* New York: Routledge.

Pyant, C.T. and Yanico, B.J. (1991) 'Relationship of racial identity and gender-role attitudes to Black women's psychological well-being.' *Journal of Counseling Psychology 38*, 3, 315–322.

Ramirez, M.M. (1984) 'Chicano career myths: the effects of an experimental intervention on students' career maturity and career myths.' Unpublished dissertation, University of Nebraska, Lincoln, NE.

Root, M.P.P. (ed) (1996) *The Multiracial Experience: Racial Borders as the New Frontier.* Thousand Oaks, CA: Sage.

SalahuDin, S.N. and Bollman, S.R. (1994) 'Identity development and self-esteem of young adolescents in foster care.' *Child and Adolescent Social Work Journal 11*, 2, 123–135.

Spencer, M.B. (1983) 'Children's cultural values and parental child rearing strategies.' *Developmental Review 3*, 4, 351–370.

Spencer, M.B. (1999) 'Social and cultural influences on school adjustment: the application of an identity-focused cultural ecological perspective.' *Educational Psychologist 34*, 1, 43–57.

Steinhauer, P.D. (1991) *The Least Detrimental Alternative: A Systematic Guide to Case Planning and Decision Making for Children in Care.* Toronto: University of Toronto Press.

Stevenson, H.C. (1994) 'Validation of the scale of racial socialization for African American adolescents: steps toward multidimensionality.' *Journal of Black Psychology 20*, 4, 445–468.

Stevenson, H.C. (1995) 'Relationship of adolescent perceptions of racial socialization to racial identity.' *Journal of Black Psychology 21*, 1, 49–70.

Stevenson, H.C. (1997) 'Managing anger: protective, proactive, or adaptive racial socialization identity profiles and African-American manhood development.' *Journal of Prevention and Intervention in the Community 16*, 1–2.

Stevenson, H.C. (1998) 'Raising safe villages: cultural-ecological factors that influence the emotional adjustment of adolescents.' *Journal of Black Psychology 24*, 1, 44–59.

Stevenson, H.C., Reed, J. and Bodison, P. (1996) 'Kinship social support and adolescent racial socialization beliefs: extending the self to family.' *Journal of Black Psychology 22*, 4, 498–508.

Stevenson, H.C., Reed, J., Bodison, P. and Bishop, A. (1997) 'Racism stress management: racial socialization beliefs and the experience of depression and anger in African American youth.' *Youth and Society 29*, 2, 197–222.

Sung, B.L. (1985) 'Bicultural conflicts in Chinese immigrant children.' *Journal of Comparative Family Studies 16*, 2, 255–269.

Tajfel, H. (1981) *Human Groups and Social Categories.* Cambridge: Cambridge University Press.

Taub, D.J. and McEwen, M.K. (1992) 'The relationship of racial identity attitudes to autonomy and mature interpersonal relationships in Black and White undergraduate women.' *Journal of College Student Development 33*, 5, 439–446.

Thornton, M.C., Chatters, L.M., Taylor, R.J. and Allen, W.R. (1990) 'Sociodemographic and environmental correlates of racial socialization by Black parents.' *Child Development 61*, 2, 401–409.

US Bureau of the Census (1992) *Marital Status and Living Arrangements: March 1992* (Current Population Reports, Population Characteristics Series P20–468). Washington, DC: US Government Printing Office.

Ward, J.V. (1990) 'Racial identity formation and transformation.' In C. Gilligan, N.P. Lyons and T.J. Hamner (eds) *Making Connections: The Relational Worlds of Adolescent Girls at Emma Willard School.* Cambridge, MA: Harvard University Press.

The Contributors

Dr Rajeev Gopal Banhatti, MBBS, MD(Psych), MRCPsych, is a consultant child and adolescent psychiatrist at the Child, Adolescent and Family Services in Northampton, UK. He trained in Pune, India, at the BJ Medical College as a general psychiatrist before arriving in the UK in 1991 to acquire training in child psychiatry. He worked in York and Folkestone before moving to Northampton. His family (wife Seema and children Ruchi and Suhrud) use Marathi, English and occasionally Hindi to talk to each other at home. His main hobbies include listening to music (especially the blues), reading and having a good time with family and friends. Apart from ethnicity his special interests include attention deficit and hyperactivity disorder (ADHD), attachment, cognitive behavioural therapy (CBT) and eye movement desensitization and reprocessing (EMDR). He is a level 1 trained EMDR therapist.

Dr Nick J. Banks, PhD, is a chartered clinical psychologist and senior lecturer in counselling and psychotherapy at the Centre for the Study of Human Relations, University of Nottingham. He holds a committed interest in the development of research, theory and practice related to black children and families. He is active in research on social work issues related to fostering and adoption and abuse in its many forms; he also acts as an expert witness.

Dr Surya Bhate, MBBS, DPM, FRCPsych, is consultant and senior lecturer in child and adolescent forensic psychiatry, The Tees and North East Yorkshire Trust. He graduated in medicine from Nagpur University, India, and trained in psychiatry in India as well as in the UK with Sir Martin Roth and later with Professor Israel Kolvin. He worked as a consultant in adolescent psychiatry in Leicester for seven years before moving to the north-east of England where he has developed the forensic services for children, young people and their families in response to the Reed Committee recommendations. He has been a member of various committees including the chairmanship of the Royal College of Psychiatrists' Committee for Overseas Doctors. He has published on the subjects of school phobia, depression and racism in medicine.

John Burnham is employed by the Birmingham Children's Hospital (NHS) Trust as a consultant family therapist working at the Parkview Clinic for children, young people and families. Together with Queenie Harris he co-organizes the therapeutic and training services in the Family Clinic and Sexual Abuse Project. In the independent sector he works at the Kensington Consultation Centre in London as a supervisor and director of the Diploma in Systemic Teaching, Training and Supervision.

Professor Ana Mari Cauce, identity formation specialist, was born in Havana, Cuba, and emigrated to the United States at the age of 3, settling in Miami. She graduated from the University of Washington, earning degrees in English literature and in psychology in 1977, before going on to Yale University, where she earned her doctoral degree in psychology, concentrating on child clinical and community psychology. After spending a brief period as an assistant professor at the University of Delaware, Dr Cauce moved to Seattle, where she has been an assistant associate and now a full professor in the Department of Psychology, where she holds the Earl R. Carlson Professorship. She also has a joint appointment in the Department of American Ethic Studies, and she presently serves as chair of the department. Since she began her graduate work, Dr Cauce has been particularly interested in normative and non-normative development in ethnic minority youth and in at-risk youth more generally. She has written more than 50 articles and chapters and has been recipient of grants from the WT Grant Foundation, the National Institute of Mental Health, the National Institute of Child Health and Human Development, and the National Institute of Alcoholism and Alcohol Abuse. She is the recipient of numerous awards, including Recognition from the American Psychological Association for Excellence in Research on Minority Issues and the University of Washington's Distinguished Teaching Award. At present she is also co-chair of the Family Consortium on Culture and Context.

Dr Kedar Nath Dwivedi, MBBS, MD, DPM, FRCPsych, is a consultant in child, adolescent and family psychiatry at the Child, Adolescent and Family Consultation Service and the Ken Stewart Family Centre, Northampton, and is also a clinical teacher in the Faculty of Medicine, University of Leicester. He graduated in medicine from the Institute of Medical Sciences, Varanasi, India, and served as assistant professor in Preventive and Social Medicine in Simla before arriving in the UK in 1974. Since then he has worked in psychiatry and is a member of more than a dozen professional associations, including the Transcultural Psychiatry Society, and has contributed extensively to the literature (nearly 50 publications) including editing or coediting of books such as *Groupwork with Children and Adolescents* (Jessica Kingsley, 1993), *A Handbook of Childhood Anxiety Management* (Arena, 1997), *Depression in Children and Adolescents* (Whurr, 1997), *Enhancing Parenting Skills* (Wiley, 1997), *Therapeutic Use of Stories* (Routledge, 1997) and *Post-traumatic Stress Disorder in Children and Adolescents* (Whurr, 2000). He is the director of courses on group work with children and adolescents in Northampton and the honorary secretary of the Overseas Working Group of the Royal College of Psychiatrists. He is also interested in eastern, particularly Buddhist, approaches to mental health.

Mrs Radha Dwivedi, MA (Pali), Cert. in Youth and Community Work, works as an outreach worker for ethnic minorities in the Northampton Child, Adolescent and Family Services. She graduated in sociology, Pali and Hindi and obtained a master's degree in Pali from the Banaras Hindu University in Varanasi. She arrived in the UK in 1975 and has worked in voluntary capacities, as an adult education tutor, and in youth service, social services and a health authority.

Dr Raina Tasneem Fateh is a family clinician and family therapist. She is also the coordinator of the Asian Service at the Marlborough Family Service, Brent, Kensington, Chelsea and Westminster Mental Health Trust, London.

Gerry German, BA, Dip. Educ, Dip. Philosophy of Educ., has long experience of teaching in Jamaica and London. He has worked as a comprehensive school head in Clwyd, as principal education officer in Nigeria and with the Commission for Racial Equality, London, for twelve years as principal education officer. He was honorary secretary of the Working Group against Racism in Children's Resources for many years and also provides (on a voluntary basis) advice, support and representational services to people with problems in employment. He is now director of the Communities Empowerment Network providing similar services to people experiencing problems in education, especially exclusions from school.

Dr Queenie Harris, FRCPsych, DPM, MBBS, is a consultant child and adolescent psychiatrist who (until her recent retirement from the NHS) worked at the Parkview Clinic, Birmingham. She also worked at the City Hospital, Birmingham, a large inner-city general hospital. She was also a senior clinical lecturer in child and adolescent psychiatry, and together with John Burnham co-organized the therapeutic and training services in the Family Clinic and Sexual Abuse Project at Parkview Clinic. She has been an examiner to various postgraduate systemic therapy degree courses in London. She arrived in the UK in the early 1960s, soon after qualifying in medicine in south India. She works as a consultant child and adolescent psychiatrist in the Charles Burns Family Clinic at the West Midlands Centre for Children, Young People, and Families and at the City Hospital, Birmingham. Her special interests are in systemic therapy, child sexual abuse and transcultural psychiatry/practice. She continues to work in private practice at the Woodbourne Priory Hospital, Birmingham.

Dr Nurun Islam was a family therapist at the Marlborough Family Service, Brent, Kensington, Chelsea and Westminster Mental Health Trust, London. She is now in general practitioner training.

Farra Khan is a family therapist at the Marlborough Family Service, Brent, Kensington, Chelsea and Westminster Mental Health Trust, London. She is also a student counsellor.

Cecilia Ko is a family clinician and family therapist at the Marlborough Family Service, Brent, Kensington, Chelsea and Westminster Mental Health Trust, London.

Dr Inga-Britt Krause is of Danish origin and holds a PhD in social anthropology, for which she studied at the London School of Economics. She has carried out ethnographic fieldwork among Hindus in Nepal and with the Punjabi community in Bedford, UK. In Bedford she worked with psychiatrists and general practitioners on concepts of mental health and illness. She trained as a family therapist at the Marlborough Family Service, Brent, Kensington, Chelsea and Westminster Mental

Health Trust, London, where she later helped set up a specialist Asian service. She is currently training and development consultant at the Tavistock and Portman Mental Health Trust. Her publications include several papers and two books: *Therapy Across Culture* (Sage, 1998) and *Culture and System in Family Therapy* (Karnac, 2002).

Dr Annie Lau, FRCPsych, was born in Australia and grew up in Singapore and Malaysia. She graduated in medicine in Canada and worked at the Royal Ottawa Hospital before arriving in the UK in 1978. She works as a consultant in child and adolescent psychiatry and is medical director in North East London Mental Health Trust. She continues to be actively involved in contributing to the literature, teaching in transcultural issues in individual and family life, and leading on staff development workshops in race and cultural awareness.

Marigold Lee is a family clinician and family therapist at the Marlborough Family Service, Brent, Kensington, Chelsea and Westminster Mental Health Trust, London.

Dr Begum Maitra, MMBS, DPM, MRCPsych, MD, is a consultant child psychiatrist at the Child and Family Consultation Centre in Hammersmith, London, and a Jungian analyst. Her training and clinical experience in India, and her subsequent experience in the UK, have fostered an interest in the impact of cultural systems on psychiatric practice and on health service provision. A significant portion of her work involves the assessment of children at risk and their families, and she teaches and writes on the complex issues around cross-cultural assessment.

Rabia Malik, PhD, is lecturer in psychosocial studies at the University of East London and a family therapist at the Marlborough Family Service, Brent, Kensington, Chelsea and Westminster Mental Health Trust, London.

Dr Harish Mehra, DipSW, MA (Race and Ethnic Studies), PhD, works as a strategic planning officer for equalities in Birmingham Social Services Department. He arrived in the UK in 1973 and was employed in industry for a few years before working as a social worker in Coventry. He became training officer with Sandwell Social Services, then the principal officer (ethnic minorities) with Northampton Social Services Department followed by principal at the Education Welfare Service, Birmingham. He is also a journalist and has written nine books including *Racism in Britain* (1997), *Racism in Education* (2000), *Dreamland* (2001) plus six books in Punjabi. He has been given awards by the East Midlands Arts Council and by the Punjabi Sath Lambra, Panjab, India, for his contribution to Punjabi literature. His articles on various issues are frequently published in the Punjabi press in the UK, Canada and India. He is the general secretary of the Asian Rationalist Society and is committed to fighting injustice.

Ann Miller, BA (Hons), AFBPS, is a consultant clinical psychologist and family therapist at the Marlborough Family Service in London, Brent, Kensington, Chelsea and Westminster Mental Health Trust, where she is particularly interested in relating training to intercultural work. She originally studied in Australia and has had wide teaching experience in family therapy both in the UK and abroad. She was coeditor of *Gender and Power in Families* (Routledge, 1990) and *Clinical Psychology Race and Culture: A Handbook for Trainers* (BPS Books, 2000).

Dr James Rodriguez, MSW, PhD, obtained his doctorate in educational psychology from the University of Washington and is now a postdoctoral fellow with the Family Research Consortium, a programme funded by the National Institute of Mental Health to support research on families in diverse contexts. He received his undergraduate degree from the City College of New York in communications and sociology in 1987, and his MSW degree from Columbia University in 1990. A consistent theme throughout his varied professional and academic experiences has been work with people of diverse ethnic backgrounds. His research interests include ethnic identity development, racial and ethnic socialization, and the importance of parents and place (neighbourhood and community context) in the psychosocial development of children and youth. He has five years' postgraduate experience as a school social worker, pre-kindergarten through 12th grade, primarily in ethnic minority communities in New York City, Los Angeles and Seattle. He has also worked in public child welfare and in hospital settings.

Linda A. Wilson, BA, MSW, was the project executive for the Practice Replication Project of Casey Family Programs, headquartered in Seattle. She has returned to Casey Family Programs after her recent retirement to serve as the interim director of the Seattle Division Operations. Her past responsibilities included the overall management of division operations and the operations department. She brings an extensive background in children's services with a focus on cross-cultural programming. She has taught at community colleges and as a lecturer at the University of Washington. She has sat on boards and commissions dealing with issues of children, and has provided extensive training to other organizations on cross-cultural competence and the issues and needs of children of colour. Her bachelor's degree is from the University of Michigan and her master's degree in social work is from Columbia University. She has certificates in management from the University of Washington School of Social Work and MIT's Sloan School of Management.

Jeremy Woodcock, BA, MSc, DipFT, Adv. DipSFTSP, is the director of family therapy training at the University of Bristol. He is also a consultant psychotherapist with the Medical Foundation for the Care of Victims of Torture, a human rights organization based in London, where he worked for many years and established the family and marital therapy service.

Dr Harry Zeitlin, BSc, MPhil, MD, PRCP, FRCPsych, is Professor of Child and Adolescent Psychiatry, North Essex Child and Family Consultation Service. He graduated from London University and trained in psychiatry at the Maudsley Hospital. He has written on various subjects including the links between child and adult disorder, child abuse and drug and substance abuse. He has a special interest in teaching on forensic and transcultural psychiatry.

Subject Index

Author Index